DEVELOPER'S GUIDE TO MICROSOFT® ENTERPRISE LIBRARY

DEVELOPER'S GUIDE TO
Microsoft® Enterprise Library

Solutions for Enterprise Development

Alex Homer
  with
  Nicolas Botto
  Bob Brumfield
  Olaf Conijn
  Grigori Melnik
  Erik Renaud
  Fernando Simonazzi
  Chris Tavares

Contents

Foreword

You are holding in your hands a book that will make your life as an enterprise developer a whole lot easier.

It's a guide on Microsoft Enterprise Library and it's meant to *guide* you through how to apply .NET for enterprise development. Enterprise Library, developed by the patterns & practices group, is a collection of reusable components, each addressing a specific cross cutting concern—be it system logging, or data validation, or exception management. Many of these can be taken advantage of easily. These components are architecture agnostic and can be applied in a multitude of different contexts.

The book walks you through functional blocks of the Enterprise Library, which include data access, caching, cryptography, exception handling, logging, security, and validation. It contains a large collection of exercises, tricks and tips.

Developing robust, reusable, and maintainable application requires knowledge of design patterns, software architectures and solid coding skills. We can help you develop those skills with Enterprise Library since it encapsulates proven and recommended practices of developing enterprise applications on the .NET platform. Though this guide does not go into the depth of discussions of architecture and patterns, it provides a solid basis for you to discover and implement these patterns from a reusable set of components. That's why I also encourage you to check out the Enterprise Library source code and read it.

This guide is not meant to be a complete reference on Enterprise Library. For that, you should go to MSDN. Instead, the guide covers most commonly used scenarios and illustrates how Enterprise Library can be applied in implementing those. The powerful message manifesting from the guide is the importance of code reuse. In today's world of complex large software systems, high-quality pluggable components are a must. After all, who can afford to write and then maintain dozens of different frameworks in a system— all to accomplish the same thing? Enterprise Library allows you to take advantage of the proven code complements to manage a wide range of task and leaves you free to concentrate on the core business logic and other "working parts" of your application.

Another important emphasis that the guide makes is on software designs, which are easy to configure, testable and maintainable. Enterprise Library has a flexible configuration subsystem driven from either external config files, or programmatically, or both. Leading by example, Enterprise Library itself is designed in a loosely-coupled manner. It promotes key design principles of the separation of concerns, single responsibility principle, principle of least knowledge and the DRY principle (Don't Repeat Yourself). Having said this, don't expect this particular guide to be a comprehensive reference on design patterns. It is not. It provides just enough to demonstrate how key patterns are used with Enterprise Library. Once you see and understand them, try to extrapolate them to other problems, contexts, scenarios.

The authors succeeded in writing a book that is targeted at both those who are seasoned Enterprise Library developers and who would like to learn about the improvements in version 5.0, and those, who are brand new to Enterprise Library. Hopefully, for the first group, it will help orientate you and also get a quick refresher of some of the key concepts. For the second group, the book may lower your learning curve and get you going with Enterprise Library quickly.

Lastly, don't just read this book. It is meant to be a practical tutorial. And learning comes only through practice. Experience Enterprise Library. Build something with it. Apply the concepts learnt in practice. And don't forget to share your experience.

In conclusion, I am excited about both the release of Enterprise Library 5.0 and this book. Especially, since they ship and support some of our great new releases—Visual Studio 2010, .NET Framework 4.0 and Silverlight 4, which together will make you, the developer, ever more productive.

Scott Guthrie
Corporate Vice-President
Microsoft .NET Developer Platform
Redmond, Washington

Preface

About This Guide

When you casually pick up a book in your local bookstore or select one from the endless collection available on your favorite Web site, you're probably wondering what the book actually covers, what you'll learn from it, whether the content is likely to be interesting and useful, and—of course—whether it is actually any good. We'll have a go at answering the first three of these questions here. The final question is one only you can answer. Of course, we would be pleased to hear your opinion through our community Web site at http://entlib.codeplex.com/.

WHAT DOES THIS GUIDE COVER?

As you can probably tell from the title, this guide concentrates on how you can get started with Enterprise Library. It will help you learn how to use Enterprise Library in your applications to manage your crosscutting concerns, simplify and accelerate your development cycle, and take advantage of proven practices. Enterprise Library is a collection of prewritten code components that have been developed and fine-tuned over many years. You can use them out of the box, modify them as required, and distribute them with your applications. You can even use Enterprise Library as a learning resource. It includes the source code that demonstrates Microsoft®.NET programming techniques and the use of common design patterns that can improve the design and maintainability of your applications. By the way, if you are not familiar with the term crosscutting concerns, don't worry; we'll explain it as we go along.

Enterprise Library is an extensive collection, with a great many moving parts. To the beginner knowing how to best take advantage of it is not completely intuitive. Therefore, in this guide we'll help you to quickly understand what Enterprise Library is, what it contains, how you can select and use just the specific features you require, and how easy it is to get started using them. You will see how you can quickly and simply add Enterprise Library to your applications, configure it to do exactly what you need, and then benefit from the simple-to-use, yet extremely compelling opportunities it provides for writing less code that achieves more.

The first chapter of this guide discusses Enterprise Library in general, and provides details of the individual parts so that you become familiar with the framework as a whole.

The aim is for you to understand the basic principles of each of the application blocks in Enterprise Library, and how you can choose exactly which blocks and features you require. Chapter 1 also discusses the fundamentals of using the blocks, such as how to configure them, how to instantiate the components, and how to use these components in your code.

The remaining seven chapters discuss in detail the application blocks that provide the basic crosscutting functionality such as data access, caching, logging, and exception handling. These chapters explain the concepts that drove development of the blocks, the kinds of tasks they can accomplish, and how they help you implement many well-known design patterns. And, of course, they explain—by way of code extracts and sample programs—how you actually use the blocks in your applications. After you've read each chapter, you should be familiar with the block and be able to use it to perform a range of functions quickly and easily, in both new and existing applications.

Finally, the appendices present more detailed information on specific topics that you don't need to know about in detail to use Enterprise Library, but are useful as additional resources and will help you understand how features such as dependency injection, interception, and encryption fit into the Enterprise Library world.

You can also download and work through the Hands-On Labs for Enterprise Library, which are available at http://go.microsoft.com/fwlink/?LinkId=188936.

WHAT THIS GUIDE DOES NOT COVER

The aim of this guide is to help you learn how to benefit from the capabilities of Enterprise Library. It does not describe the common design patterns in depth, or attempt to teach you about application architecture in general. Instead, it concentrates on getting you up to speed quickly and with minimum fuss so you can use Enterprise Library to manage your crosscutting concerns.

One of the core tenets of modern application design is that you should reduce the coupling or dependencies between components and objects, and Enterprise Library version 5.0 helps you achieve this goal through use of the Dependency Injection (DI) design pattern. However, you do not have to be a DI expert to use Enterprise Library; all of the complexity is managed internally by the core mechanisms within the framework. While we do explain the basic use of DI in terms of Enterprise Library, that is not a fundamental feature of this guide.

Enterprise Library is designed to be extensible. You can extend it simply by writing custom plug-in providers, by modifying the core code of the library, or even by creating entirely new blocks. In this guide, we provide pointers to how you can do this and explain the kinds of providers that you may be tempted to create, but it is not a topic that we cover in depth. These topics are discussed more fully in the documentation installed with Enterprise Library and available online at http://go.microsoft.com/fwlink/?LinkId=188874, and in the many other resources available from our community Web site at http://www.codeplex.com/entlib.

For more information about the Dependency Injection (DI) design pattern and the associated patterns, see "Inversion of Control Containers and the Dependency Injection pattern" at http://martinfowler.com/articles/injection.html.

HOW WILL THIS GUIDE HELP YOU?

If you build applications that run on the Microsoft .NET Framework, whether they are enterprise-level business applications or even relatively modest Windows® Forms, Windows Presentation Foundation (WPF), Windows Communication Foundation (WCF), or ASP.NET applications, you can benefit from Enterprise Library. This guide helps you to quickly grasp what Enterprise Library can do for you, presents examples that show it in action, and make it easier for you to start experimenting with Enterprise Library.

The sample applications are easy to assimilate, fully commented, and contain code that demonstrates all of the main features. You can copy this code directly into your applications if you wish, or just use it as a guide when you need to implement the common functionality it provides. The samples are console-based applications that contain separate procedures for each function they demonstrate. You can download these samples from http://go.microsoft.com/fwlink/?LinkId=189009.

Finally, what is perhaps the most important feature of this guide is that it will hopefully allay any fears you may have about using other people's code in your applications. By understanding how to select exactly the features you need, and installing the minimum requirements to implement these features, you will see that what might seem like a huge and complicated framework is actually a really useful set of individual components and features from which you can pick and choose—a candy store for the architect and developer.

What Do You Need to Get Started?

The prerequisites for using this guide are relatively simple. You'll need to be relatively experienced in Visual Basic, and understand general object-oriented programming techniques. The system requirements and prerequisites for using Enterprise Library are:

- Supported architectures: x86 and x64.
- Operating system: Microsoft Windows® 7 Professional, Enterprise, or Ultimate; Windows Server® 2003 R2; Windows Server 2008 with Service Pack 2; Windows Server 2008 R2; Windows Vista® with Service Pack 2; or Windows XP with Service Pack 3.
- Microsoft .NET Framework 3.5 with Service Pack 1 or Microsoft .NET Framework 4.0.
- For a rich development environment, the following are recommended:
    - Microsoft Visual Studio® 2008 Development System with Service Pack 1 (any edition) or Microsoft Visual Studio 2010 Development System (any edition).
- To run the unit tests, the following are also required:
    - Microsoft Visual Studio 2008 Professional, Visual Studio 2008 Team Edition, Visual Studio 2010 Premium, Visual Studio 2010 Professional, or Visual Studio 2010 Ultimate Edition.
    - Moq v3.1 assemblies.

- For the Data Access Application Block, the following is also required:
  - A database server running a database that is supported by a .NET Framework 3.5 with Service Pack 1 or .NET Framework 4.0 data provider. This includes Microsoft SQL Server® 2000 or later, SQL Server 2005 Compact Edition, and Oracle 9i or later. The database server can also run a database that is supported by the .NET Framework 3.5 with Service Pack 1 or the .NET Framework 4.0 data providers for OLE DB or ODBC.
- For the Logging Application Block, the following are also required:
  - Stores to maintain log messages. If you are using the MSMQ trace listener to store log messages, you need the Microsoft Message Queuing (MSMQ) component installed. If you are using the Database trace listener to store log messages, you need access to a database server. If you are using the Email trace listener to store log messages, you need access to an SMTP server.

Other than that, all you require is some spare time to sit and read, and to play with the example programs. Hopefully you will find the contents interesting (and perhaps even entertaining), as well as a useful source for learning about Enterprise Library.

THE TEAM WHO BROUGHT YOU THIS GUIDE

Idea/Vision	Grigori Melnik
Main Author	Alex Homer
Contributing Authors	Nicolas Botto, Bob Brumfield, Olaf Conijn, Grigori Melnik, Erik Renaud, Fernando Simonazzi, and Chris Tavares.
Reviewers	Scott Densmore, Tom Hollander, Hernan de Lahitte, Ajoy Krishnamoorthy, Ade Miller, and Don Smith.
Graphic Artists	Patrick Lanfear and Tom Draper.
Editors	RoAnn Corbisier and Nancy Michell.

THE ENTERPRISE LIBRARY 5.0 DEVELOPMENT TEAM

Product/Program Management	Grigori Melnik (Microsoft Corporation).
Architecture/ Development	Bob Brumfield and Chris Tavares (Microsoft Corporation); Fernando Simonazzi (Clarius Consulting); Nicolas Botto (Digit Factory); and Olaf Conijn (Olaf Conijn BV).
Testing	Carlos Farre, Masashi Narumoto, and Rohit Sharma (Microsoft Corporation); Nicolas Botto (Digit Factory); Lavanya Selvaraj, Magdelene Sona, Mani Krishnaswami, Meenakshi Krishnamoorthi, Santhosh Panneerselvam, and Ravindra Varman (Infosys Technologies Ltd); Erik Renaud and François Tanguay (nVentive Inc); and Rick Carr (DCB Software Testing, Inc).
User Experience	Damon van Vessem, Heidi Adkisson, Jen Amsterlaw, and Kelly Franznick (Blink Interactive); and Brad Cunningham (Interknowlodgy).
Documentation	Alex Homer (Microsoft Corporation) and Dennis DeWitt (Linda Werner &Associates Inc).

Editing/Production	RoAnn Corbisier and Steve Elston (Microsoft Corporation); Nancy Michell (Content Master Ltd.); John Hubbard (Eson) Ted Brian Neveln (Ballard Indexing Services) and Patrick Lanfear and Tom Draper (Twist Creative LLC).
Release Management	Richard Burte (ChannelCatalyst.com, Inc.) and Jennifer Burch (DCB Software Testing, Inc).
Administrative Support	Tracy Emory (Microsoft Corporation).
Advisory Council	Brian Button (Asynchrony Solutions); Kyle Huntley (Avanade); David Starr (Pluralsight); Wallin Ludwik (Volvo); Bill Wilder (Fidelity); Andrej Golcov (Hermes SoftLab); John Askew, Nicholas Blumhardt, Martin Bennedik, and Serge Baranovsky (Independent); Evgeny Sorokin and Ksenia Mukhortova (Intel); Scott Nichols (Idaho Central); Eng Chong Lim and Isabel Niu (McDonald's Corporation); Aaron Hanks, Glenn Block, Hugo Batista, Jason Hogg, Jason Olson, John Czernuszka, Joshy Joseph, Lenny Fenster, Massimo Mascaro, Matthew Podwysocki, Tom Hollander, Piyush Gupta, and Scott Densmore (Microsoft Corporation); Matthew Buonomano and Nikola Malovic (Monster.com); Daniel Piessens and Phill Van Hoven (Red Prairie); and Walter Wu (Royal Bank of Canada).
Community	Attendees at patterns & practices summits, PDC, TechReady, and TechEd conferences who provided informal feedback; and Enterprise Library users who commented on this guide on CodePlex, through our blogs, surveys and via e-mail.

Thank you!

1   Welcome to the Library

Meet the Librarian

Before we begin our exploration of Microsoft® Enterprise Library and the wondrous range of capabilities and opportunities it encompasses, you need to meet the Librarian. Sometimes we call him Tom, sometimes we call him Chris, and sometimes we call him Grigori. But, despite this somewhat unnerving name variability, he—in collaboration with an advisory board of experts from the industry and other internal Microsoft product groups, and a considerable number of other community contributors—is the guardian and protector of the Microsoft Enterprise Library.

Since its inception as a disparate collection of individual application blocks, the Librarian has guided, prodded, inspired, and encouraged his team to transform it into a comprehensive, powerful, easy-to-use, and proven library of code that can help to minimize design and maintenance pain, maximize development productivity, and reduce costs. And now in version 5.0, it contains even more built-in goodness that should make your job easier. It's even possible that, with the time and effort you will save, Enterprise Library can reduce your golf handicap, help you master the ski slopes, let you spend more time with your kids, or just make you a better person. However, note that the author, the publisher, and their employees cannot be held responsible if you just end up watching more TV or discovering you actually have a life.

What You Get with Enterprise Library

Enterprise Library is made up of a series of application blocks, each aimed at managing specific crosscutting concerns. In case this concept is unfamiliar, crosscutting concerns are those annoying tasks that you need to accomplish in several places in your application. When trying to manage crosscutting concerns there is often the risk that you will implement slightly different solutions for each task at each location in your application, or that you will just forget them altogether. Writing entries to a system log file or Windows® Event Log, caching data, and validating user input are typical crosscutting concerns. While there are several approaches to managing them, the Enterprise Library application blocks make it a whole lot easier by providing generic and configurable functionality that you can centralize and manage.

What are application blocks? *The definition we use is "pluggable and reusable software components designed to assist developers with common enterprise development challenges." Application blocks help address the kinds of problems developers commonly face from one line-of-business project to the next. Their design encapsulates the Microsoft recommended practices for Microsoft .NET Framework-based applications, and developers can add them to .NET-based applications and configure them quickly and easily.*

As well as the application blocks, Enterprise Library contains configuration tools, plus a set of core functions that manage tasks applicable to all of the blocks. Some of these functions—routines for handling configuration and serialization, for example—are exposed and available for you to use in your own applications.

And, on the grounds that you need to learn how to use any new tool that is more complicated than a hammer or screwdriver, Enterprise Library includes a range of sample applications, descriptions of key scenarios for each block, hands-on labs, and comprehensive reference documentation. You even get all of the source code and the unit tests that the team created when building each block (the team follows a test-driven design approach by writing tests before writing code). So you can understand how it works, see how the team followed good practices to create it, and then modify it if you want it to do something different. Figure 1 shows the big picture for Enterprise Library.

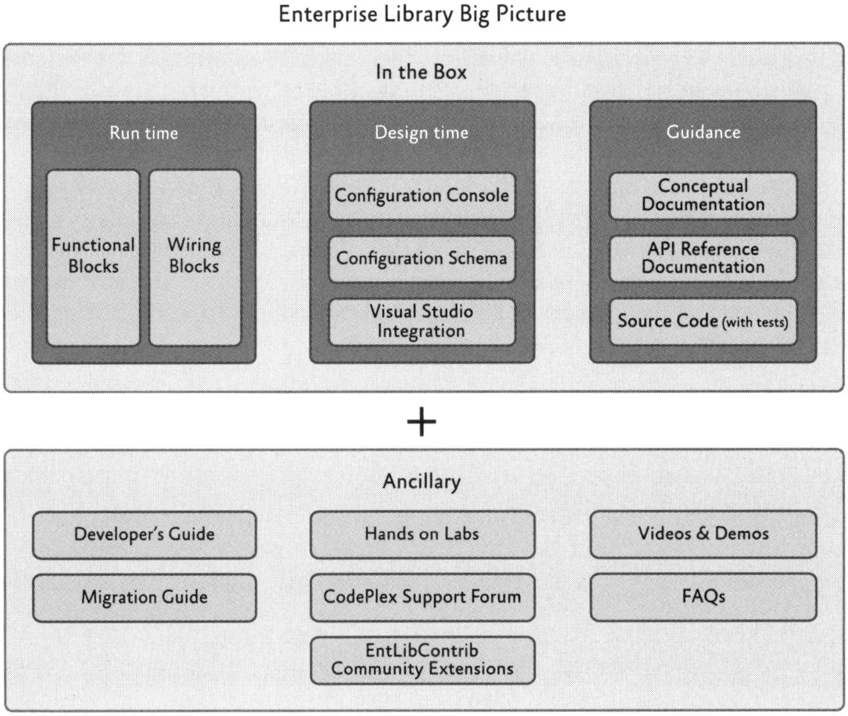

Enterprise Library Big Picture

FIGURE 1
Enterprise Library—the big picture

Things You Can Do with Enterprise Library

If you look at the installed documentation, you'll see that Enterprise Library today actually contains nine application blocks. However, there are actually only seven blocks that "do stuff"—these are referred to as *functional* blocks. The other two are concerned with "wiring up stuff" (the *wiring* blocks). What this really means is that there are seven blocks that target specific crosscutting concerns such as caching, logging, data access, and validation. The other two, the Unity Dependency Injection mechanism and the Policy Injection Application Block, are designed to help you implement more loosely coupled, testable, and maintainable systems. There's also some shared core pieces used in all the blocks. This is shown in Figure 2.

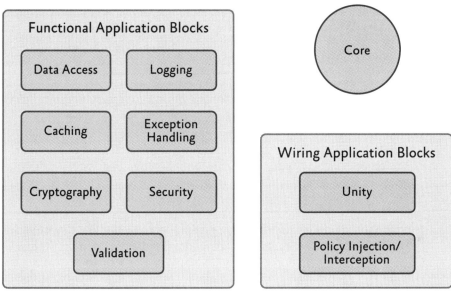

FIGURE 2
The parts of Enterprise Library

In this book we'll be concentrating on the seven functional blocks. If you want to know more about how you can use Unity and the Policy Injection Application Block, check out the appendices for this guide. They describe the capabilities of Unity as a dependency injection mechanism and the use of policy injection in more detail.

The following list describes the crosscutting scenarios you'll learn about in this book:

- **Caching**. The Caching Application Block lets you incorporate a local cache in your applications that uses an in-memory cache and, optionally, a database or isolated storage backing store. The block provides all the functionality needed to retrieve, add, and remove cached data, and supports configurable expiration and scavenging policies. You can also extend it by creating your own pluggable

providers or by using third-party providers—for example, to support distributed caching and other features. Caching can provide considerable improvements in performance and efficiency in many application scenarios.

- **Credential Management**. The Security Application Block lets you easily
implement common authorization-related functionality, such as caching the
user's authorization and authentication data and integrating with the Microsoft
.NET Framework security features.
- **Data Access**. The Data Access Application Block simplifies many common data
access tasks such as reading data for display, passing data through application
layers, and submitting changed data back to the database system. It includes
support for both stored procedures and in-line SQL, can expose the data as a
sequence of objects for client-side querying, and provides access to the most
frequently used features of ADO.NET in simple-to-use classes.
- **Encryption**. The Cryptography Application Block makes it easy to incorporate
cryptographic functionality such as encrypting and decrypting data, creating a
hash from data, and comparing hash values to verify that data has not been
altered. Using this block can help you avoid common pitfalls when developing
custom mechanisms that might introduce security vulnerabilities.
- **Exception Handling**. The Exception Handling Application Block lets you
quickly and easily design and implement a consistent strategy for managing
exceptions that occur in various architectural layers of your application. It can
log exception information, hide sensitive information by replacing the original
exception with another exception, and maintain contextual information for an
exception by wrapping the original exception inside another exception.
- **Logging**. The Logging Application Block simplifies the implementation of
common logging functions such as writing information to the Windows Event
Log, an e-mail message, a database, Windows Message Queuing, a text file, a
Windows Management Instrumentation (WMI) event, or a custom location.
- **Validation**. The Validation Application Block provides a range of features for
implementing structured and easy-to-maintain validation mechanisms using
attributes and rule sets, and integrating with most types of application interface technologies.

Why You Should Use Enterprise Library

As you can see from the previous section, Enterprise Library provides a comprehensive
set of features that can help you to manage your crosscutting concerns though a reusable
set of components and core functionality. Of course, like many developers, you may suf-
fer from the well-known NIH (not invented here) syndrome. But, seriously, isn't it about
time that every developer on your team stopped writing his or her own logging framework? It's a commonly accepted fact that the use of standard and proven code libraries
and components can save development time, minimize costs, reduce the use of precious
test resources, and decrease the overall maintenance effort. In the words of the Librarian,
"These days you cannot afford not to reuse."

You can download the Nucleus Research 2009 Report on Microsoft patterns &
practices, which reviews the key components, benefits, and includes direct feedback
from software architects and developers who have adopted patterns & practices
deliverables in their projects and products from http://msdn.microsoft.com/en-us/
practices/ee406167.aspx.

And it's not as though Enterprise Library is some new kid on the block that might
morph into something completely different next month. Enterprise Library as a concept
has been around for many years, and has passed through five full releases of the library as
well as intermediate incremental releases.

Enterprise Library continues to evolve along with the capabilities of the .NET Framework. As the .NET Framework has changed over time, some features that were part of
Enterprise Library were subsumed into the core, while Enterprise Library changed to take
advantage of the new features available in both the .NET Framework and the underlying
system. Examples include new programming language capabilities and improved performance and capabilities in the .NET configuration and I/O mechanisms. Yet, even in version
5.0, the vast majority of the code is entirely backwards compatible with applications
written to use Enterprise Library 2.0.

You can also use Enterprise Library as learning material—not only to implement design patterns in your application, but also to learn how the development team applies
patterns when writing code. Enterprise Library embodies many design patterns, and demonstrates good architectural and coding techniques. The source code for the entire library
is provided, so you can explore the implementations and reuse the techniques in your own
applications.

And, finally, it is free! Or rather, it is distributed under the Microsoft Public License
(MSPL) that grants you a royalty-free license to build derivative works, and distribute
them free—or even sell them. You must retain the attribution headers in the source files,
but you can modify the code and include your own custom extensions. Do you really need
any other reasons to try Enterprise Library?

You'll notice that, even though we didn't print "Don't Panic!" in large friendly letters
on the cover, this book does take a little time to settle down into a more typical style
of documentation, and start providing practical examples. However, you can be sure
that—from here on in—you'll find a whole range of guidance and examples that will
help you master Enterprise Library quickly and easily. There are other resources to help
if you're getting started with Enterprise Library (such as hands-on-labs), and there's
help for existing users as well (such as the breaking changes and migration information
for previous versions) available at http://www.codeplex.com/entlib/. You can also visit
the source code section of the site to see what the Enterprise Library team is working
on as you read this guide.

Some Fundamentals of Enterprise Library

Before we dive into our tour of the application blocks and features of Enterprise Library, you need to grasp some fundamentals. In this chapter, the Librarian will help you explore topics such as how to install and deploy the library, and how to perform initial configuration. After that, you'll be free to skip to any of the other chapters and learn more about the ways that each block helps you to simplify your code and manage your crosscutting concerns. For more information about the topics covered in this chapter, see the product documentation installed with Enterprise Library, or the online documentation available at http://go.microsoft.com/fwlink/?LinkId=188874.

CHOOSING WHICH BLOCKS TO INSTALL

Enterprise Library is a "pick and mix" candy store, where you choose just the features you want to use and simply disregard the rest. Of course, before you can choose your favorite candies from the tempting displays in the candy store, you need to find a paper bag to hold them. You can think of this as a prerequisite for picking and mixing, and a basic feature that you will use every time—irrespective of whether you choose gummy bears, chocolate-covered hazelnuts, or mint imperials.

Likewise, with Enterprise Library, there are prerequisites and basic features. The main prerequisite before you start development is to install the binaries and support files onto your machine. The basic features that you need every time you use Enterprise Library are the core assemblies that implement access to configuration, object creation, and ancillary features used by all of the blocks.

However, when you install Enterprise Library, you can choose which of the application blocks you want to install; though it is generally a good idea to install them all unless you are sure you will not use specific blocks. Some blocks have dependencies on other blocks, and installing all of them while developing your applications will simplify configuration and ensure that you do not have to re-run the installer to add other blocks later on. When you come to deploy your application, you only need to deploy the blocks you are using and their dependent blocks.

For example, the Exception Handling block depends on the Logging block for logging exception information. Table 1 shows the full list of these dependencies.

TABLE 1 **Application block optional dependencies**

Application Block	Optional dependencies
Caching Block	May use the Data Access block to cache data in a database.
	May use the Cryptography block to encrypt cached data.
Exception Handling Block	May use the Logging block to log exception information.
	May use the Data Access block to log exception information to a database.
Logging Block	May use the Data Access block to log to a database.
Security Block	May use the Caching block to cache credentials.
	May use the Data Access block to cache credentials in a database.
	May use the Cryptography block to encrypt cached credentials.

The configuration tools will automatically add the required block to your application configuration file with the default configuration when required. For example, when you add a Logging handler to an Exception Handling block policy, the configuration tool will add the Logging block to the configuration with the default settings.

The seven application blocks we cover in this guide are the functional blocks that are specifically designed to help you manage a range of crosscutting concerns. All of these blocks depend on the core features of Enterprise Library, which in turn depend on the Unity dependency injection and interception mechanism (the Unity Application Block) to perform object creation and additional basic functions.

INSTALLING ENTERPRISE LIBRARY

To begin using Enterprise Library you must first install it. You can download the current version from http://msdn.microsoft.com/entlib/. Simply run the Microsoft Installer (MSI) package to begin the installation, and select the blocks and features you want to install. This installs the precompiled binaries ready for you to use, along with the accompanying tools and resources such as the configuration editor and scripts to install the samples and instrumentation.

If you want to examine the source code, and perhaps even modify it to suit your own requirements, be sure to select the option to install the source code when you run the installer. The source code is included within the main installer as a separate package, which allows you to make as many working copies of the source as you want and go back to the original version easily if required. If you choose to install the source, then it's also a good idea to select the option to have the installer compile the library for you so that you are ready to start using it straight away. However, if you are happy to use the precompiled assemblies, you do not need to install or compile the source code.

After the installation is complete, you will see a Start menu entry containing links to the Enterprise Library tools, source code installer, and documentation. The tools include batch files that install instrumentation, database files, and other features. There are also batch files that you can use to compile the entire library source code, and to copy all the assemblies to the **bin** folder within the source code folders, if you want to rebuild the library from the source code.

ASSEMBLIES AND REFERENCES

It's not uncommon, when people first look at Enterprise Library, to see a look of mild alarm spread across their faces. Yes, there are quite a few assemblies, but remember:

- You only need to use those directly connected with your own scenario.
- Several are required for only very special situations.
- The runtime assemblies you will use in your applications are mostly less than 100 KB in size; and the largest of all is only around 500 KB.
- In most applications, the total size of all the assemblies you will use will be between 1 and 2 MB.

The assemblies you should add to any application that uses Enterprise Library are the common (core) assembly, the Unity dependency injection mechanism (if you are using the default Unity container), and the container service location assembly:

- Microsoft.Practices.EnterpriseLibrary.Common.dll
- Microsoft.Practices.Unity.dll
- Microsoft.Practices.Unity.Interception.dll
- Microsoft.Practices.ServiceLocation.dll

You will also need the assembly **Microsoft.Practices.Unity.Configuration.dll**
*if you wish to reference specific Unity configuration classes in your code. However,
in the majority of cases, you will not require this assembly.*

In addition to the required assemblies, you must reference the assemblies that implement the Enterprise Library features you will use in your application. There are several assemblies for each application block. Generally, these comprise a main assembly that has the same name as the block (such as **Microsoft.Practices.EnterpriseLibrary.Logging.dll**), plus additional assemblies that implement specific handlers or capabilities for the block. You only need these additional assemblies if you want to use the features they add. For example, in the case of the Logging block, there is a separate assembly for logging to a database (**Microsoft.Practices.EnterpriseLibrary.Logging.Database.dll**). If you do not log to a database, you do not need to reference this additional assembly.

GAC or Bin, Signed or Unsigned?

All of the assemblies are provided as precompiled signed versions that you can install into the global assembly cache (GAC) if you wish. However, if you need to run different versions of Enterprise Library assemblies side by side, this may be problematic and you may prefer to locate them in folders close to your application.

You can then reference the compiled assemblies in your projects, which automatically copies them to the **bin** folder. In a Web application, you can simply copy them directly to your application's **bin** folder. This approach gives you simple portability and easy installation.

Alternatively, you can install the source code for Enterprise Library and use the scripts provided to compile unsigned versions of the assemblies. This is useful if you decide to modify the source code to suit your own specific requirements. You can strong name and sign the assemblies using your own credentials afterwards if required.

For more information about side-by-side operation and other deployment issues, see the documentation installed with Enterprise Library and available online at http://go.microsoft.com/fwlink/?LinkId=188874.

Importing Namespaces

After you reference the appropriate assemblies in your projects, you will probably want to add **Imports** statements to your project files to simplify your code and avoid specifying objects using the full namespace names. Start by importing the two core namespaces that you will require in every project that uses Enterprise Library:

- Microsoft.Practices.EnterpriseLibrary.Common
- Microsoft.Practices.EnterpriseLibrary.Common.Configuration

Depending on how you decide to work with Enterprise Library in terms of instantiating the objects it contains, you may need to import two more namespaces. We'll come to this when we look at object instantiation in Enterprise Library a little later in this chapter.

You will also need to import the namespaces for the specific application blocks you are using. Most of the Enterprise Library assemblies contain several namespaces to organize the contents. For example, as you can see in Figure 3, the main assembly for the Logging block (one of the more complex blocks) contains a dozen subsidiary namespaces. If you use classes from these namespaces, such as specific filters, listeners, or formatters, you may need to import several of these namespaces.

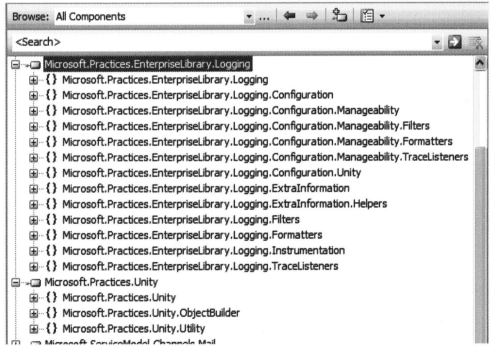

FIGURE 3
Namespaces in the Logging block

Configuring Enterprise Library

Before the original individual application blocks were combined into Enterprise Library, one of the biggest challenges for users was configuration. You had to edit the sections of the application configuration file manually, which proved to be error-prone and just plain annoying. In Enterprise Library, you have a choice of tools for performing configuration and a wealth of opportunities for defining and managing your configuration information.

This flexibility comes about because Enterprise Library uses configuration sources to expose configuration information to the application blocks and the core features of the library. The configuration sources can read configuration from standard .NET configuration files (such as App.config and Web.config), from other files, from a database (using the example SQL Configuration Source available from http://entlib.codeplex.com), and can also take into account Group Policy rules for a machine or a domain.

In addition, you can use the fluent interface or the .NET configuration API to create and populate configuration sources programmatically, merge parts of your configuration with a central shared configuration, generate merged configuration files, and generate different configurations for individual run-time environments. For more information about these more advanced configuration scenarios, see Appendix D, "Enterprise Library Configuration Scenarios."

THE CONFIGURATION TOOLS

Enterprise Library includes a stand-alone configuration console, and a configuration editor that integrates with Microsoft Visual Studio®. The stand-alone console is provided as versions specifically aimed at the 32-bit (x86) platform and versions compiled for any platform. For each of these platforms, there is a separate version of the console for the 3.5 and 4.0 versions of the .NET Framework. You can even copy it (and the assemblies it uses) to a machine that does not have Enterprise Library installed if you just want to perform post-deployment configuration and system administration. Figure 4 shows the configuration console with some of the application blocks covered in this book installed into the configuration.

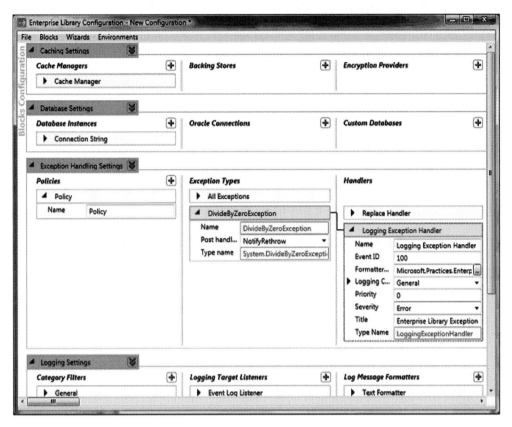

FIGURE 4
The Enterprise Library configuration console

The Visual Studio configuration editor displays an interface very similar to that shown in Figure 4, but allows you to edit your configuration files with a simple right-click in Solution Explorer.

USING THE CONFIGURATION TOOLS

The most common scenario for basic configuration of an application is to store the configuration information in a local configuration file (such as Web.config or App.config). You can create a new Enterprise Library configuration in the configuration console and then save it to disk, or you can open an existing configuration file and edit it to add Enterprise Library to your application.

Even if you use the more advanced approaches described in Appendix D, "Enterprise Library Configuration Scenarios," the techniques for defining your Enterprise Library configuration are basically the same. The general procedure for configuring an application is as follows:

1. Open the stand-alone configuration tool from your **Start** menu, or right-click on a configuration file in Visual Studio Solution Explorer and click **Edit Enterprise Library V5 Configuration**.

2. Click the **Blocks** menu and select the block you want to add to the configuration. This adds the block with the default settings.
   - If you want to use the configuration console to edit values in the **<appSettings>** section of your configuration file, select **Add Application Settings**.
   - If you want to enable instrumentation for Enterprise Library, select **Add Instrumentation Settings**.
   - If you want to use an alternative source for your configuration, such as a custom XML file, select **Add Configuration Settings**.

3. To view the configuration settings for each section, block, or provider, click the right-facing arrow next to the name of that section, block, or provider. Click it again, or press the Spacebar key, to collapse this section.

4. To view the properties pane for each main configuration section, click the downward-facing double arrow. Click it again to close the properties pane.

5. To add a provider to a block, depending on the block or the type of provider, you either right-click the section in the left column and select the appropriate **Add** item on the shortcut menu, or click the plus-sign icon in the appropriate column of the configuration tool. For example, to add a new exception type to a policy in the Exception Handling block, right-click the **Policy** item and click **Add Exception Type**.

*When you rename items, the heading of that item changes to match the name. For example, if you renamed the default **Policy** item in the Exception Handling block, the item will show the new name instead of "Policy."*

6. Edit the properties of the section, block, or provider using the controls in that section for that block. You will see information about the settings required, and what they do, in the subsequent chapters of this guide. For full details of all of the settings that you can specify, see the documentation installed with Enterprise Library for that block.

7. To delete a section or provider, right-click the section or provider and click **Delete** on the shortcut menu. To change the order of providers when more than one is configured for a block, right-click the section or provider and click the **Move Up** or **Move Down** command on the shortcut menu.

8. To set the default provider for a block, such as the default **Database** for the Data Access block, click the down-pointing double arrow icon next to the block name and select the default provider name from the drop-down list. In this section you can also specify the type of provider used to encrypt this section, and whether the block should demand full permissions.

For more details about encrypting configuration, see the next section of this chapter. For information about running the block in partial trust environments, which requires you to turn off the **Require Permission** *setting, see the documentation installed with Enterprise Library.*

9. To use a wizard to simplify configuration for a common task, such as configuring logging to a database, open the **Wizards** menu and select the one you require. The wizard will display a series of dialogs that guide you through setting the required configuration.

10. If you want to configure different settings for an application based on different deployment scenarios or environments, open the **Environments** menu and click **New Environment**. This adds a drop-down list, **Overrides on Environment,** to each section. If you select **Override Properties** in this list, you can specify the settings for each new environment that you add to the configuration. This feature is useful if you have multiple environments that share the same basic configuration but require different property settings. It allows you to create a base configuration file (.config) and an environment delta file that contains the differences (.dconfig). See Appendix D, "Enterprise Library Configuration Scenarios" for information on configuring and using multiple environments.

11. As you edit the configuration, the lower section of the tool displays any warnings or errors in your configuration. You must resolve all errors before you can save the configuration.

12. When you have finished configuring your application, use the commands on the **File** menu to save it as a file in your application folder with the appropriate name; for example, use Web.config for a Web application and App.config for a Windows Forms application.

You can, of course, edit the configuration files using a text or XML editor, but this is likely to be a more tedious process compared to using the configuration console. However, it may be a useful approach for minor changes to the configuration when the application is running on a server where the configuration console is not installed. Enterprise Library also contains an XML configuration schema that you can use to enable IntelliSense® and simplify hand editing of the configuration files.

To enable the Enterprise Library XML schema in Visual Studio, open the configuration file, open the **XML** *menu, and click* **Schemas**. *In the XML Schemas dialog, locate the Enterprise Library schema and change the value in the* **Use** *column to* **Use this schema**. *Then click* **OK**.

ENCRYPTING CONFIGURATION SECTIONS

Probably the most common approach for storing configuration information for your applications that use Enterprise Library is to use an App.config or Web.config file stored in the root folder of your application. That's fine, but you may be concerned that anyone who happens to stroll past the server (either physically, or virtually over the Internet) will be able to open the file and see sensitive details. These might include connection strings for the Data Access block, validation rules for the Validation block, or connection information used by the Logging block to communicate with Windows Message Queuing.

While in theory, you will protect your configuration files by physically securing the server and not leaving it running under a logged-on administrator account, you can (and probably should) add an extra layer of protection by encrypting sections of your configuration files. The configuration tools can do this for you automatically; all you need to do is set the **ProtectionProvider** property of the specific block or configuration section that you want to encrypt. For more information, see Appendix E, "Encrypting Configuration Files."

Instantiating and Using Enterprise Library Objects

After you have referenced the assemblies you need, imported the required namespaces, and configured your application, you can start to think about creating instances of the Enterprise Library objects you want to use in your applications. As you will see in each of the following chapters, the Enterprise Library application blocks are optimized for use as loosely coupled components in almost any type of application. In addition, the change in this release to using a dependency injection container to generate instances of Enterprise Library objects means that you can realize the benefits of contemporary design patterns and solution architectures more easily.

> *By default, Enterprise Library uses the Unity dependency injection mechanism, which is provided as part of Enterprise Library. However, it's possible to configure Enterprise Library to use any dependency injection container—or other underlying mechanism— that exposes the required configuration information though an implementation of the* **IServiceLocator** *interface. See Appendix B, "Dependency Injection in Enterprise Library," and http://commonservicelocator.codeplex.com for more information.*

In Appendix A, "Dependency Injection with Unity," we take a more in-depth look at what a dependency injection container actually is, and how it can assist you in applying design patterns that follow the dependency inversion principle (DIP); in particular, how the Dependency Injection (DI) pattern can help you to create more decoupled applications that are easier to build, test, and maintain. However, you don't need to understand this or learn about DI to be able to use Enterprise Library. You can create instances of Enterprise Library objects easily and quickly with a single line of code.

ENTERPRISE LIBRARY OBJECTS, FACADES, AND FACTORIES

Each of the application blocks in Enterprise Library contains one or more core objects that you typically use to access the functionality of that block. An example is the Exception Handling Application Block, which provides a facade named **Exception Manager** that exposes the methods you use to pass exceptions to the block for handling. The following table lists the commonly used objects for each block.

Application Block	Non-static Instance or Factory
Caching	ICacheManager
Cryptography	CryptographyManager
Data Access	Database
Exception Handling	ExceptionManager
Logging	LogWriter TraceManager
Security	ISecurityCacheProvider IAuthorizationProvider
Validation	ValidatorFactory ConfigurationValidatorFactory AttributeValidatorFactory ValidationAttributeValidatorFactory

There are also task-specific objects in some blocks that you can create directly in your code in the traditional way using the operator. For example, you can create individual validators from the Validation Application Block, or log entries from the Logging Application Block. We show how to do this in the examples for each application block chapter.

To use the features of an application block, all you need to do is create an instance of the appropriate object, facade, or factory listed in the table above and then call its methods. The behavior of the block is controlled by the configuration you specified, and often you can carry out tasks such as exception handling, logging, caching, and encrypting values with just a single line of code. Even tasks such as accessing data or validating instances of your custom types require only a few lines of simple code. So, let's look at how you create instances of the Enterprise Library objects you want to use.

CREATING INSTANCES OF ENTERPRISE LIBRARY TYPES

In this release of Enterprise Library, there are two recommended approaches to creating instances of the Enterprise Library objects. The decision as to which you use is based solely on the way you decide to architect your application. You can use the simple approach of obtaining instances using the Enterprise Library service locator, which provides access to the Unity container that holds the Enterprise Library configuration information. Alternatively, if you are already a DI convert, you can take charge of the entire process by creating and populating a container and using it to create and manage both Enterprise Library objects and your own custom types. We'll look at both approaches next.

The Simple Approach — Using the Enterprise Library Service Locator

When you initially create an instance of an Enterprise Library type in your application code, the underlying mechanism reads your configuration information into a container and exposes it to your code through a service locator that is initialized as part of the Enterprise Library configuration mechanism. This service locator provides methods that you can call at any point in your application code to obtain configured instances of any Enterprise Library type.

For example, if you are using the Logging Application Block, you can obtain a reference to a **LogWriter** using a single line of code, and then call its **Write** method to write your log entry to the configured targets, as shown here.

```
Dim writer = EnterpriseLibraryContainer.Current.GetInstance(Of LogWriter)()
writer.Write("I'm a log entry created by the Logging block!")
```

> *Notice that this code uses type inference by omitting the variable type name keyword. The variable will assume the type returned by the assignment; this technique can make your code more maintainable.*

If you configured more than one instance of a type for a block, such as more than one Database for the Data Access Application Block, you can specify the name when you call the **GetInstance** method. For example, you may configure an Enterprise Library **Database** instance named Customers that specifies a Microsoft SQL Server® database, and a separate **Database** instance named Products that specifies another type of database. In this case, you specify the name of the object you want to resolve when you call the **Get Instance** method, as shown here.

```
Dim customerDb _
    = EnterpriseLibraryContainer.Current.GetInstance(Of Database)("Customers")
```

You don't have to initialize the block, read configuration information, or do anything other than call the methods of the service locator. For many application scenarios, this simple approach is ideal for obtaining instances of the Enterprise Library types you want to use.

The Sophisticated Approach — Accessing the Container Directly

If you want to take advantage of design patterns such as Dependency Injection and Inversion of Control in your application, you will probably already be considering the use of a dependency injection mechanism to decouple your components and layers, and to resolve types. If this is the case, the more sophisticated approach to incorporating Enterprise Library into your applications will fit well with your solution architecture.

Instead of allowing Enterprise Library to create, populate, and expose a default container that holds just Enterprise Library configuration information, you can create the container and populate it yourself—and hold onto a reference to the container for use in your application code. This not only allows you to obtain instances of Enterprise Library objects, it also lets you use the container to implement dependency injection for your own custom types. Effectively, the container itself becomes your service locator.

For example, you can create registrations and mappings in the container that specify features such as the dependencies between the components of your application, mappings between types, the values of parameters and properties, interception for methods, and deferred object creation.

You may be thinking that all of these wondrous capabilities will require a great deal of code and effort to achieve; however, they don't. To initialize and populate the default Unity container with the Enterprise Library configuration information and make it available to your application, only a single line of code is required. It is shown here:

```
Dim theContainer = New UnityContainer() _
            .AddNewExtension(Of EnterpriseLibraryCoreExtension)()
```

Now that you have a reference to the container, you can obtain an instance of any Enterprise Library type by calling the container methods directly. For example, if you are using the Logging Application Block, you can obtain a reference to a **LogWriter** using a single line of code, and then call its **Write** method to write your log entry to the configured targets.

```
Dim writer = theContainer.Resolve(Of LogWriter)()
writer.Write("I'm a log entry created by the Logging block!")
```

And if you configured more than one instance of a type for a block, such as more than one database for the Data Access Application Block, you can specify the name when you call the **Resolve** method, as shown here:

```
Dim customerDb = theContainer.Resolve(Of Database)("Customers")
```

*You may have noticed the similarity in syntax between the **Resolve** method and the **GetInstance** method we used earlier. Effectively, when you are using the default Unity container, the **GetInstance** method of the service locator simply calls the **Resolve** method of the Unity container. It therefore makes sense that the syntax and parameters are similar. Both the container and the service locator expose other methods that allow you to get collections of objects, and there are both generic and non-generic overloads that allow you to use the methods in languages that do not support generics.*

One point to note if you choose this more sophisticated approach to using Enterprise Library in your applications is that you should import two additional namespaces into your code. These namespaces include the container and core extension definitions:

- Microsoft.Practices.EnterpriseLibrary.Common.Configuration.Unity
- Microsoft.Practices.Unity

Pros and Cons of Object Instantiation

If you haven't already decided which approach to follow for creating Enterprise Library objects, the following table will help you to understand the advantages and disadvantages of each one.

Object instantiation technique	Advantages	Considerations
Using the Enterprise Library service locator	Requires no initialization code. The service locator is made available automatically. You can resolve types anywhere in your application code. You don't need to hold onto a reference to the container.	You can only resolve Enterprise Library types (as interfaces, abstract types, or concrete types that are registered automatically). You cannot manipulate, or add registrations or mappings to the container.
Using the container as the service locator	You can directly access all the functionality of the Unity container. You can iterate over the contents and read or manipulate the registrations and mappings (though you should not attempt to change the Enterprise Library configuration information). You can add and remove your own registrations and mappings, allowing you to take full advantage of DI techniques.	Requires initialization, though this is simply one line of code executed at application startup, or simple configuration settings, when you use the default Unity container. Request-based applications such as ASP.NET and Web services require additional code to store the container reference and resolve the dependencies of the request class (such as the Page).

One of the prime advantages of the more sophisticated approach of accessing the container directly is that you can use it to resolve dependencies of your own custom types. For example, assume you have a class named **TaxCalculator** that needs to perform logging and implement a consistent policy for handling exceptions that you apply across your entire application. Your class will contain a constructor that accepts an instance of an **ExceptionManager** and a **LogWriter** as dependencies.

```
Public Class TaxCalculator

  Private _exceptionManager As ExceptionManager
  Private _logWriter As LogWriter

  Public Sub New(em As ExceptionManager, lw As LogWriter)
    Me._exceptionManager = em
    Me._logWriter = lw
  End Sub
  ...
End Class
```

If you use the **Enterprise Library service locator** approach, you could simply obtain these instances within the class constructor or methods when required, rather than passing them in as parameters. However, a more commonly used approach is to generate and reuse the instances in your main application code, and pass them to the **TaxCalculator** when you create an instance.

```
Dim exManager _
  = EnterpriseLibraryContainer.Current.GetInstance(Of ExceptionManager)()
Dim writer _
  = EnterpriseLibraryContainer.Current.GetInstance(Of LogWriter)()
Dim calc As New TaxCalculator(exManager, writer)
```

Alternatively, if you have **created and held a reference to the container**, you just need to resolve the **TaxCalculator** type through the container. Unity will instantiate the type, examine the constructor parameters, and automatically inject instances of the **Exception Manager** and a **LogWriter** into them. It returns your new **TaxCalculator** instance with all of the dependencies populated.

```
Dim calc As TaxCalculator = theContainer.Resolve(Of TaxCalculator)()
```

More Reasons to be Sophisticated

It is clear from the preceding examples that managing the container yourself offers considerable advantages in all but the simplest applications or scenarios. And the example you've seen for using dependency injection only scratches the surface of what you can do using the more sophisticated approach. For example, if you have a reference to the container, you can:

- Manage the lifetime of your custom types. They can be resolved by the container as singletons, with a lifetime based on the lifetime of the object that created them, or as a new instance per execution thread.
- Implement patterns such as plug-in and service locator by mapping interfaces and abstract types to concrete implementations of your custom types.
- Defer creation of the resolved custom type until it is actually required.
- Specify dependencies and values for parameters and properties of the resolved instances of your custom types.
- Apply interception to your custom types to modify their behavior, implement management of crosscutting concerns, or add additional functionality.
- Set up hierarchies of dependencies that are automatically populated to achieve maximum decoupling between components, assist in debugging, simplify testing, and reduce maintenance cost and effort.

When you use the default Unity container, you have a powerful general-purpose dependency injection mechanism in your arsenal. You can define and modify registrations and mappings in the container programmatically at run time, or you can define them using configuration files. Appendix A, "Dependency Injection with Unity," contains more information about using Unity.

To give you a sense of how easy it is to use, the following code registers a mapping between an interface named **IMyService** and a concrete type named **CustomerService**, specifying that it should be a singleton.

```
theContainer.RegisterType(Of IMyService, CustomerService)( _
                    New ContainerControlledLifetimeManager())
```

Then you can resolve the single instance of the concrete type using the following code.

```
Dim myServiceInstance As IMyService = theContainer.Resolve(Of IMyService)()
```

This returns an instance of the **CustomerService** type, though you can change the actual type returned at run time by changing the mapping in the container. Alternatively, you can create multiple registrations or mappings for an interface or base class with different names and specify the name when you resolve the type.

Unity can also read its configuration from your application's App.config or Web.config file (or any other configuration file). This means that you can use the sophisticated approach to creating Enterprise Library objects and your own custom types, while being able to change the behavior of your application just by editing the configuration file.

If you want to load type registrations and mappings into a Unity container from a configuration file, you must add the assembly Microsoft.Practices.Unity.Configuration. dll to your project, and optionally import the namespace Microsoft.Practices.Unity. Configuration into your code. This assembly and namespace contains the extension to the Unity container for loading configuration information.

For example, the following extract from a configuration file initializes the container and adds the same custom mapping to it as the **RegisterType** example shown above.

```
<unity>
  <alias alias="CoreExtension"
        type="Microsoft.Practices.EnterpriseLibrary.Common.Configuration
            .Unity.EnterpriseLibraryCoreExtension,
            Microsoft.Practices.EnterpriseLibrary.Common" />
  <namespace name="Your.Custom.Types.Namespace" />
  <assembly name="Your.Custom.Types.Assembly.Name" />
  <container>
    <extension type="CoreExtension" />
    <register type="IMyService" mapTo="CustomerService">
      <lifetime type="singleton" />
    </register>
  </container>
</unity>
```

Then, all you need to do is load this configuration into a new Unity container. This requires just one line of code, as shown here.

```
Dim theContainer = New UnityContainer().LoadConfiguration()
```

> *Other techniques we demonstrate in Appendix A, "Dependency Injection with Unity," include using attributes to register type mappings and dependencies, defining named registrations, and specifying dependencies and values for parameters and properties.*

The one point to be aware of when you use the more sophisticated technique for creating objects is that your application is responsible for managing the container, holding a reference to it, and making that reference available to code that must access the container. In forms-based applications that automatically maintain global state (for example, applications built using technologies such as Windows Forms, Windows Presentation Foundation (WPF), and Silverlight®), you can use an application-wide variable for this.

However, in request-based applications built using technologies such as ASP.NET, ASMX, and Windows Communication Foundation (WCF), you generally require additional code to maintain the container and make it available for each request. We discuss some of the ways that you can achieve this in Appendix B, "Dependency Injection in Enterprise Library," and you will find full details in the documentation installed with Enterprise Library and available online at http://go.microsoft.com/fwlink/?LinkId=188874.

GETTING OBJECTS FROM PREVIOUS VERSIONS OF ENTERPRISE LIBRARY

If you have used versions of Enterprise Library prior to version 5.0, you may be more familiar with the previous approach to creating objects within your application code. Earlier versions generally supported or recommended the use of a series of static facades. While these facades are still supported in version 5.0 for backward compatibility with existing applications, they are no longer the recommended approach and may be deprecated in future releases.

Figure 5 summarizes all the approaches you can use to get access to the features of Enterprise Library. 1 and 2 are the recommended approaches for Enterprise Library 5.0; 3 and 4 are still supported to make it easier to upgrade your existing applications that use a previous version of Enterprise Library.

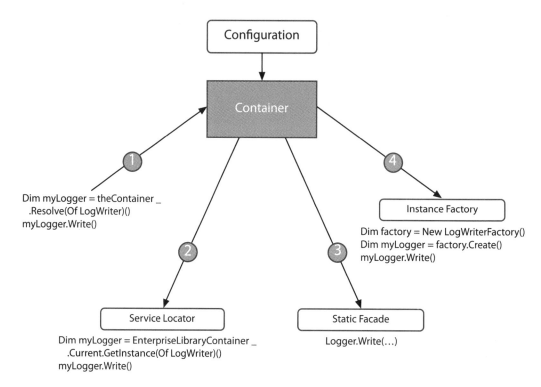

FIGURE 5
Four ways, one library

The Example Applications

To help you understand how you can use Enterprise Library and each of the seven application blocks covered in this guide, we provide a series of simple example applications that you can run and examine. Each is a console-based application and, in most cases, all of the relevant code that uses Enterprise Library is found within a series of routines in the Program.vb file. This makes it easy to see how the different blocks work, and what you can achieve with each one.

The examples use the simplest approach (the service locator and **GetInstance** method described earlier in the chapter) for creating the Enterprise Library objects they require, and have the configuration information for the blocks they use stored in the App.config file. Each of the options in the examples exercises specific features of the relevant block and displays the results. You can open the solutions for these examples in Visual Studio, or just run the executable file in the bin\debug folder and view the source files in a text editor if you prefer.

To obtain the example applications, go to
http://go.microsoft.com/fwlink/?LinkId=189009.

Summary

This brief introduction to Enterprise Library will help you to get started if you are not familiar with its capabilities and the basics of using it in applications. This chapter described what Enterprise Library is, where you can get it, and how it can make it much easier to manage your crosscutting concerns. This book concentrates on the application blocks in Enterprise Library that "do stuff" (as opposed to those that "wire up stuff"). The blocks we concentrate on in this book include the Caching, Cryptography, Data Access, Exception Handling, Logging, Security, and Validation Application Blocks.

The aim of this chapter was also to help you get started with Enterprise Library by explaining how you deploy and reference the assemblies it contains, how you configure your applications to use Enterprise Library, how you instantiate Enterprise Library objects, and the example applications we provide. Some of the more advanced features and configuration options were omitted so that you may concentrate on the fundamental requirements. However, each appendix in this guide provides more detailed information, while Enterprise Library contains substantial reference documentation, samples, and other resources that will guide you as you explore these more advanced features.

2 Much ADO about Data Access

Introduction

When did you last write an enterprise-level application where you didn't need to handle data? And when you were handling data there was a good chance it came from some kind of relational database. Working with databases is the single most common task most enterprise applications need to accomplish, so it's no surprise that the Data Access Application Block is the most widely used of all of the Enterprise Library blocks—and no coincidence that we decided to cover it in the first of the application block chapters in this book.

A great many of the millions of Enterprise Library users around the world first cut their teeth on the Data Access block. Why? Because it makes it easy to implement the most commonly used data access operations without needing to write the same repetitive code over and over again, and without having to worry about which database the application will target. As long as there is a Data Access block provider available for your target database, you can use the same code to access the data. You don't need to worry about the syntax for parameters, the idiosyncrasies of the individual data access methods, or the different data types that are returned.

This means that it's also easy to switch your application to use a different database, without having to rewrite code, recompile, and redeploy. Administrators and operators can change the target database to a different server; and even to a different database (such as moving from Oracle to Microsoft® SQL Server® or the reverse), without affecting the application code. In the current release, the Data Access Application Block contains providers for SQL Server, SQL Server Compact Edition, and Oracle databases. There are also third-party providers available for the IBM DB2, MySql, Oracle (ODP.NET), PostgreSQL, and SQLite databases. For more information on these, see http://codeplex.com/entlibcontrib.

What Does the Data Access Application Block Do?

The Data Access Application Block abstracts the actual database you are using, and exposes a series of methods that make it easy to access that database to perform common tasks. It is designed to simplify the task of calling stored procedures, but also provides full support for the use of parameterized SQL statements. As an example of how easy the block is to use, when you want to fill a **DataSet** you simply create an instance of the appropriate **Database** class, use it to get an appropriate command instance (such as **DbCommand**), and pass this to the **ExecuteDataSet** method of the **Database** class. You don't need to create a **DataAdapter** or call the **Fill** method. The **ExecuteDataSet** method manages the connection, and carries out all the tasks required to populate your **DataSet**. In a similar way, the **Database** class allows you to obtain a **DataReader**, execute commands directly, and update the database from a **DataSet**. The block also supports transactions to help you manage multiple operations that can be rolled back if an error occurs.

In addition to the more common approaches familiar to users of ADO.NET, the Data Access block also provides techniques for asynchronous data access for databases that support this feature, and provides the ability to return data as a sequence of objects suitable for client-side querying using techniques such as Language Integrated Query (LINQ). However, the block is *not* intended to be an Object/Relational Mapping (O/RM) solution. It uses mappings to relate parameters and relational data with the properties of objects, but does not implement an O/RM modeling solution.

The major advantage of using the Data Access block, besides the simplicity achieved through the encapsulation of the boilerplate code that you would otherwise need to write, is that it provides a way to create provider-independent applications that can easily be moved to use a different source database type. In most cases, unless your code takes advantage of methods specific to a particular database, the only change required is to update the contents of your configuration file with the appropriate connection string. You don't have to change the way you specify queries (such as SQL statements or stored procedure names), create and populate parameters, or handle return values. This also means reduced requirements for testing, and the configuration changes can even be accomplished through Group Policy.

DATA OPERATIONS SUPPORTED BY THE DATA ACCESS BLOCK

The following table lists by task the most commonly used methods that the Data Access Application Block exposes to retrieve and update data. Some of the method names will be familiar to those used to using ADO.NET directly.

Task	Methods
Filling a DataSet and updating the database from a DataSet.	**ExecuteDataSet**. Creates, populates, and returns a DataSet. **LoadDataSet**. Populates an existing DataSet. **UpdateDataSet**. Updates the database using an existing DataSet.
Reading multiple data rows.	**ExecuteReader**. Creates and returns a provider-independent DbDataReader instance.
Executing a Command.	**ExecuteNonQuery**. Executes the command and returns the number of rows affected. Other return values (if any) appear as output parameters. **ExecuteScalar**. Executes the command and returns a single value.
Retrieving data as a sequence of objects.	**ExecuteSprocAccessor**. Returns data selected by a stored procedure as a sequence of objects for client-side querying. **ExecuteSqlStringAccessor**. Returns data selected by a SQL statement as a sequence of objects for client-side querying.
Retrieving XML data (SQL Server only).	**ExecuteXmlReader**. Returns data as a series of XML elements exposed through an XmlReader. Note that this method is specific to the SqlDatabase class (not the underlying Database class).
Creating a Command.	**GetStoredProcCommand**. Returns a command object suitable for executing a stored procedure. **GetSqlStringCommand**. Returns a command object suitable for executing a SQL statement (which may contain parameters).
Working with Command parameters.	**AddInParameter**. Creates a new input parameter and adds it to the parameter collection of a Command. **AddOutParameter**. Creates a new output parameter and adds it to the parameter collection of a command. **AddParameter**. Creates a new parameter of the specific type and direction and adds it to the parameter collection of a command. **GetParameterValue**. Returns the value of the specified parameter as an Object type. **SetParameterValue**. Sets the value of the specified parameter.
Working with transactions.	**CreateConnection**. Creates and returns a connection for the current database that allows you to initiate and manage a transaction over the connection.

You can see from this table that the Data Access block supports almost all of the common scenarios that you will encounter when working with relational databases. Each data access method also has multiple overloads, designed to simplify usage and integrate—when necessary—with existing data transactions. In general, you should choose the overload you use based on the following guidelines:

- Overloads that accept an ADO.NET **DbCommand** object provide the most flexibility and control for each method.
- Overloads that accept a stored procedure name and a collection of values to be used as parameter values for the stored procedure are convenient when your application calls stored procedures that require parameters.

- Overloads that accept a **CommandType** value and a string that represents the command are convenient when your application executes inline SQL statements, or stored procedures that require no parameters.
- Overloads that accept a transaction allow you to execute the method within an existing transaction.
- If you use the **SqlDatabase** type, you can execute several of the common methods asynchronously by using the **Begin** and **End** versions of the methods.
- You can use the **Database** class to create **Accessor** instances that execute data access operations both synchronously and asynchronously, and return the results as a series of objects suitable for client-side querying using technologies such as LINQ.

How Do I Use the Data Access Block?

Before you start to use the Data Access block, you must add it to your application. You configure the block to specify the databases you want to work with, and add the relevant assemblies to your project. Then you can create instances of these databases in your code and use them to read and write data.

CONFIGURING THE BLOCK AND REFERENCING THE REQUIRED ASSEMBLIES

The first step in using the Data Access block is to configure the databases you want to access. The block makes use of the standard **<connectionStrings>** section of the App. config, Web.config, or other configuration file to store the individual database connection strings, with the addition of a small Enterprise Library-specific section that defines which of the configured databases is the default. You can configure all of these settings using the Enterprise Library configuration console, as shown in Figure 1.

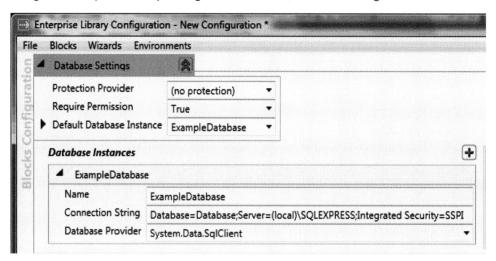

FIGURE 1
Creating a new configuration for the Data Access Application Block

After you configure the databases you need, you must instantiate them in your application code. Add references to the assemblies you will require, and add **Imports** statements to your code for the namespaces containing the objects you will use. In addition to the Enterprise Library assemblies you require in every Enterprise Library project (listed in Chapter 1, "Introduction"), you must reference or add to your bin folder the assembly **Microsoft.Practices.EnterpriseLibrary.Data.dll**. This assembly includes the classes for working with SQL Server databases.

If you are working with a SQL Server Compact Edition database, you must also reference or add the assembly **Microsoft.Practices.EnterpriseLibrary.Data.SqlCe.dll**. If you are working with an Oracle database, you can use the Oracle provider included with Enterprise Library and the ADO.NET Oracle provider, which requires you to reference or add the assembly **System.Data.OracleClient.dll**. However, keep in mind that the **OracleClient** provider is deprecated in version 4.0 of the .NET Framework, although it is still supported by Enterprise Library. For future development, consider choosing a different Oracle driver, such as that available from the Enterprise Library Contrib site at http://codeplex.com/entlibcontrib.

To make it easier to use the objects in the Data Access block, you can add references to the relevant namespaces, such as Microsoft.Practices.EnterpriseLibrary.Data and Microsoft.Practices.EnterpriseLibrary.Data.Sql to your project.

CREATING DATABASE INSTANCES

You can use a variety of techniques to obtain a **Database** instance for the database you want to access. The section "Instantiating Enterprise Library Objects" in Chapter 1, "Introduction" describes the different approaches you can use. The examples you can download for this chapter use the simplest approach: calling the **GetInstance** method of the service locator available from the **Current** property of the **EnterpriseLibraryContainer**, as shown here, and storing these instances in application-wide variables so that they can be accessed from anywhere in the code.

```
' Resolve the default Database object from the container.
' The actual concrete type is determined by the configuration settings.
Dim defaultDB As Database _
   = EnterpriseLibraryContainer.Current.GetInstance(Of Database)()

' Resolve a Database object from the container using the connection string name.
Dim namedDB As Database _
   = EnterpriseLibraryContainer.Current.GetInstance(Of Database)("ExampleDatabase")
```

The code above shows how you can get an instance of the default database and a named instance (using the name in the connection strings section). Using the default database is a useful approach because you can change which of the databases defined in your configuration is the default simply by editing the configuration file, without requiring recompilation or redeployment of the application.

Notice that the code above references the database instances as instances of the **Database** base class. This is required for compatibility if you want to be able to change the database type at some later stage. However, it means that you can only use the features available across all of the possible database types (the methods and properties defined in the **Database** class).

Some features are only available in the concrete types for a specific database. For example, the **ExecuteXmlReader** method is only available in the **SqlDatabase** class. If you want to use such features, you must cast the database type you instantiate to the appropriate concrete type. The following code creates an instance of the **SqlDatabase** class.

```
' Resolve a SqlDatabase object from the container using the default database.
Dim sqlServerDB As Database _
    = TryCast(EnterpriseLibraryContainer.Current.GetInstance(Of Database)(), _
            SqlDatabase)
```

In addition to using configuration to define the databases you will use, the Data Access block allows you to create instances of concrete types that inherit from the **Database** class directly in your code, as shown here. All you need to do is provide a connection string that specifies the appropriate ADO.NET data provider type (such as **SqlClient**).

```
' Assume the method GetConnectionString exists in your application and
' returns a valid connection string.
Dim myConnectionString As String = GetConnectionString()
Dim db As SqlDatabase = New SqlDatabase(myConnectionString)
```

THE EXAMPLE APPLICATION

Now that you have your new **Database** object ready to go, we'll show you how you can use it to perform a variety of tasks. You can download an example application (a simple console-based application) that demonstrates all of the scenarios you will see in the remainder of this chapter. You can run this directly from the bin\debug folder, or open the solution named **DataAccess** in Microsoft Visual Studio® to see all of the code as you run the examples.

The two connection strings for the database we provide with this example are:

```
Data Source=.\SQLEXPRESS;
AttachDbFilename=|DataDirectory|\DataAccessExamples.mdf;
Integrated Security=True;User Instance=True
Data Source=.\SQLEXPRESS;Asynchronous Processing=true;AttachDbFilename=
|DataDirectory|\DataAccessExamples.mdf;
Integrated Security=True;User Instance=True
```

*If you have configured a different database using the scripts provided with the example, you may find that you get an error when you run this example. It is likely that you have an invalid connection string in your App.config file for your database. In addition, use the Services MMC snap-in in your Administrative Tools folder to check that the SQL Server (SQLEXPRESS) database service (the service is named **MSSQL$SQLEXPRESS**) is running.*

In addition, the final example for this block uses the Distributed Transaction Coordinator (DTC) service. This service may not be set to auto-start on your machine. If you receive an error that the DTC service is not available, open the Services MMC snap-in from your Administrative Tools menu and start the service manually; then run the example again.

READING MULTIPLE DATA ROWS

One of the most common operations when working with a database is reading multiple rows of data. In a .NET application, you usually access these rows as a **DataReader** instance, or store them in a **DataTable** (usually within a **DataSet** you create). In this section we'll look at the use of the **ExecuteReader** method that returns a **DataReader**. You will see how to use a **DataSet** with the Data Access block methods later in this chapter.

Reading Rows Using a Query with No Parameters

Simple queries consisting of an inline SQL statement or a stored procedure, which take no parameters, can be executed using the **ExecuteReader** method overload that accepts a **CommandType** value and a SQL statement or stored procedure name as a string.

The following code shows the simplest approach for a stored procedure, where you can also omit the **CommandType** parameter. The default is **CommandType.Stored Procedure** (unlike ADO.NET, where the default is **CommandType.Text**).

```
' Call the ExecuteReader method by specifying just the stored procedure name.
Using reader As IDataReader = namedDB.ExecuteReader("MyStoredProcName")
  ' Use the values in the rows as required.
End Using
```

To use an inline SQL statement, you must specify the appropriate **CommandType** value, as shown here.

```
' Call the ExecuteReader method by specifying the command type
' as a SQL statement, and passing in the SQL statement
Using reader As IDataReader = namedDB.ExecuteReader(CommandType.Text, _
                        "SELECT TOP 1 * FROM OrderList")
  ' Use the values in the rows as required - here we are just displaying them.
  DisplayRowValues(reader)
End Using
```

The example named *Return rows using a SQL statement with no parameters* uses this code to retrieve a **DataReader** containing the first order in the sample database, and then displays the values in this single row. It uses a simple auxiliary routine that iterates through all the rows and columns, writing the values to the console screen.

```
Sub DisplayRowValues(ByVal reader As IDataReader)
  While reader.Read()
    Dim i As Integer = 0
    While i < reader.FieldCount
      Console.WriteLine("{0} = {1}", reader.GetName(i), reader(i).ToString())
      System.Math.Max(System.Threading.Interlocked.Increment(i), i - 1)
    End While
    Console.WriteLine()
  End While
End Sub
```

The result is a list of the columns and their values in the **DataReader**, as shown here.

```
Id = 1
Status = DRAFT
CreatedOn = 01/02/2009 11:12:06
Name = Adjustable Race
LastName = Abbas
FirstName = Syed
ShipStreet = 123 Elm Street
ShipCity = Denver
ShipZipCode = 12345
ShippingOption = Two-day shipping
State = Colorado
```

Reading Rows Using an Array of Parameter Values

While you may use simple no-parameter stored procedures and SQL statements in some scenarios, it's far more common to use queries that accept input parameters that select rows or specify how the query will execute within the database server. If you use only input parameters, you can wrap the values up as an **Object** array and pass them to the stored procedure or SQL statement. Note that this means you must add them to the array in the same order as they are expected by the query, because you are not using names for these parameters—you are only supplying the actual values. The following code shows how you can execute a stored procedure that takes a single string parameter.

```
' Call the ExecuteReader method with the stored procedure
' name and an Object array containing the parameter values
Using reader As IDataReader = defaultDB.ExecuteReader("ListOrdersByState", _
                                    New Object() {"Colorado"})
   DisplayRowValues(reader)
End Using
```

The example named *Return rows using a stored procedure with parameters* uses this code to query the sample database, and generates the following output.

```
Id = 1
Status = DRAFT
CreatedOn = 01/02/2009 11:12:06
Name = Adjustable Race
LastName = Abbas
FirstName = Syed
ShipStreet = 123 Elm Street
ShipCity = Denver
ShipZipCode = 12345
ShippingOption = Two-day shipping
State = Colorado

Id = 2
Status = DRAFT
CreatedOn = 03/02/2009 01:12:06
Name = All-Purpose Bike Stand
LastName = Abel
FirstName = Catherine
ShipStreet = 321 Cedar Court
ShipCity = Denver
ShipZipCode = 12345
ShippingOption = One-day shipping
State = Colorado
```

Reading Rows Using Queries with Named Parameters

The technique in the previous example of supplying just an array of parameter values is easy and efficient, but has some limitations. It does not allow you to specify the direction (such as input or output), or the data type—which may be an issue if the data type of a parameter does not exactly match (or cannot be implicitly converted into) the correct type discovered for a stored procedure. If you create an array of parameters for your query, you can specify more details about the types of the parameters and the way they should be used.

In addition, some database systems allocate parameters used in SQL statements or stored procedures simply by position. However, many database systems, such as SQL Server, allow you to use named parameters. The database matches the names of the parameters sent with the command to the names of the parameters defined in the SQL statement or stored procedure. This means that you are not confined to adding parameters to your command in a specific order. However, be aware that if you use named parameters and then change the database type to one that does not support named parameters, any parameters that are supplied out of order will probably cause errors. (This may be difficult to detect if all of the parameters are of the same data type!)

To work with named parameters or parameters of defined types, you must access the **Command** object that will be used to execute the query, and manipulate its collection or parameters. The Data Access block makes it easy to create and access the **Command** object by using two methods of the **Database** class: **GetSqlStringCommand** and **GetStoredProcCommand**. These methods return an instance of the appropriate command class for the configured database as a provider-independent **DbCommand** type reference.

After you create the appropriate type of command, you can use the many variations of the **Database** methods to manipulate the collection of parameters. You can add parameters with a specific direction using the **AddInParameter** or **AddOutParameter** method, or by using the **AddParameter** method and providing a value for the **Parameter Direction** parameter. You can change the value of existing parameters already added to the command using the **GetParameterValue** and **SetParameterValue** methods.

The following code shows how easy it is to create a command, add an input parameter, and execute both a SQL statement and a stored procedure. Notice how the code specifies the command to which the **Database** class should add the parameter (there could be more than one connection defined for the database), the name, the data type, and the value of the new parameter.

```
' Read data with a SQL statement that accepts one parameter.
Dim sqlStatement As String _
    = "SELECT TOP 1 * FROM OrderList WHERE State LIKE @state"
' Create a suitable command type and add the required parameter.
Using sqlCmd As DbCommand = defaultDB.GetSqlStringCommand(sqlStatement)
  defaultDB.AddInParameter(sqlCmd, "state", DbType.String, "New York")

  ' Call the ExecuteReader method with the command.
  Using sqlReader As IDataReader = namedDB.ExecuteReader(sqlCmd)
    DisplayRowValues(sqlReader)
  End Using

End Using


' Now read the same data with a stored procedure that accepts one parameter.
Dim storedProcName As String = "ListOrdersByState"

' Create a suitable command type and add the required parameter.
Using sprocCmd As DbCommand = defaultDB.GetStoredProcCommand(storedProcName)
  defaultDB.AddInParameter(sprocCmd, "state", DbType.String, "New York")

  ' Call the ExecuteReader method with the command.
  Using sprocReader As IDataReader = namedDB.ExecuteReader(sprocCmd)
    DisplayRowValues(sprocReader)
  End Using

End Using
```

The example named *Return rows using a SQL statement or stored procedure with named parameters* uses the code you see above to execute a SQL statement and a stored procedure against the sample database. The code provides the same parameter value to each, and both queries return the same single row, as shown here.

```
Id = 4
Status = DRAFT
CreatedOn = 07/02/2009 05:12:06
Name = BB Ball Bearing
LastName = Abel
FirstName = Catherine
ShipStreet = 888 Main Street
ShipCity = New York
ShipZipCode = 54321
ShippingOption = Three-day shipping
State = New York
```

RETRIEVING DATA AS OBJECTS

Modern programming techniques typically concentrate on data as objects. This approach is useful if you use Data Transfer Objects (DTOs) (see http://msdn.microsoft.com/en-us/library/ms978717.aspx) to pass data around you application layers, implement a data access layer using O/RM techniques, or want to take advantage of new client-side data querying techniques such as LINQ.

The Data Access block is not, in itself, an O/RM solution; but it contains features that allow you to extract data using a SQL statement or a stored procedure as the query, and have the data returned to you as a sequence of objects that implements the **IEnumerable** interface. This allows you to execute queries, or obtain lists or arrays of objects that represent the original data in the database.

About Accessors

The block provides two core classes for performing this kind of query: the **SprocAccessor** and the **SqlStringAccessor**. You can create and execute these accessors in one operation using the **ExecuteSprocAccessor** and **ExecuteSqlAccessor** methods of the **Database** class, or create a new accessor directly and then call its **Execute** method.

Accessors use two other objects to manage the parameters you want to pass into the accessor (and on to the database as it executes the query), and to map the values in the rows returned from the database to the properties of the objects it will return to the client code. Figure 2 shows the overall process.

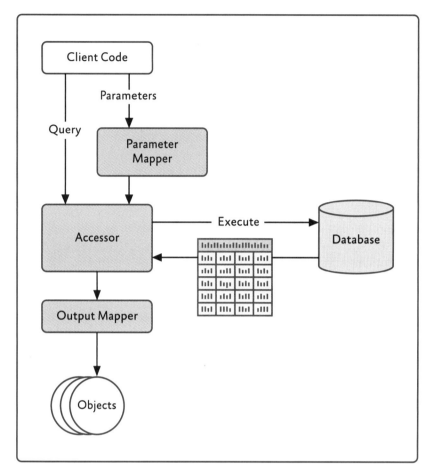

FIGURE 2
Overview of data accessors and the related types

The accessor will attempt to resolve the parameters automatically using a default mapper if you do not specify a parameter mapper. However, this feature is only available for stored procedures executed against SQL Server and Oracle databases. It is not available when using SQL statements, or for other databases and providers, where you must specify a custom parameter mapper that can resolve the parameters.

If you do not specify an output mapper, the block uses a default map builder class that maps the column names of the returned data to properties of the objects it creates. Alternatively, you can create a custom mapping to specify the relationship between columns in the row set and the properties of the objects.

Inferring the details required to create the correct mappings means that the default parameter and output mappers can have an effect on performance. You may prefer to create your own custom mappers and retain a reference to them for reuse when possible to maximize performance of your data access processes when using accessors.

For a full description of the techniques for using accessors, see the Enterprise Library documentation on MSDN® at http://go.microsoft.com/fwlink/?LinkId=188874, or installed with Enterprise Library. This chapter covers only the simplest approach: using the **ExecuteSprocAccessor** method of the **Database** class.

Creating and Executing an Accessor

The following code shows how you can use an accessor to execute a stored procedure and then manipulate the sequence of objects that is returned. You must specify the object type that you want the data returned as—in this example it is a simple class named **Product** that has the three properties: **ID**, **Name**, and **Description**.

The stored procedure takes a single parameter that is a search string, and returns details of all products in the database that contain this string. Therefore, the code first creates an array of parameter values to pass to the accessor, and then calls the **ExecuteSprocAccessor** method. It specifies the **Product** class as the type of object to return, and passes to the method the name of the stored procedure to execute and the array of parameter values.

```
' Create an object array and populate it with the required parameter values.
Dim params() As Object = New Object() {"%bike%"}

' Create and execute a sproc accessor that uses default
' parameter and output mappings.
Dim productData = defaultDB.ExecuteSprocAccessor(Of Product)("GetProductList", _
                                                    params)


' Perform a client-side query on the returned data. Be aware that
' the orderby and filtering is happening on the client, not the database.
Dim results = From productItem In productData _
            Where Not productItem.Description Is Nothing _
            Order By productItem.Name _
            Select New Product(productItem.Name, productItem.Description)


' Display the results
For Each item In results
  Console.WriteLine("Product Name: {0}", item.Name)
  Console.WriteLine("Description: {0}", item.Description)
  Console.WriteLine()
Next
```

The accessor returns the data as a sequence that, in this example, the code handles using a LINQ query to remove all items where the description is empty, sort the list by name, and then create a new sequence of objects that have just the **Name** and **Description** properties. For more information on using LINQ to query sequences, see http://msdn.microsoft.com/en-us/library/bb397676.

Keep in mind that returning sets of data that you manipulate on the client can have an impact on performance. In general, you should attempt to return data in the format required by the client, and minimize client-side data operations.

The example *Return data as a sequence of objects using a stored procedure* uses the code you see above to query the sample database and process the resulting rows. The output it generates is shown here.

```
Product Name: All-Purpose Bike Stand
Description: Perfect all-purpose bike stand for working on your bike at home.
Quick-adjusting clamps and steel construction.

Product Name: Bike Wash - Dissolver
Description: Washes off the toughest road grime; dissolves grease, environmentally
safe. 1-liter bottle.

Product Name: Hitch Rack - 4-Bike
Description: Carries 4 bikes securely; steel construction, fits 2" receiver hitch.
```

For an example of creating an accessor and then calling the **Execute** method, see the section "Retrieving Data as Objects Asynchronously" later in this chapter.

Creating and Using Mappers

In some cases, you may need to create a custom parameter mapper to pass your parameters to the query that the accessor will execute. This typically occurs when you need to execute a SQL statement to work with a database system that does not support parameter resolution, or when a default mapping cannot be inferred due to a mismatch in the number or types of the parameters. The parameter mapper class must implement the **IParameterMapper** interface and contain a method named **AssignParameters** that takes a reference to the current **Command** instance and the array of parameters. The method simply needs to add the required parameters to the **Command** object's **Parameters** collection.

More often, you will need to create a custom output mapper. To help you do this, the block provides a class called **MapBuilder** that you can use to create the set of mappings you require between the columns of the data set returned by the query and the properties of the objects you need.

By default, the accessor will expect to generate a simple sequence of a single type of object (in our earlier example, this was a sequence of the **Product** class). However, you can use an accessor to return a more complex graph of objects if you wish. For example, you might execute a query that returns a series of **Order** objects and the related **Order Lines** objects for all of the selected orders. Simple output mapping cannot cope with this scenario, and neither can the **MapBuilder** class. In this case, you would create a result set mapper by implementing the **IResultSetMapper** interface. Your custom row set mapper must contain a method named **MapSet** that receives a reference to an object that implements the **IDataReader** interface. The method should read all of the data available through the data reader, processes it to create the sequence of objects you require, and return this sequence.

RETRIEVING XML DATA

Some years ago, XML was the coolest new technology that was going to rule the world and change the way we think about data. In some ways, it did, though the emphasis on XML has receded as the relational database model continues to be the basis for most enterprise systems. However, the ability to retrieve data from a relational database as XML is useful in many scenarios, and is supported by the Data Access block.

SQL Server supports a mechanism called SQLXML that allows you to extract data as a series of XML elements, or in a range of XML document formats, by executing specially formatted SQL queries. You can use templates to precisely control the output, and have the server format the data in almost any way you require. For a description of the capabilities of SQLXML, see http://msdn.microsoft.com/en-us/library/aa286527(v=MSDN.10).aspx.

The Data Access block provides the **ExecuteXmlReader** method for querying data as XML. It takes a SQL statement that contains the **FOR XML** statement and executes it against the database, returning the result as an **XmlReader**. You can iterate through the resulting XML elements or work with them in any of the ways supported by the XML classes in the .NET Framework. However, as SQLXML is limited to SQL Server (the implementations of this type of query differ in other database systems), it is only available when you specifically use the **SqlDatabase** class (rather than the **Database** class).

The following code shows how you can obtain a **SqlDatabase** instance, specify a suitable SQLXML query, and execute it using the **ExecuteXmlReader** method.

```
' Resolve a SqlDatabase object from the container using the default database.
Dim sqlServerDB As SqlDatabase _
  = TryCast(EnterpriseLibraryContainer.Current.GetInstance(Of Database)(), _
          SqlDatabase)


' Specify a SQL query that returns XML data.
Dim xmlQuery As String _
    = "SELECT * FROM OrderList WHERE State = @state FOR XML AUTO"


' Create a suitable command type and add the required parameter
' NB: ExecuteXmlReader is only available for SQL Server databases
Using xmlCmd As DbCommand = sqlServerDB.GetSqlStringCommand(xmlQuery)
  xmlCmd.Parameters.Add(New SqlParameter("state", "Colorado"))
  Using reader As XmlReader = sqlServerDB.ExecuteXmlReader(xmlCmd)
    ' Iterate through the elements in the XmlReader
    While Not reader.EOF
      If reader.IsStartElement() Then
        Console.WriteLine(reader.ReadOuterXml())
      End If
    End While
  End Using
End Using
```

The code above also shows a simple approach to extracting the XML data from the **XmlReader** returned from the **ExecuteXmlReader** method. One point to note is that, by default, the result is an XML fragment, and not a valid XML document. It is, effectively, a sequence of XML elements that represent each row in the results set. Therefore, at minimum, you must wrap the output with a single root element so that it is well-formed. For more information about using an **XmlReader**, see "Reading XML with the XmlReader" in the online MSDN documentation at http://msdn.microsoft.com/en-us/library/9d83k261.aspx.

The example *Return data as an XML fragment using a SQL Server XML query* uses the code you see above to query a SQL Server database. It returns two XML elements in the default format for a FOR XML AUTO query, with the values of each column in the data set represented as attributes, as shown here.

```
<OrderList Id="1" Status="DRAFT" CreatedOn="2009-02-01T11:12:06"
Name="Adjustable Race" LastName="Abbas" FirstName="Syed"
ShipStreet="123 Elm Street" ShipCity="Denver" ShipZipCode="12345"
ShippingOption="Two-day shipping" State="Colorado" />
<OrderList Id="2" Status="DRAFT" CreatedOn="2009-02-03T01:12:06"
Name="All-Purpose Bike Stand" LastName="Abel" FirstName="Catherine"
ShipStreet="321 Cedar Court" ShipCity="Denver" ShipZipCode="12345"
ShippingOption="One-day shipping" State="Colorado" />
```

You might use this approach when you want to populate an XML document, transform the data for display, or persist it in some other form. You might use an XSLT style sheet to transform the data to the required format. For more information on XSLT, see "XSLT Transformations" at http://msdn.microsoft.com/en-us/library/14689742.aspx.

RETRIEVING SINGLE SCALAR VALUES

A common requirement when working with a database is to extract a single scalar value based on a query that selects either a single row or a single value. This is typically the case when using lookup tables or checking for the presence of a specific entity in the database. The Data Access block provides the **ExecuteScalar** method to handle this requirement. It executes the query you specify, and then returns the value of the first column of the first row of the result set as an **Object** type. This means that it provides much better performance than the **ExecuteReader** method, because there is no need to create a **DataReader** and stream the results to the client as a row set. To maximize this efficiency, you should aim to use a query that returns a single value or a single row.

The **ExecuteScalar** method has a set of overloads similar to the **ExecuteReader** method we used earlier in this chapter. You can specify a **CommandType** (the default is **StoredProcedure**) and either a SQL statement or a stored procedure name. You can also pass in an array of **Object** instances that represent the parameters for the query. Alternatively, you can pass to the method a **Command** object that contains any parameters you require.

The following code demonstrates passing a **Command** object to the method to execute both an inline SQL statement and a stored procedure. It obtains a suitable

Command instance from the current **Database** instance using the **GetSqlStringCommand** and **GetStoredProcCommand** methods. You can add parameters to the command before calling the **ExecuteScalar** method if required. However, to demonstrate the way the method works, the code here simply extracts the complete row set. The result is a single **Object** that you must cast to the appropriate type before displaying or consuming it in your code.

```
' Create a suitable command type for a SQL statement.
Using sqlCmd As DbCommand _
              = defaultDB.GetSqlStringCommand("SELECT [Name] FROM States")

  ' Call the ExecuteScalar method of the command.
  Console.WriteLine("Result using a SQL statement: {0}", _
                    defaultDB.ExecuteScalar(sqlCmd).ToString())
End Using


' Create a suitable command type for a stored procedure.
' NB: For efficiency, aim to return only a single value or a single row.
Using sprocCmd As DbCommand = defaultDB.GetStoredProcCommand("GetStatesList")

  ' Call the ExecuteScalar method of the command.
  Console.WriteLine("Result using a stored procedure: {0}", _
                    defaultDB.ExecuteScalar(sprocCmd).ToString())
End Using
```

You can see the code listed above running in the example *Return a single scalar value from a SQL statement or stored procedure*. The somewhat unexciting result it produces is shown here.

```
Result using a SQL statement: Alabama
Result using a stored procedure: Alabama
```

RETRIEVING DATA ASYNCHRONOUSLY

Having looked at all of the main ways you can extract data using the Data Access block, we'll move on to look at some more exciting scenarios (although many would perhaps fail to consider anything connected with data access exciting...). Databases are generally not renowned for being the fastest of components in an application—in fact many people will tell you that they are major bottleneck in any enterprise application. It's not that they are inefficient, it's usually just that they contain many millions of rows, and the queries you need to execute are relatively complex. Of course, it may just be that the query is badly written and causes poor performance, but that's a different story.

One way that applications can minimize the performance hit from data access is to perform it asynchronously. This means that the application code can continue to execute, and the user interface can remain interactive during the process. Asynchronous data access may not suit every situation, but it can be extremely useful.

For example, you might be able to perform multiple queries concurrently and combine the results to create the required data set. Or query multiple databases, and only use the data from the one that returned the results first (which is also a kind of failover feature). However, keep in mind that asynchronous data access has an effect on connection and data streaming performance over the wire. Don't expect a query that returns ten rows to show any improvement using an asynchronous approach—it is more likely to take longer to return the results!

The Data Access block provides asynchronous **Begin** and **End** versions of many of the standard data access methods, including **ExecuteReader**, **ExecuteScalar**, **Execute XmlReader**, and **ExecuteNonQuery**. It also provides asynchronous **Begin** and **End** versions of the **Execute** method for accessors that return data as a sequence of objects. You will see both of these techniques here.

Preparing for Asynchronous Data Access

Before you can execute a query asynchronously, you must specify the appropriate setting in the connection string for the database you want to use. By default, asynchronous data access is disabled for connections, which prevents them from suffering the performance hit associated with asynchronous data retrieval. To use asynchronous methods over a connection, the connection string must include **Asynchronous Processing=true** (or just **async=true**), as shown in this extract from a **<connectionStrings>** section of a configuration file.

```
<connectionStrings>
  <add name="AsyncExampleDatabase"
       connectionString="Asynchronous Processing=true; Data Source=.\SQLEXPRESS;
                         Initial Catalog=MyDatabase; Integrated Security=True;"
       providerName="System.Data.SqlClient" />
  ...
</connectionStrings>
```

In addition, asynchronous processing in the Data Access block is only available for SQL Server databases. The **Database** class includes a property named **SupportsAsync** that you can query to see if the current **Database** instance does, in fact, support asynchronous operations. The example for this chapter contains a simple check for this.

One other point to note is that asynchronous data access usually involves the use of a callback that runs on a different thread from the calling code. A common approach to writing callback code in modern applications is to use Lambda expressions rather than a separate callback handler routine. However, Visual Basic in version 9 (in Visual Studio® 2008 and version 3.5 of the .NET Framework) does not fully support Lambda expressions for callbacks, so you may need to use separate callback routines in this scenario. This callback usually cannot directly access the user interface in a Windows® Forms or Windows Presentation Foundation (WPF) application. You will, in most cases, need to use a delegate to call a method in the original UI class to update the data returned by the callback.

Other points to note about asynchronous data access are the following:

- You can use the standard .NET methods and classes from the **System. Threading** namespace, such as wait handles and manual reset events, to manage asynchronous execution of the Data Access block methods. You can also cancel a pending or executing command by calling the **Cancel** method of the command you used to initiate the operation. For more information, see "Asynchronous Command Execution in ADO.NET 2.0" on MSDN at http://msdn.microsoft.com/en-us/library/ms379553(VS.80).aspx.

- The **BeginExecuteReader** method does not accept a **CommandBehavior** parameter. By default, the method will automatically set the **Command Behavior** property on the underlying reader to **CloseConnection** unless you specify a transaction when you call the method. If you do specify a transaction, it does not set the **CommandBehavior** property.

- Always ensure you call the appropriate **EndExecute** method when you use asynchronous data access, even if you do not actually require access to the results, or call the **Cancel** method on the connection. Failing to do so can cause memory leaks and consume additional system resources.

- Using asynchronous data access with the Multiple Active Results Set (MARS) feature of ADO.NET may produce unexpected behavior, and should generally be avoided.

- Asynchronous data access is only available if the database is SQL Server 7.0 or later. Also, for SQL Server 7.0 and SQL Server 2000, the database connection must use TCP. It cannot use shared memory. To ensure that TCP is used for SQL Server 7.0 and SQL Server 2000, use **localhost**, **tcp:server_name**, or **tcp:ip_address** for the server name in the connection string.

Asynchronous code is notoriously difficult to write, test, and debug for all edge cases, and you should only consider using it where it really can provide a performance benefit. For guidance on performance testing and setting performance goals see "patterns & practices Performance Testing Guidance for Web Applications" at http://perftesting guide.codeplex.com/.

Retrieving Row Set Data Asynchronously

The following code shows how you can perform asynchronous data access to retrieve a row set from a SQL Server database. The code creates a **Command** instance and adds two parameters, and then calls the **BeginExecuteReader** method of the **Database** class to start the process. Although you can use complex Lambda expressions in Visual Studio 2010 and Visual Basic 10, you cannot do so if you are using Visual Basic version 9 in Visual Studio 2008. Instead, you can create a separate callback function and specify it when you call the **BeginExecuteReader** method, as shown here.

```
Try
  ' Create command to execute stored procedure and add parameters.
  Dim cmd As DbCommand = asyncDB.GetStoredProcCommand("ListOrdersSlowly")
```

```vb
  asyncDB.AddInParameter(cmd, "state", DbType.String, "Colorado")
  asyncDB.AddInParameter(cmd, "status", DbType.String, "DRAFT")


  ' Execute the query asynchronously specifying the command and
  ' the callback to execute when data access completes.
  asyncDB.BeginExecuteReader(cmd, AddressOf ExecuteReadData, asyncDB)

Catch ex As Exception
  Console.WriteLine("Error while starting data access: {0}", ex.Message)
End Try
...


'-------------------------------------------------
' Callback executed when the data access completes.
Sub ExecuteReadData(ByVal asyncResult As IAsyncResult)
  Try
    ' Extract Database instance from async state passed to callback
    Dim db as Database = CType(asyncResult.AsyncState, Database)
    Using reader As IDataReader = db.EndExecuteReader(asyncResult)
      DisplayRowValues(reader)
    End Using
  Catch ex As Exception
    Console.WriteLine("Error after data access completed: {0}", ex.Message)
  End Try
End Sub
```

The Lambda expression then calls the **EndExecuteReader** method to obtain the results of the query execution.

The **AsyncState** parameter can be used to pass any required state information into the callback routine. For example, when you use a separate callback, you would pass a reference to the current **Database** instance as the **AsyncState** parameter so that the callback code can call the **EndExecuteReader** (or other appropriate **End** method) to obtain the results. If you use a Lambda expression instead, the current **Database** instance is available within the expression and, therefore, you do not need to populate the **AsyncState** parameter.

The callback executes the **EndExecuteReader** method to obtain the results of the query. At this point you can consume the row set in your application or, as the code above does, just display the values. Notice that the callback expression should handle any errors that may occur during the asynchronous operation.

The example *Execute a command that retrieves data asynchronously* uses the code shown above to fetch two rows from the database and display the contents. As well as the code above, it uses a simple routine that displays a "Waiting..." message every second as the code executes. The result is shown here.

```
Database supports asynchronous operations
Waiting... Waiting... Waiting... Waiting... Waiting...

Id = 1
Status = DRAFT
CreatedOn = 01/02/2009 11:12:06
Name = Adjustable Race
LastName = Abbas
FirstName = Syed
ShipStreet = 123 Elm Street
ShipCity = Denver
ShipZipCode = 12345
ShippingOption = Two-day shipping
State = Colorado

Id = 2
Status = DRAFT
CreatedOn = 03/02/2009 01:12:06
Name = All-Purpose Bike Stand
LastName = Abel
FirstName = Catherine
ShipStreet = 321 Cedar Court
ShipCity = Denver
ShipZipCode = 12345
ShippingOption = One-day shipping
State = Colorado
```

Of course, as we don't have a multi-million-row database handy to query, the example uses a stored procedure that contains a **WAIT** statement to simulate a long-running data access operation. It also uses **ManualResetEvent** objects to manage the threads so that you can see the results more clearly. Open the sample in Visual Studio, or view the Program.vb file, to see the way this is done.

Retrieving Data as Objects Asynchronously

You can also execute data accessors asynchronously when you want to return your data as a sequence of objects rather than as rows and columns. The example *Execute a command that retrieves data as objects asynchronously* demonstrates this technique. You can create your accessor and associated mappers in the same way as shown in the previous section of this chapter, and then call the **BeginExecute** method of the accessor. This works in much the same way as when using the **BeginExecuteReader** method described in the previous example.

You pass to the **BeginExecute** method the lambda expression or callback to execute when the asynchronous data access process completes, along with the **AsyncState** and an array of **Object** instances that represent the parameters to apply to the stored procedure or SQL statement you are executing. The lambda expression or callback method can obtain a reference to the accessor that was executed from the **AsyncState** (casting it to an instance of the **DataAccessor** base type so that the code will work with any accessor implementation), and then call the **EndExecute** method of the accessor to obtain a reference to the sequence of objects the accessor retrieved from the database.

UPDATING DATA

So far, we've looked at retrieving data from a database using the classes and methods of the Data Access block. Of course, while this is typically the major focus of many applications, you will often need to update data in your database. The Data Access block provides features that support data updates. You can execute update queries (such as INSERT, DELETE, and UPDATE statements) directly against a database using the **Execute NonQuery** method. In addition, you can use the **ExecuteDataSet**, **LoadDataSet**, and **UpdateDataSet** methods to populate a **DataSet** and push changes to the rows back into the database. We'll look at both of these approaches here.

Executing an Update Query

The Data Access block makes it easy to execute update queries against a database. By update queries, we mean inline SQL statements, or SQL statements within stored procedures, that use the **UPDATE**, **DELETE**, or **INSERT** keywords. You can execute these kinds of queries using the **ExecuteNonQuery** method of the **Database** class.

Like the **ExecuteReader** method we used earlier in this chapter, the **Execute NonQuery** method has a broad set of overloads. You can specify a **CommandType** (the default is **StoredProcedure**) and either a SQL statement or a stored procedure name. You can also pass in an array of **Object** instances that represent the parameters for the query. Alternatively, you can pass to the method a **Command** object that contains any parameters you require. There are also **Begin** and **End** versions that allow you to execute update queries asynchronously.

The following code from the example application for this chapter shows how you can use the **ExecuteNonQuery** method to update a row in a table in the database. It updates the **Description** column of a single row in the **Products** table, checks that the update succeeded, and then updates it again to return it to the original value (so that you can run the example again). The first step is to create the command and add the required parameters, as you've seen in earlier examples, and then call the **ExecuteNonQuery** method with the command as the single parameter. Next, the code changes the value of the command parameter named **description** to the original value in the database, and then executes the compensating update.

```
Dim oldDescription As String _
    = "Carries 4 bikes securely; steel construction, fits 2"" receiver hitch."
Dim newDescription As String = "Bikes tend to fall off after a few miles."

' Create command to execute stored procedure and add parameters.
Dim cmd As DbCommand = defaultDB.GetStoredProcCommand("UpdateProductsTable")
defaultDB.AddInParameter(cmd, "productID", DbType.Int32, 84)
defaultDB.AddInParameter(cmd, "description", DbType.String, newDescription)
```

```
' Execute the query and check if one row was updated.
If defaultDB.ExecuteNonQuery(cmd) = 1 Then
  ' Update succeeded.
Else
  Console.WriteLine("ERROR: Could not update just one row.")
End If


' Change the value of the second parameter
defaultDB.SetParameterValue(cmd, "description", oldDescription)

' Execute query and check if one row was updated
If defaultDB.ExecuteNonQuery(cmd) = 1 Then
  ' Update succeeded.
Else
  Console.WriteLine("ERROR: Could not update just one row.")
End If
```

Notice the pattern used to execute the query and check that it succeeded. The **ExecuteNonQuery** method returns an integer value that is the number of rows updated (or, to use the more accurate term, affected) by the query. In this example, we are specifying a single row as the target for the update by selecting on the unique ID column. Therefore, we expect only one row to be updated—any other value means there was a problem.

If you are expecting to update multiple rows, you would check for a non-zero returned value. Typically, if you need to ensure integrity in the database, you could perform the update within a connection-based transaction, and roll it back if the result was not what you expected. We look at how you can use transactions with the Data Access block methods in the section "Working with Connection-Based Transactions" later in this chapter.

The example *Update data using a Command object*, which uses the code you see above, produces the following output.

```
Contents of row before update:
Id = 84
Name = Hitch Rack - 4-Bike
Description = Carries 4 bikes securely; steel construction, fits 2" receiver hitch.

Contents of row after first update:
Id = 84
Name = Hitch Rack - 4-Bike
Description = Bikes tend to fall off after a few miles.

Contents of row after second update:
Id = 84
```

```
Name = Hitch Rack - 4-Bike
Description = Carries 4 bikes securely; steel construction, fits 2" receiver hitch.
```

Working with DataSets

If you need to retrieve data and store it in a way that allows you to push changes back into the database, you will usually use a **DataSet**. The Data Access block supports simple operations on a normal (non-typed) **DataSet**, including the capability to fill a **DataSet** and then update the original database table from the **DataSet**.

To fill a **DataSet**, you use the **ExecuteDataSet** method, which returns a new instance of the **DataSet** class populated with a table containing the data for each row set returned by the query (which may be a multiple-statement batch query). The tables in this **DataSet** will have default names such as **Table**, **Table1**, and **Table2**.

If you want to load data into an existing **DataSet**, you use the **LoadDataSet** method. This allows you to specify the name(s) of the target table(s) in the **DataSet**, and lets you add additional tables to an existing **DataSet** or refresh the contents of specific tables in the **DataSet**.

Both of these methods, **ExecuteDataSet** and **LoadDataSet**, have a similar broad set of overloads to the **ExecuteReader** and other methods you've seen earlier in this chapter. You can specify a **CommandType** (the default is **StoredProcedure**) and either a SQL statement or a stored procedure name. You can also pass in an array of **Object** instances that represent the parameters for the query. Alternatively, you can pass to the method a **Command** object that contains any parameters you require.

For example, the following code lines show how you can use the **ExecuteDataSet** method with a SQL statement; with a stored procedure and a parameter array; and with a command pre-populated with parameters. The code assumes you have created the Data Access block **Database** instance named **db**.

```
Dim productDataSet As DataSet

' Using a SQL statement.
Dim sql As String = "SELECT CustomerName, CustomerPhone FROM Customers"
productDataSet = db.ExecuteDataSet(CommandType.Text, sql)

' Using a stored procedure and a parameter array.
productDataSet = db.ExecuteDataSet("GetProductsByCategory", _
                                   New Object() { "%bike%" })

' Using a stored procedure and a named parameter.
Dim cmd As DbCommand = db.GetStoredProcCommand("GetProductsByCategory")
db.AddInParameter(cmd, "CategoryID", DbType.Int32, 7)
productDataSet = db.ExecuteDataSet(cmd)
```

Updating the Database from a DataSet

To update data in a database from a **DataSet**, you use the **UpdateDataSet** method, which returns a total count of the number of rows affected by the update, delete, and insert operations. The overloads of this method allow you to specify the source **DataSet** containing the updated rows, the name of the table in the database to update, and references to the three **Command** instances that the method will execute to perform UPDATE, DELETE, and INSERT operations on the specified database table.

In addition, you can specify a value for the **UpdateBehavior**, which determines how the method will apply the updates to the target table rows. You can specify one of the following values for this parameter:

- **Standard**. If the underlying ADO.NET update process encounters an error, the update stops and no subsequent updates are applied to the target table.
- **Continue**. If the underlying ADO.NET update process encounters an error, the update will continue and attempt to apply any subsequent updates.
- **Transactional**. If the underlying ADO.NET update process encounters an error, all the updates made to all rows will be rolled back.

Finally, you can—if you wish—provide a value for the **UpdateBatchSize** parameter of the **UpdateDataSet** method. This forces the method to attempt to perform updates in batches instead of sending each one to the database individually. This is more efficient, but the return value for the method will show only the number of updates made in the final batch, and not the total number for all batches. Typically, you are likely to use a batch size value between 10 and 100. You should experiment to find the most appropriate batch size; it depends on the type of database you are using, the query you are executing, and the number of parameters for the query.

The examples for this chapter include one named *Fill a DataSet and update the source data*, which demonstrates the **ExecuteDataSet** and **UpdateDataSet** methods. It uses the simple overloads of the **ExecuteDataSet** and **LoadDataSet** methods to fill two **DataSet** instances, using a separate routine named **DisplayTableNames** (not shown here) to display the table names and a count of the number of rows in these tables. This shows one of the differences between these two methods. Note that the **LoadDataSet** method requires a reference to an existing **DataSet** instance, and an array containing the names of the tables to populate.

```
Dim selectSQL As String _
    = "SELECT Id, Name, Description FROM Products WHERE Id > 90"


' Fill a DataSet from the Products table using the simple approach.
Dim simpleDS As DataSet = defaultDB.ExecuteDataSet(CommandType.Text, selectSQL)
DisplayTableNames(simpleDS, "ExecuteDataSet")


' Fill a DataSet from the Products table using the LoadDataSet method.
' This allows you to specify the name(s) for the table(s) in the DataSet.
Dim loadedDS As New DataSet("ProductsDataSet")
defaultDB.LoadDataSet(CommandType.Text, selectSQL, loadedDS, _
                      New String() {"Products"})
DisplayTableNames(loadedDS, "LoadDataSet")
```

This produces the following result.

```
Tables in the DataSet obtained using the ExecuteDataSet method:
 - Table named 'Table' contains 6 rows.

Tables in the DataSet obtained using the LoadDataSet method:
 - Table named 'Products' contains 6 rows.
```

The example then accesses the rows in the **DataSet** to delete a row, add a new row, and change the **Description** column in another row. After this, it displays the updated contents of the **DataSet** table.

```
' get a reference to the Products table in the DataSet.
Dim dt As DataTable = loadedDS.Tables("Products")

' Delete a row in the DataSet table.
dt.Rows(0).Delete()

' Add a new row to the DataSet table.
Dim rowData As Object() = New Object() {-1, "A New Row", _
               "Added to the table at " + DateTime.Now.ToShortTimeString()}
dt.Rows.Add(rowData)

' Update the description of a row in the DataSet table.
rowData = dt.Rows(1).ItemArray
rowData(2) = "A new description on " + DateTime.Now.ToShortTimeString()
dt.Rows(1).ItemArray = rowData

' Display the contents of the DataSet.
DisplayRowValues(dt)
```

This produces the following output. To make it easier to see the changes, we've omitted the unchanged rows from the listing. Of course, the deleted row does not show in the listing, and the new row has the default ID of -1 that we specified in the code above.

```
Rows in the table named 'Products':

Id = 99
Name = HL Mountain Frame - Silver, 44
Description = A new description at 14:25

...

Id = -1
Name = A New Row
Description = Added to the table at 14:25
```

The next stage is to create the commands that the **UpdateDataSet** method will use to update the target table in the database. The code declares three suitable SQL statements, and then builds the commands and adds the requisite parameters to them. Note that each parameter may be applied to multiple rows in the target table, so the actual value must be dynamically set based on the contents of the **DataSet** row whose updates are currently being applied to the target table.

This means that you must specify, in addition to the parameter name and data type, the name and the version (**Current** or **Original**) of the row in the **DataSet** to take the value from. For an INSERT command, you need the current version of the row that contains the new values. For a DELETE command, you need the original value of the ID to locate the row in the table that will be deleted. For an UPDATE command, you need the original value of the ID to locate the row in the table that will be updated, and the current version of the values with which to update the remaining columns in the target table row.

```vb
Dim addSQL As String _
    = "INSERT INTO Products (Name, Description) VALUES (@name, @description);"
Dim updateSQL As String = "UPDATE Products SET Name = @name, " _
                    & "Description = @description WHERE Id = @id"
Dim deleteSQL As String = "DELETE FROM Products WHERE Id = @id"

' Create the commands to update the original table in the database
Dim insertCommand As DbCommand = defaultDB.GetSqlStringCommand(addSQL)
defaultDB.AddInParameter(insertCommand, "name", DbType.String, "Name", _
                    DataRowVersion.Current)
defaultDB.AddInParameter(insertCommand, "description", DbType.String, _
                    "Description", DataRowVersion.Current)

Dim updateCommand As DbCommand = defaultDB.GetSqlStringCommand(updateSQL)
defaultDB.AddInParameter(updateCommand, "name", DbType.String, "Name", _
                    DataRowVersion.Current)
defaultDB.AddInParameter(updateCommand, "description", DbType.String, _
                    "Description", DataRowVersion.Current)
defaultDB.AddInParameter(updateCommand, "id", DbType.String, "Id", _
                    DataRowVersion.Original)

Dim deleteCommand As DbCommand = defaultDB.GetSqlStringCommand(deleteSQL)
defaultDB.AddInParameter(deleteCommand, "id", DbType.Int32, "Id", _
                    DataRowVersion.Current)
```

Finally, you can apply the changes by calling the **UpdateDataSet** method, as shown here.

```
' Apply the updates in the DataSet to the original table in the database.
Dim rowsAffected As Integer = defaultDB.UpdateDataSet(loadedDS, "Products", _
                insertCommand, updateCommand, deleteCommand, _
                UpdateBehavior.Standard)
Console.WriteLine("Updated a total of {0} rows in the database.", rowsAffected)
```

The code captures and displays the number of rows affected by the updates. As expected, this is three, as shown in the final section of the output from the example.

```
Updated a total of 3 rows in the database.
```

MANAGING CONNECTIONS

For many years, developers have fretted about the ideal way to manage connections in data access code. Connections are scarce, expensive in terms of resource usage, and can cause a big performance hit if not managed correctly. You must obviously open a connection before you can access data, and you should make sure it is closed after you have finished with it. However, if the operating system does actually create a new connection, and then closes and destroys it every time, execution in your applications would flow like molasses.

Instead, ADO.NET holds a pool of open connections that it hands out to applications that require them. Data access code must still go through the motions of calling the methods to create, open, and close connections, but ADO.NET automatically retrieves connections from the connection pool when possible, and decides when and whether to actually close the underlying connection and dispose it. The main issues arise when you have to decide when and how your code should call the **Close** method. The Data Access block helps to resolve these issues by automatically managing connections as far as is reasonably possible.

When you use the Data Access block to retrieve a **DataSet**, the **ExecuteDataSet** method automatically opens and closes the connection to the database. If an error occurs, it will ensure that the connection is closed. If you want to keep a connection open, perhaps to perform multiple operations over that connection, you can access the **Active Connection** property of your **DbCommand** object and open it before calling the **ExecuteDataSet** method. The **ExecuteDataSet** method will leave the connection open when it completes, so you must ensure that your code closes it afterwards.

In contrast, when you retrieve a **DataReader** or an **XmlReader**, the **ExecuteReader** method (or, in the case of the **XmlReader**, the **ExecuteXmlReader** method) must leave the connection open so that you can read the data. The **ExecuteReader** method sets the **CommandBehavior** property of the reader to **CloseConnection** so that the connection is closed when you dispose the reader. Commonly, you will use a **Using** construct to ensure that the reader is disposed, as shown here:

```
Using reader As IDataReader = db.ExecuteReader(cmd)
   ' use the reader here
End Using
```

This code, and code later in this section, assumes you have created the Data Access block **Database** *instance named* **db** *and a* **DbCommand** *instance named* **cmd***.*

Typically, when you use the **ExecuteXmlReader** method, you will explicitly close the connection after you dispose the reader. This is because the underlying **XmlReader** class does not expose a **CommandBehavior** property. However, you should still use the same approach as with a **DataReader** (a **Using** statement) to ensure that the **XmlReader** is correctly closed and disposed.

```
Using reader As XmlReader = db.ExecuteXmlReader(cmd)
  ' use the reader here
End Using
```

Finally, if you want to be able to access the connection your code is using, perhaps to create connection-based transactions in your code, you can use the Data Access block methods to explicitly create a connection for your data access methods to use. This means that you must manage the connection yourself, usually through a **Using** statement as shown below, which automatically closes and disposes the connection:

```
Using con As DbConnection = defaultDB.CreateConnection()
con.Open()
  Try
    ' perform data access here
  Catch
    ' handle any errors here
  End Try
End Using
```

WORKING WITH CONNECTION-BASED TRANSACTIONS

A common requirement in many applications is to perform multiple updates to data in such a way that they all succeed, or can all be undone (rolled back) to leave the databases in a valid state that is consistent with the original content. The traditional example is when your bank carries out a monetary transaction that requires them to subtract a payment from one account and add the same amount to another account (or perhaps slightly less, with the commission going into their own account).

Transactions should follow the four ACID principles. These are **Atomicity** (all of the tasks of a transaction are performed or none of them are), **Consistency** (the database remains in a consistent state before and after the transaction), **Isolation** (other operations cannot access or see the data in an intermediate state during a transaction), and **Durability** (the results of a successful transaction are persisted and will survive system failure).

You can execute transactions when all of the updates occur in a single database by using the features of your database system (by including the relevant commands such as BEGIN TRANSACTION and ROLLBACK TRANSACTION in your stored procedures). ADO.NET also provides features that allow you to perform connection-based transactions over a single connection. This allows you to perform multiple actions on different tables in the same database, and manage the commit or rollback in your data access code.

All of the methods of the Data Access block that retrieve or update data have overloads that accept a reference to an existing transaction as a **DbTransaction** type. As an example of their use, the following code explicitly creates a transaction over a connection. It assumes you have created the Data Access block **Database** instance named **db** and two **DbCommand** instances named **cmdA** and **cmdB**.

```
Using conn As DbConnection = db.CreateConnection()
  conn.Open()
  Dim trans As DbTransaction = conn.BeginTransaction()
  Try
    ' execute commands, passing in the current transaction to each one
    db.ExecuteNonQuery(cmdA, trans)
    db.ExecuteNonQuery(cmdB, trans)
    trans.Commit()    ' commit the transaction
  Catch
    trans.Rollback()  ' rollback the transaction
  End Try
End Using
```

The examples for this chapter include one named *Use a connection-based transaction*, which demonstrates the approach shown above. It starts by displaying the values of two rows in the **Products** table, and then uses the **ExecuteNonQuery** method twice to update the **Description** column of two rows in the database within the context of a connection-based transaction. As it does so, it displays the new description for these rows. Finally, it rolls back the transaction, which restores the original values, and then displays these values to prove that it worked.

```
Contents of rows before update:

Id = 53
Name = Half-Finger Gloves, L
Description = Full padding, improved finger flex, durable palm, adjustable closure.

Id = 84
Name = Hitch Rack - 4-Bike
Description = Carries 4 bikes securely; steel construction, fits 2" receiver hitch.

----------------------------------------------------------------------------
Updated row with ID = 53 to 'Third and little fingers tend to get cold.'.
Updated row with ID = 84 to 'Bikes tend to fall off after a few miles.'.
----------------------------------------------------------------------------
```

```
Contents of row after rolling back transaction:

Id = 53
Name = Half-Finger Gloves, L
Description = Full padding, improved finger flex, durable palm, adjustable closure.

Id = 84
Name = Hitch Rack - 4-Bike
Description = Carries 4 bikes securely; steel construction, fits 2" receiver hitch.
```

WORKING WITH DISTRIBUTED TRANSACTIONS

If you need to access different databases as part of the same transaction (including data-bases on separate servers), of if you need to include other data sources such as Microsoft Message Queuing (MSMQ) in your transaction, you must use a distributed transaction coordinator (DTC) mechanism such as Windows Component Services. In this case, you just perform the usual data access actions, and configure your components to use the DTC. Commonly, this is done through attributes added to the classes that perform the data access.

However, ADO.NET supports the concept of automatic or lightweight transactions through the **TransactionScope** class. You can specify that a series of actions require trans-actional support, but ADO.NET will not generate an expensive distributed transaction until you actually open more than one connection within the transaction scope. This means that you can perform multiple transacted updates to different tables in the same database over a single connection. As soon as you open a new connection, ADO.NET automatically creates a distributed transaction (using Windows Component Services), and enrolls the original connections and all new connections created within the transaction scope into that distributed transaction. You then call methods on the transaction scope to either commit all updates, or to roll back (undo) all of them.

Therefore, once you create the transaction scope or explicitly create a transaction, you use the Data Access block methods in exactly the same way as you would outside of a transaction. You do not need to pass the transaction scope to the methods as you would when using ADO.NET methods directly. For example, the methods of the Data Access Application Block automatically detect if they are being executed within the scope of a transaction. If they are, they enlist in the transaction scope and reuse the existing connection (because opening a new one would force Component Services to start a distributed transaction), and do not close the connection when they complete. The trans-action scope will close and dispose the connection when it is disposed.

Typically, you will use the **TransactionScope** class in the following way:

```
Using scope = New TransactionScope(TransactionScopeOption.RequiresNew)
  ' perform data access here
End Using
```

For more details about using a DTC and transaction scope, see "Distributed Transactions (ADO.NET)" at http://msdn.microsoft.com/en-us/library/ms254973.aspx and "System. Transactions Integration with SQL Server (ADO.NET)" at http://msdn.microsoft.com/en-us/library/ms172070.aspx.

The examples for this chapter contain one named *Use a TransactionScope for a distributed transaction*, which demonstrates the use of a **TransactionScope** with the Data Access block. It performs the same updates to the **Products** table in the database as you saw in the previous example of using a connection-based transaction. However, there are subtle differences in the way this example works.

In addition, as it uses the Windows Distributed Transaction Coordinator (DTC) service, you must ensure that this service is running before you execute the example; depending on your operating system it may not be set to start automatically. To start the service, open the Services MMC snap-in from your Administrative Tools menu, right-click on the Distributed Transaction Coordinator service, and click **Start**. To see the effects of the **TransactionScope** and the way that it promotes a transaction, open the Component Services MMC snap-in from your Administrative Tools menu and expand the **Component Services** node until you can see the **Transaction List** in the central pane of the snap-in.

When you execute the example, it creates a new **TransactionScope** and executes the **ExecuteNonQuery** method twice to update two rows in the database table. At this point, the code stops until you press a key. This gives you the opportunity to confirm that there is no distributed transaction—as you can see if you look in the transaction list in the Component Services MMC snap-in.

After you press a key, the application creates a new connection to the database (when we used a connection-based transaction in the previous example, we just updated the parameter values and executed the same commands over the same connection). This new connection, which is within the scope of the existing **TransactionScope** instance, causes the DTC to start a new distributed transaction and enroll the existing lightweight transaction into it; as shown in Figure 3.

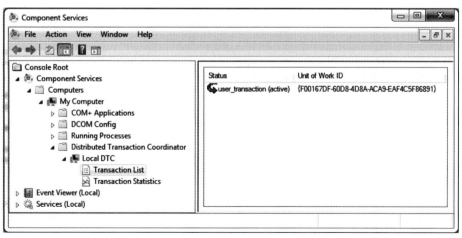

FIGURE 3
Viewing DTC transactions

The code then waits until you press a key again, at which point it exits from the using clause that created the **TransactionScope**, and the transaction is no longer in scope. As the code did not call the **Complete** method of the **TransactionScope** to preserve the changes in the database, they are rolled back automatically. To prove that this is the case, the code displays the values of the rows in the database again. This is the complete output from the example.

```
Contents of rows before update:

Id = 53
Name = Half-Finger Gloves, L
Description = Full padding, improved finger flex, durable palm, adjustable closure.

Id = 84
Name = Hitch Rack - 4-Bike
Description = Carries 4 bikes securely; steel construction, fits 2" receiver hitch.


----------------------------------------------------------------------------
Updated row with ID = 53 to 'Third and little fingers tend to get cold.'.
No distributed transaction. Press any key to continue...

Updated row with ID = 84 to 'Bikes tend to fall off after a few miles.'.
New distributed transaction created. Press any key to continue...
----------------------------------------------------------------------------


Contents of row after disposing TransactionScope:

Id = 53
Name = Half-Finger Gloves, L
Description = Full padding, improved finger flex, durable palm, adjustable closure.

Id = 84
Name = Hitch Rack - 4-Bike
Description = Carries 4 bikes securely; steel construction, fits 2" receiver hitch.
```

This default behavior of the **TransactionScope** ensures that an error or problem that stops the code from completing the transaction will automatically roll back changes. If your code does not seem to be updating the database, make sure you remembered to call the **Complete** method!

Extending the Block to Use Other Databases

The Data Access block contains providers for SQL Server, Oracle, and SQL Server Compact Edition. However, you can extend the block to use other databases if you wish. Writing a new provider is not a trivial task, and you may find that there is already a third party provider available for your database. For example, at the time of writing, the Enterprise Library Community Contribution site listed providers for MySql and SQLite databases. For more information, visit the *EntLib Contrib Project* site at http://codeplex. com/entlibcontrib/.

If you decide to create a new provider, you can create a new class derived from the Enterprise Library **Database** class and override its methods to implement the appropriate functionality. One limiting factor is that there must be an ADO.NET provider available for your database. The **Database** class in Enterprise Library relies on this to perform data access operations.

You must also be aware of the differences between database functionality, and manage these differences in your code. For example, you must handle return values, parameter prefixes (such as "@"), data type conversions, and other relevant factors. However, you can add additional methods to your provider to take advantage of features of your target database that are not available for other database types. For example, the SQL Server provider in the Data Access block exposes a method that uses the SQLXML functionality in SQL Server to extract data in XML format.

For more information on creating additional database providers for the Data Access block, see the Enterprise Library online guidance at http://go.microsoft.com/ fwlink/?LinkId=188874 or the installed documentation.

Summary

This chapter discussed the Data Access Application Block; one of the most commonly used blocks in Enterprise Library. The Data Access block provides two key advantages for developers and administrators. Firstly, it abstracts the database so that developers and administrators can switch the application from one type of database to another with only changes to the configuration files required. Secondly, it helps developers by making it easier to write the most commonly used sections of data access code with less effort, and it hides some of the complexity of working directly with ADO.NET.

In terms of abstracting the database, the block allows developers to write code in such a way that (for most functions) they do not need to worry which database (such as SQL Server, SQL Server CE, or Oracle) their applications will use. They write the same code for all of them, and configure the application to specify the actual database at run time. This means that administrators and operations staff can change the targeted database without requiring changes to the code, recompilation, retesting, and redeployment.

In terms of simplifying data access code, the block provides a small number of methods that encompass most data access requirements, such as retrieving a **DataSet**, a **DataReader**, a scalar (single) value, one or more values as output parameters, or a series of XML elements. It also provides methods for updating a database from a **DataSet**, and integrates with the ADO.NET **TransactionScope** class to allow a range of options for working with transactions. However, the block does not limit your options to use more advanced ADO.NET techniques, as it allows you to access the underlying objects such as the connection and the **DataAdapter**.

The chapter also described general issues such as managing connections and integration with transactions, and explored the actual capabilities of the block in more depth. Finally, we looked briefly at how you can use the block with other databases, including those supported by third-party providers.

3   Error Management Made Exceptionally Easy

Introduction

Let's face it, exception handling isn't the most exciting part of writing application code. In fact, you could probably say that managing exceptions is one of those necessary tasks that absorb effort without seeming to add anything useful to your exciting new application. So why would you worry about spending time and effort actually designing a strategy for managing exceptions? Surely there are much more important things you could be doing.

In fact, a robust and well-planned exception handling plan is a vital feature of your application design and implementation. It should not be an afterthought. If you don't have a plan, you can find yourself trying to track down all kinds of strange effects and unexpected behavior in your code. And, worse than that, you may even be sacrificing security and leaving your application and systems open to attack. For example, a failure may expose error messages containing sensitive information such as: "Hi, the application just failed, but here's the name of the server and the database connection string it was using at the time." Not a great plan.

The general expectations for exception handling are to present a clear and appropriate message to users, and to provide assistance for operators, administrators, and support staff who must resolve problems that arise. For example, the following actions are usually part of a comprehensive exception handling strategy:

- Notifying the user with a friendly message
- Storing details of the exception in a production log or other repository
- Alerting the customer service team to the error
- Assisting support staff in cross-referencing the exception and tracing the cause

So, having decided that you probably should implement some kind of structured exception handling strategy in your code, how do you go about it? A good starting point, as usual, is to see if there are any recommendations in the form of well-known patterns that you can implement. In this case, there are. The primary pattern that helps you to build secure applications is called Exception Shielding. Exception Shielding is the process of ensuring that your application does not leak sensitive information, no matter what runtime or system event may occur to interrupt normal operation. And on a more granular level, it can prevent your assets from being revealed across layer, tier, process, or service boundaries.

Two more exception handling patterns that you should consider implementing are the Exception Logging pattern and the Exception Translation pattern. The Exception Logging pattern can help you diagnose and troubleshoot errors, audit user actions, and track malicious activity and security issues. The Exception Translation pattern describes wrapping exceptions within other exceptions specific to a layer to ensure that they actually reflect user or code actions within the layer at that time, and not some miscellaneous details that may not be useful.

In this chapter, you will see how the Enterprise Library Exception Handling block can help you to implement these patterns, and become familiar with the other techniques that make up a comprehensive exception management strategy. You'll see how to replace, wrap, and log exceptions; and how to modify exception messages to make them more useful. And, as a bonus, you'll see how you can easily implement exception shielding for Windows® Communication Foundation (WCF) Web services.

When Should I Use the Exception Handling Block?

The Exception Handling block allows you to configure how you want to manage exceptions, and centralize your exception handling code. It provides a selection of plug-in exception handlers and formatters that you can use, and you can even create your own custom implementations. You can use the block when you want to implement exception shielding, modify exceptions in a range of ways, or chain exceptions (for example, by logging an exception and then passing it to another layer of your application). The configurable approach means that administrators can change the behavior of the exception management mechanism simply by editing the application configuration without requiring any changes to the code, recompilation, or redeployment.

> *The Exception Handling block was never intended for use everywhere that you catch exceptions. The block is primarily designed to simplify exception handling and exception management at your application or layer boundaries.*

How Do I Use the Exception Handling Block?

Like all of the Enterprise Library application blocks, you start by configuring your application to use the block, as demonstrated in Chapter 1, "Introduction." Then you add one or more exception policies and, for each policy, specify the type of exception it applies to. Finally, you add one or more exception handlers to each policy. The simplest approach is a policy that specifies the base type, **Exception**, and uses one of the handlers provided with the block. However, you'll see the various handlers, and other options, demonstrated in the examples in this chapter.

What Exception Policies Do I Need?

The key to handling exceptions is to apply the appropriate policies to each type of exception. You can pretend you are playing the well-known TV quiz game that just might make you a millionaire:

Question: **How should I handle exceptions?**	
A: Wrap them	B: Replace them
C: Log and re-throw them	D: Allow them to propagate

You can, of course, phone a friend or ask the audience if you think it will help. However, unlike most quiz games, all of the answers are actually correct (which is why we don't offer prizes). If you answered A, B, or C, you can move on to the section "About Exception Handling Policies." However, if you answered D: Allow them to propagate, read the following section.

ALLOWING EXCEPTIONS TO PROPAGATE

If you cannot do anything useful when an exception occurs, such as logging exception information, modifying the exception details, or retrying the failed process, there is no point in catching the exception in the first place. Instead, you just allow it to propagate up through the call stack, and catch it elsewhere in your code—either to resolve the issue or to display error messages. Of course, at this point, you can apply an exception policy; and so you come back to how you should choose and implement an appropriate exception handling strategy.

ABOUT EXCEPTION HANDLING POLICIES

Each policy you configure for the Exception Handling block can specify one or more exception types, such as **DivideByZeroException**, **SqlException**, **InvalidCastException**, the base class **Exception**, or any custom exception type you create that inherits from **System.Exception**. The block compares exceptions that it handles with each of these types, and chooses the one that is most specific in the class hierarchy.

For each policy, you configure:

- **One or more exception handlers** that the block will execute when a matching exception occurs. You can choose from four out-of-the-box handlers: the **Replace** handler, the **Wrap** handler, the **Logging** handler, and the **Fault Contract** exception handler. Alternatively, you can create custom exception handlers and choose these (see "Extending your Exception Handling" near the end of this chapter for more information).
- **A post-handling action** value that specifies what happens after the Exception Handling block executes the handlers you specify. Effectively, this setting tells the calling code whether to continue executing. You can choose from:

- **NotifyRethrow** (the default). Return **True** to the calling code to indicate that it should throw an exception, which may be the one that was actually caught or the one generated by the policy.
- **ThrowNewException**. The Exception Handling block will throw the exception that results from executing all of the handlers.
- **None**. Returns **False** to the calling code to indicate that it should continue executing.

Figure 1 shows an example policy named **MyTestExceptionPolicy** in the Enterprise Library configuration console. This policy handles the three exception types—**Divide ByZeroException**, **Exception** (shown as **All Exceptions** in the configuration tool), and **InvalidCastException**—and contains a mix of handlers for each exception type. The tool automatically adds the logging section to the configuration with the default settings when you add a **Logging** exception handler to your exception handling configuration.

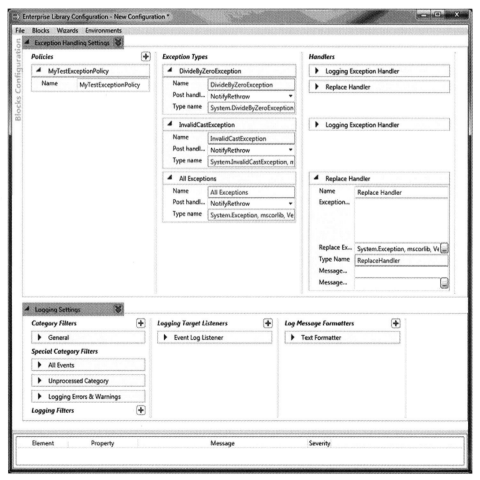

FIGURE 1
Configuration of the MyTestExceptionPolicy exception handling policy

Notice how you can specify the properties for each type of exception handler. For example, in the previous screenshot you can see that the **Replace Handler** has properties for the exception message and the type of exception you want to use to replace the original exception. Also, notice that you can localize your policy by specifying the name and type of the resource containing the localized message string.

CHOOSING AN EXCEPTION HANDLING STRATEGY

So let's get back to our quiz question, "How should I handle exceptions?" You should be able to see from the options available for exception handling policies how you can implement the common strategies for handling exceptions:

- **Replace the exception with a different one and throw the new exception**. This is an implementation of the Exception Shielding pattern. In your exception handling code, you can clean up resources or perform any other relevant processing. You use a **Replace** handler in your exception handling policy to replace the exception with a different exception containing sanitized or new information that does not reveal sensitive details about the source of the error, the application, or the operating system. Add a **Logging** handler to the exception policy if you want to log the exception. Place it before the **Replace** handler to log the original exception, or after it to log the replacement exception (if you log sensitive information, make sure your log files are properly secured). Set the post-handling action to **ThrowNewException** so that the block will throw the new exception.

- **Wrap the exception to preserve the content and then throw the new exception**. This is an implementation of the Exception Translation pattern. In your exception handling code, you can clean up resources or perform any other relevant processing. You use a **Wrap** handler in your exception-handling policy to wrap the exception within another exception that is more relevant to the caller and then throw the new exception so that code higher in the code stack can handle it. This approach is useful when you want to keep the original exception and its information intact, and/or provide additional information to the code that will handle the exception. Add a **Logging** handler to the exception policy if you want to log the exception. Place it before the **Wrap** handler to log the original exception, or after it to log the enclosing exception. Set the post-handling action to **ThrowNewException** so that the block will throw the new exception.

- **Log and, optionally, re-throw the original exception**. In your exception handling code, you can clean up resources or perform any other relevant processing. You use a **Logging** handler in your exception handling policy to write details of the exception to the configured logging store such as Windows Event Log or a file (an implementation of the Exception Logging pattern). If the exception does not require any further action by code elsewhere in th application (for example, if a retry action succeeds), set the post-handling action to **None**. Otherwise, set the post-handling action to **NotifyRethro** Your event handler code can then decide whether to throw the exceptior Alternatively, you can set it to **ThrowNewException** if you always want Exception Handling block to throw the exception for you.

Remember that the whole idea of using the Exception Handling block is to implement a strategy made up of configurable policies that you can change without having to edit, recompile, and redeploy the application. For example, the block allows you (or an administrator) to:

- **Add, remove, and change the types of handlers** (such as the Wrap, Replace, and Logging handlers) that you use for each exception policy, and change the order in which they execute.
- **Add, remove, and change the exception types that each policy will handle**, and the types of exceptions used to wrap or replace the original exceptions.
- **Modify the target and style of logging**, including modifying the log messages, for each type of exception you decide to log. This is useful, for example, when testing and debugging applications.
- **Decide what to do after the block handles the exception**. Provided that the exception handling code you write checks the return value from the call to the Exception Handling block, the post-handling action will allow you or an administrator to specify whether the exception should be thrown. Again, this is extremely useful when testing and debugging applications.

PROCESS OR HANDLE EXCEPTION?

The Exception Handling block provides two ways for you to manage exceptions. You can use the **Process** method to execute any method in your application, and have the block automatically perform management and throwing of the exception. Alternatively, if you want to apply more granular control over the process, you can use the **HandleException** method. The following will help you to understand which approach to choose.

- The **Process** method is the most common approach, and is useful in the majority of cases. You specify either a delegate (the address of a method) or a lambda expression that you want to execute. The Exception Handling block executes the method or expression, and automatically manages any exception that occurs. You will generally specify a **PostHandlingAction** of **ThrowNew Exception** so that the block automatically throws the exception that results from executing the exception handling policy. However, if you want the code to continue to execute (instead of throwing the exception), you can set the **PostHandlingAction** of your exception handling policy to **None**.
- The **HandleException** method is useful if you want to be able to detect the result of executing the exception handling policy. For example, if you set the **PostHandlingAction** of a policy to **NotifyRethrow**, you can use the return value of the **HandleException** method to determine whether or not to throw the exception. You can also use the **HandleException** method to pass an exception to the block and have it return the exception that results from executing the policy—which might be the original exception, a replacement exception, or the original exception wrapped inside a new exception.

You will see both the **Process** and the **HandleException** techniques described in the following examples, although most of them use the **Process** method.

Using the Process Method

The **Process** method has several overloads that make it easy to execute functions that return a value, and methods that do not. Typically, you will use the **Process** method in one of the following ways:

- To execute a routine or method that does not accept parameters and does not return a value:

```
exManager.Process(AddressOf method_name, "Exception Policy Name")
```

- To execute a routine that does accept parameters but does not return a value:

```
exManager.Process(Function() method_name(param1, param2), _
                "Exception Policy Name")
```

- To execute a routine that accepts parameters and returns a value:

```
Dim result As [function-result-type]
result = exManager.Process(Function() result _
                        = method_name(param1, param2), _
                        "Exception Policy Name")
```

- To execute a routine that accepts parameters and returns a value, and to also supply a default value to be returned should an exception occur and the policy that executes does not throw the exception. If you do not specify a default value and the **PostHandlingAction** is set to **None**, the **Process** method will return **Nothing** for reference types, zero for numeric types, or the default empty value for other types should an exception occur.

```
Dim result As [function-result-type]
result = exManager.Process(Function() result _
                        = method_name(param1, param2), _
                        default_result_value, _
                        "Exception Policy Name")
```

- To execute code defined within the lambda expression itself (this technique is only available with version 10 and Visual Studio® 2010):

```
' NOTE: This applies only to Visual Basic® 2010.
exManager.Process(Function(param As type) _
        ' Code lines here to execute application feature
        ' that may raise an exception that the Exception
        ' Handling block will handle using the policy named
        ' in the final parameter of the Process method.
        ' If required, the lambda expression defined here
        ' can return a value that the Process method will
        ' return to the calling code.
    End Function, _
    "Exception Policy Name")
```

*The **Process** method is optimized for use with lambda expressions, which are supported in C# 3.0 on version 3.5 of the .NET Framework and in Microsoft® Visual Studio® 2008 onwards. Visual Basic only fully supports Lambda expressions in version 10 on version 4.0 of the .NET Framework and in Visual Studio 2010. However, you can use simple lambda expressions with the Process method if you are using Visual Basic version 9 on version 3.5 of the .NET Framework and in Visual Studio 2008. If you are not familiar with lambda functions or their syntax, see http://msdn.microsoft.com/en-us/library/bb531253.aspx. For a full explanation of using the **HandleException** method, see the "Key Scenarios" topic in the online documentation for Enterprise Library 4.1 at http://msdn.microsoft.com/en-us/library/dd203198.aspx.*

Diving in with a Simple Example

The code you can download for this guide contains a sample application named **ExceptionHandling** that demonstrates the techniques described in this chapter. The sample provides a number of different examples that you can run. They illustrate each stage of the process of applying exception handling described in this chapter. However, this chapter describes an iterative process of updating a single application scenario. To make it easier to see the results of each stage, we have provided separate examples for each of them.

If you run the examples under the Visual Studio debugger, you will find that the code halts when an exception occurs—before it is sent to the Exception Handling block. You can press F5 at this point to continue execution. Alternatively, you can run the examples by pressing Ctrl-F5 (non-debugging mode) to prevent this from happening.

To see how you can apply exception handling strategies and configure exception handling policies, we'll start with a simple example that causes an exception when it executes. First, we need a class that contains a method that we can call from our main routine, such as the following in the **SalaryCalculator** class of the example application.

```
Public Function GetWeeklySalary(ByVal employeeId As String, _
                                ByVal weeks As Integer) As Decimal
  Dim connString As String = String.Empty
  Dim employeeName As String = String.Empty
  Dim salary As Decimal = 0

  Try
    ' Access the database to get the salary for this employee.
    connString = ConfigurationManager.ConnectionStrings( _
                                "EmployeeDatabase").ConnectionString
    ' Access database to get salary for employee here...
    ' In this example, just assume it's some large number.
    employeeName = "John Smith"
    salary = 1000000
    Return salary / weeks
```

```
Catch ex As Exception

    ' Provide error information for debugging.
    Dim template As String = "Error calculating salary for {0}. " _
                        & "Salary: {1}. Weeks: {2}" & vbLf _
                        & "Connection: {3}" & vbLf + "{4}"

    ' Create a new exception to return.
    Dim informationException As New Exception( _
            String.Format(template, employeeName, salary, weeks, _
                        connString, ex.Message))
    Throw informationException

  End Try
End Function
```

You can see that a call to the **GetWeeklySalary** method will cause an exception of type **DivideByZeroException** when called with a value of zero for the number of weeks parameter. The exception message contains the values of the variables used in the calculation, and other information useful to administrators when debugging the application. Unfortunately, the current code has several issues. It trashes the original exception and loses the stack trace, preventing meaningful debugging. Even worse, the global exception handler for the application presents any user of the application with all of the sensitive information when an error occurs.

If you run the example for this chapter, and select option *Typical Default Behavior without Exception Shielding*, you will see this result generated by the code in the **Catch** statement:

```
Exception type System.Exception was thrown.
Message: 'Error calculating salary for John Smith.
Salary: 1000000. Weeks: 0
Connection: Database=Employees;Server=CorpHQ;
User ID=admin;Password=2g$tXD76qr Attempted to divide by zero.'
Source: 'ExceptionHandlingExample'
No Inner exception
```

APPLYING EXCEPTION SHIELDING

It's clear that the application as it stands has a severe security hole that allows it to reveal sensitive information. Of course, we could prevent this by not adding the sensitive information to the exception message. However, the information will be useful to administrators and developers if they need to debug the application. For example, if the data connection had failed or the database contained invalid data, they would have seen this through missing values for the employee name or salary; and they could see if the configuration file contains the correct database connection string. Alternatively, in the case shown here, they can immediately tell that the database returned the required values for the operation, but the user interface allowed the user to enter the value zero for the number of weeks.

To provide this extra information, yet apply exception shielding, you may consider implementing configuration settings and custom code to allow administrators to specify when they need the additional information. However, this is exactly where the Exception Handling block comes in. You can set up an exception handling policy that administrators can modify as required, without needing to write custom code or set up custom configuration settings.

The first step is to create an exception handling policy that specifies the events you want to handle, and contains a handler that will either wrap (hide) or replace (remove) the exception containing all of the debugging information with one that contains a simple error message suitable for display to users or propagation through the layers of the application. You'll see these options implemented in the following sections. You will also see how you can log the original exception before replacing it, how you can handle specific types of exceptions, and how you can apply exception shielding to WCF services.

Wrapping an Exception

If you want to retain the original exception and the information it contains, you can wrap the exception in another exception and specify a sanitized user-friendly error message for the containing exception. This is the error message that the global error handler will display. However, code elsewhere in the application (such as code in a calling layer that needs to access and log the exception details) can access the contained exception and retrieve the information it requires before passing the exception on to another layer or to the global exception handler. This intermediate code could alternatively remove the contained exception—or use an Exception Handling block policy to replace it at that point in the application.

CONFIGURING THE WRAP HANDLER POLICY

So, the first stage is to configure the exception handling policy you require. You need to add a policy that specifies the type of exception returned from your code (in this case, we'll specify the base class **Exception**), and set the **PostHandlingAction** property for this exception type to **ThrowNewException** so that the Exception Handling block will automatically throw the new exception that wraps the original exception. Then, add a **Wrap** handler to the policy, and specify the exception message and the type of exception you want to use to wrap the original exception (we chose **Exception** here again). Figure 2 shows the completed configuration.

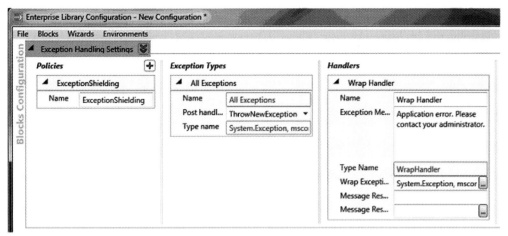

FIGURE 2
Configuration of the Wrap handler

INITIALIZING THE EXCEPTION HANDLING BLOCK

Now you must edit your code to use the Exception Handling block. You'll need to add references to the appropriate Enterprise Library assemblies and namespaces. The examples in this chapter demonstrate logging exception information and handling exceptions in a WCF application, as well as the basic processes of wrapping and replacing exceptions, so we'll add references to all of the assemblies and namespaces required for these tasks.

The assemblies you must add to your project (in addition to the assemblies required for all Enterprise Library projects) are:

- Microsoft.Practices.EnterpriseLibrary.ExceptionHandling.dll
- Microsoft.Practices.EnterpriseLibrary.ExceptionHandling.WCF.dll
- Microsoft.Practices.EnterpriseLibrary.ExceptionHandling.Logging.dll
- Microsoft.Practices.EnterpriseLibrary.Logging.dll

If you are only wrapping and replacing exceptions in your application but not logging them, you don't need to add the assemblies and references for logging. If you are not using the block to shield WCF services, you don't need to add the assemblies and references for WCF.

To make it easier to use the objects in the Exception Handling block, you can add references to the relevant namespaces to your project.

Now you can resolve an instance of the **ExceptionManager** class you'll use to perform exception management. You can use the dependency injection approach described in Chapter 1, "Introduction" and Appendices A and B, or the **GetInstance** method. This example uses the simple **GetInstance** approach.

```
' Global variable to store the ExceptionManager instance.
Dim exManager As ExceptionManager


' Resolve the default ExceptionManager object from the container.
exManager = EnterpriseLibraryContainer.Current.GetInstance(Of ExceptionManager)()
```

EDITING THE APPLICATION CODE TO USE THE NEW POLICY

Now you can update your exception handling code to use the new policy. You have two choices. If the configured exception policy does everything you need to do, you can actually remove the **Try...catch** block completely from the method that may cause an error, and—instead—use the **Process** method of the **ExceptionManager** to execute the code within the method, as shown here.

```vb
Public Function GetWeeklySalary(ByVal employeeId As String, _
                                ByVal weeks As Integer) As Decimal
    Dim employeeName As String = String.Empty
    Dim salary As Decimal = 0
    Dim weeklySalary As Decimal = 0

    exManager.Process(Function() _
        Dim connString As String = ConfigurationManager.ConnectionStrings( _
                            "EmployeeDatabase").ConnectionString _
        employeeName = "John Smith" _
        salary = 1000000 _
        weeklySalary = salary / weeks _
      End Function, _
    "ExceptionShielding")

    Return weeklySalary
End Function
```

The approach used above is only valid in Visual Basic if you are using version 10 and Visual Studio 2010. It is not valid in Visual Basic version 9 in Visual Studio 2008.

The body of your logic is placed inside a lambda function and passed to the **Process** method. If an exception occurs during the execution of the expression, it is caught and handled according to the configured policy. The name of the policy to execute is specified in the second parameter of the **Process** method.

Alternatively, you can use the **Process** method in your main code to call the method of your class. This is a useful approach if you want to perform exception shielding at the boundary of other classes or objects. If you do not need to return a value from the function or routine you execute, you can create any instance you need and work with it inside the lambda expression, as shown here.

```vb
exManager.Process(Function() _
    Dim calc As New SalaryCalculator() _
    Console.WriteLine("Result is: {0}", calc.GetWeeklySalary("jsmith", 0)) _
  End Function, _
  "ExceptionShielding")
```

The approach used above is only valid in Visual Basic if you are using Visual Studio 2010. It is not valid in Visual Basic in Visual Studio 2008.

If you want to be able to return a value from the method or routine, you can use the overload of the **Process** method that returns the lambda expression value, like this.

```
Dim calc As New SalaryCalculator()
Dim result As Decimal = exManager.Process(Function() _
          result = calc.GetWeeklySalary("jsmith", 0), "ExceptionShielding")
Console.WriteLine("Result is: {0}", result)
```

Notice that this approach creates the instance of the **SalaryCalculator** class outside of the **Process** method, and therefore it will not pass any exception that occurs in the constructor of that class to the exception handling policy. But when any other error occurs, the global application exception handler sees the wrapped exception instead of the original informational exception. If you run the example *Behavior After Applying Exception Shielding with a Wrap Handler,* the **Catch** section now displays the following. You can see that the original exception is hidden in the Inner Exception, and the exception that wraps it contains the generic error message.

```
Exception type System.Exception was thrown.
Message: 'Application Error. Please contact your administrator.'
Source: 'Microsoft.Practices.EnterpriseLibrary.ExceptionHandling'

Inner Exception: System.Exception: Error calculating salary for John Smith.
Salary: 1000000. Weeks: 0
Connection: Database=Employees;Server=CorpHQ;User ID=admin;Password=2g$tXD76qr
Attempted to divide by zero.
   at ExceptionHandlingExample.SalaryCalculator.GetWeeklySalary(String employeeI
d, Int32 weeks) in ...\ExceptionHandling\ExceptionHandling\SalaryCalculator.vb:
line 34
   at ExceptionHandlingExample.Program.<WithWrapExceptionShielding>b__0() in
...\ExceptionHandling\ExceptionHandling\Program.vb:line 109
   at Microsoft.Practices.EnterpriseLibrary.ExceptionHandling.ExceptionManagerIm
pl.Process(Action action, String policyName)
```

This means that developers and administrators can examine the wrapped (inner) exception to get more information. However, bear in mind that the sensitive information is still available in the exception, which could lead to an information leak if the exception propagates beyond your secure perimeter. While this approach may be suitable for highly technical, specific errors, for complete security and exception shielding, you should use the technique shown in the next section to replace the exception with one that does not contain any sensitive information.

> *For simplicity, this example shows the principles of exception shielding at the level of the UI view. The business functionality it uses may be in the same layer, in a separate business layer, or even on a separate physical tier. Remember that you should design and implement an exception handling strategy for individual layers or tiers in order to shield exceptions on the layer or service boundaries.*

Replacing an Exception

Having seen how easy it is to use exception handling policies, we'll now look at how you can implement exception shielding by replacing an exception with a different exception. This approach is also useful if you need to perform cleanup operations in your code, and then use the exception to expose only what is relevant. To configure this scenario, simply create a policy in the same way as the previous example, but with a **Replace** handler instead of a **Wrap** handler, as shown in Figure 3.

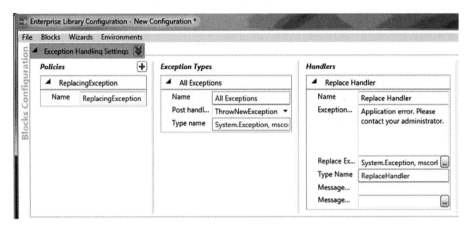

FIGURE 3
Configuring a Replace handler

When you call the method that generates an exception, you see the same generic exception message as in the previous example. However, there is no inner exception this time. If you run the example *Behavior After Applying Exception Shielding with a Replace Handler,* the Exception Handling block replaces the original exception with the new one specified in the exception handling policy. This is the result:

```
Exception type System.Exception was thrown.
Message: 'Application Error. Please contact your administrator.'
Source: 'Microsoft.Practices.EnterpriseLibrary.ExceptionHandling'
No Inner Exception
```

Logging an Exception

The previous section shows how you can perform exception shielding by replacing an exception with a new sanitized version. However, you now lose all the valuable debugging and testing information that was available in the original exception. Of course, the Librarian (remember him?) realized that you would need to retain this information and make it available in some way when implementing the Exception Shielding pattern. You preserve this information by chaining exception handlers within your exception handling policy. In other words, you add a **Logging** handler to the policy.

That doesn't mean that the **Logging** handler is only useful as part of a chain of handlers. If you only want to log details of an exception (and then throw it or ignore it, depending on the requirements of the application), you can define a policy that contains just a **Logging** handler. However, in most cases, you will use a **Logging** handler with other handlers that wrap or replace exceptions.

Figure 4 shows what happens when you add a **Logging** handler to your exception handling policy. The configuration tool automatically adds the Logging Application block to the configuration with a set of default properties that will write log entries to the Windows Application Event Log. You do, however, need to set a few properties of the **Logging** exception handler in the **Exception Handling Settings** section:

- Specify the ID for the log event your code will generate as the **Event ID** property.
- Specify the **TextExceptionFormatter** as the type of formatter the Exception Handling block will use. Click the ellipsis (**...**) button in the **Formatter Type** property and select **TextExceptionFormatter** in the type selector dialog that appears.
- Set the category for the log event. The Logging block contains a default category named **General**, and this is the default for the Logging exception handler. However, if you configure other categories for the Logging block, you can select one of these from the drop-down list that is available when you click on the **Logging Category** property of the **Logging** handler.

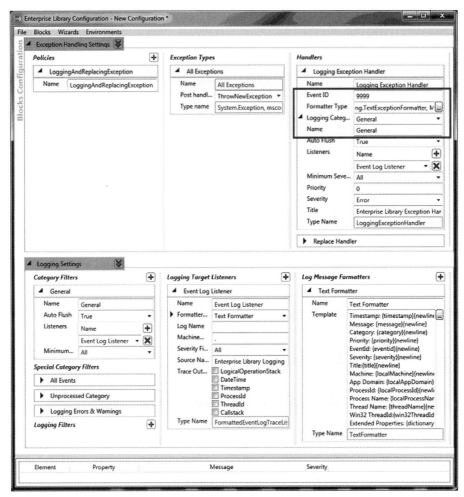

FIGURE 4
Adding a logging handler

The configuration tool adds new exception handlers to the end of the handler chain by default. However, you will obviously want to log the details of the original exception rather than the new exception that replaces it. You can right-click on the **Logging** handler and use the shortcut menu to move it up to the first position in the chain of handlers if required.

In addition, if you did not already do so, you must add a reference to the Logging Application block assembly to your project and (optionally) add a **Imports** statement to your class, as shown here.

```
Imports Microsoft.Practices.EnterpriseLibrary.Logging
```

Now, when the application causes an exception, the global exception handler continues to display the same sanitized error message. However, the **Logging** handler captures details of the original exception before the Exception Handling block policy replaces it, and writes the details to whichever logging sink you specify in the configuration for the Logging block. The default in this example is Windows Application Event Log. If you run the example *Logging an Exception to Preserve the Information it Contains*, you will see an exception like the one in Figure 5.

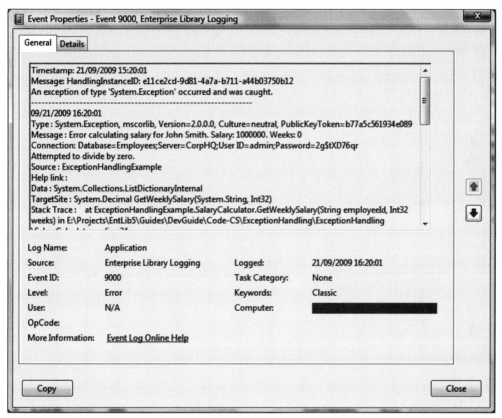

FIGURE 5
Details of the logged exception

This example shows the Exception Handling block using the default settings for the Logging block. However, as you can see in Chapter 4, "As Easy As Falling Off a Log," the Logging block is extremely configurable. So you can arrange for the Logging handler in your exception handling policy to write the information to any Windows Event Log, an e-mail message, a database, a message queue, a text file, a Windows Management Instrumentation (WMI) event, or a custom location using classes you create that take advantage of the application block extension points.

Shielding Exceptions at WCF Service Boundaries

You can use the Exception Handling block to implement exception handling policies for WCF services. A common scenario is to implement the Exception Shielding pattern at a WCF service boundary. The Exception Handling block contains a handler specifically designed for this (the **Fault Contract** exception handler), which maps the values in the exception to a new instance of a fault contract that you specify.

CREATING A FAULT CONTRACT

A fault contract for a WCF service will generally contain just the most useful properties for an exception, and exclude sensitive information such as the stack trace and anything else that may provide attackers with useful information about the internal workings of the service. The following code shows a simple example of a fault contract suitable for use with the **Fault Contract** exception handler:

```
<DataContract()> _
Public Class SalaryCalculationFault

  Dim theID As Guid
  Dim theMessage As String

  Public Sub New()
  End Sub

  Public Sub New(ByVal FaultID As Guid, ByVal FaultMessage As String)
    theID = FaultID
    theMessage = FaultMessage
  End Sub

  <DataMember()> _
  Public Property FaultID() As Guid
    Get
      Return theID
    End Get
    Set(ByVal value As Guid)
      theID = value
    End Set
  End Property

  <DataMember()> _
  Public Property FaultMessage() As String
    Get
      Return theMessage
    End Get
    Set(ByVal value As String)
```

```
        theMessage = value
      End Set
    End Property
End Class
```

CONFIGURING THE EXCEPTION HANDLING POLICY

Figure 6 shows a sample configuration for the **Fault Contract** exception handler. This specifies the type **SalaryCalculationFault** as the target fault contract type, and the exception message that the policy will generate to send to the client. Note that, when using the **Fault Contract** exception handler, you should always set the **PostHandlingAction** property to **ThrowNewException** so that the Exception Handling block throws an exception that forces WCF to return the fault contract to the client.

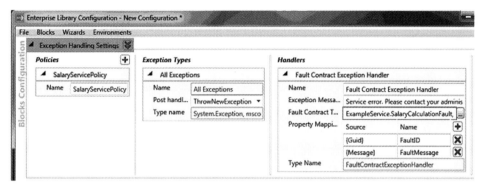

FIGURE 6
The Fault Contract exception handler configuration

Notice that we specified **Property Mappings** for the handler that map the **Message** property of the exception generated within the service to the **FaultMessage** property of the **SalaryCalculationFault** class, and map the unique Handling Instance ID of the exception (specified by setting the **Source** to "**{Guid}**") to the **FaultID** property, as shown in Figure 6.

EDITING THE SERVICE CODE TO USE THE NEW POLICY

After you specify your fault contract and configure the **Fault Contract** exception handler, you must edit your service code to use the new exception policy. If you did not already do so, you must also add a reference to the assembly that contains the **Fault Contract** exception handler to your project and (optionally) add a **Imports** statement to your service class, as shown here:

```
Imports Microsoft.Practices.EnterpriseLibrary.ExceptionHandling.WCF
```

You can now call the **Process** method of the **ExceptionManager** class from code in your service in exactly the same way as shown in the previous examples of wrapping and replacing exceptions in a Windows Forms application. Alternatively, you can add attributes to the methods in your service class to specify the policy they should use when an exception occurs, as shown in this code:

```
<ServiceContract> _
Public Interface ISalaryService

  <OperationContract> _
  <FaultContract(GetType(SalaryCalculationFault))> _
  Function GetWeeklySalary(employeeId As String, weeks As Integer) _
                                    As Decimal

End Interface

<ExceptionShielding("SalaryServicePolicy")> _
Public Class SalaryService
  Implements ISalaryService

  Public Function GetWeeklySalary(employeeId As String, weeks As Integer) _
                                    As Decimal _
    Implements ISalaryService.GetWeeklySalary
    Dim calc As New SalaryCalculator()
    Return calc.GetWeeklySalary(employeeId, weeks)
  End Function

End Class
```

You add the **ExceptionShielding** attribute to a service implementation class or to a service contract interface, and use it to specify the name of the exception policy to use. If you do not specify the name of a policy in the constructor parameter, or if the specified policy is not defined in the configuration, the Exception Handling block will automatically look for a policy named **WCF Exception Shielding**.

THE FAULT CONTRACT EXCEPTION HANDLER

The Exception Handling block executes the **Fault Contract** exception handler that you specify in your policy when an exception occurs. Effectively, the **Fault Contract** handler is a specialized version of the **Replace** handler. It takes the original exception, generates an instance of the fault contract, populates it with values from the exception, and then throws a **FaultException***(OfYourFaultContractType)* exception. The handler performs the following actions:

- It generates a new instance of the fault contract class you specify for the **FaultContractType** property of the **Fault Contract** exception handler.
- It extracts the values from the properties of the exception that you pass to the method.
- It sets the values of the new fault contract instance to the values extracted from the original exception. It uses mappings between the exception property names and the names of the properties exposed by the fault contract to assign the exception values to the appropriate properties. If you do not specify a

mapping, it matches the source and target properties that have the same name. The result is that, instead of a general service failure message, the client receives a fault message containing the appropriate information about the exception.

The example *Applying Exception Shielding at WCF Application Boundaries* uses the service described above and the Exception Handling block WCF Fault Contract handler to demonstrate exception shielding. You can run this example in one of three ways:

- Inside Visual Studio by starting it with *F5* (debugging mode) and then pressing *F5* again when the debugger halts at the exception in the **SalaryCalculator** class.
- Inside Visual Studio by right-clicking SalaryService.svc in Solution Explorer and selecting **View in Browser** to start the service, then pressing *Ctrl-F5* (non-debugging mode) to run the application.
- By starting the **SalaryService** in Visual Studio (as described in the previous bullet) and then running the executable file **ExceptionHandlingExample.exe** in the **bin\debug** folder directly.

The result is shown below. You can see that the exception raised by the **SalaryCalculator** class causes the service to return an instance of the **SalaryCalculationFault** type that contains the fault ID and fault message. However, the Exception Handling block captures this exception and replaces the sensitive information in the message with text that suggests the user contact their administrator. Research shows that users really appreciate this type of informative error message.

```
Getting salary for 'jsmith' from WCF Salary Service...
Exception type System.ServiceModel.FaultException`1[ExceptionHandlingExample.Sal
aryService.SalaryCalculationFault] was thrown.
Message: 'Service error. Please contact your administrator.'
Source: 'mscorlib'
No Inner Exception

Fault contract detail:
Fault ID: bafb7ec2-ed05-4036-b4d5-56d6af9046a5
Message: Error calculating salary for John Smith. Salary: 1000000. Weeks: 0
Connection: Database=Employees;Server=CorpHQ;User ID=admin;Password=2g$tXD76qr
Attempted to divide by zero.
```

You can also see, below the details of the exception, the contents of the original fault contract, which are obtained by casting the exception to the type **FaultException(OfSalary CalculationFault)** and querying the properties. You can see that this contains the original exception message generated within the service. Look at the code in the example file, and run it, to see more details.

Handling Specific Exception Types

So far, all of the examples have used an exception policy that handles a single exception type (in the examples, this is **Exception** so that the policy will apply to any type of exception passed to it). However, you can specify multiple exception types within a policy, and specify different handlers—including chains of handlers—for each exception type. Figure 7 shows a section of the configuration console with three exception types defined for the policy named **NotifyingRethrow** (which is used in the next example). Each exception type has different exception handlers specified.

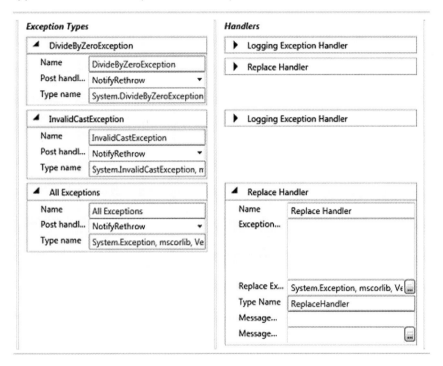

FIGURE 7
Three exception types defined

The advantage of this capability should be obvious. You can create policies that will handle different types of exceptions in different ways and, for each exception type, can have different messages and post-handling actions as well as different handler combinations. And, best of all, administrators can modify the policies post deployment to change the behavior of the exception handling as required. They can add new exception types, modify the types specified, change the properties for each exception type and the associated handlers, and generally fine-tune the strategy to suit day-to-day operational requirements.

Of course, this will only work if your application code throws the appropriate exception types. If you generate informational exceptions that are all of the base type **Exception**, as we did in earlier examples in this chapter, only the handlers for that exception type will execute.

Executing Code around Exception Handling

So far, all of the examples have used the Process method to execute the code that may cause an exception. They simply used the **Process** method to execute the target class method, as shown here.

```
Dim calc As New SalaryCalculator()
Dim result As Decimal = exManager.Process(Function() _
        result = calc.GetWeeklySalary("jsmith", 0), "ExceptionShielding")
Console.WriteLine("Result is: {0}", result)
```

However, as you saw earlier in this chapter, the **Process** method does not allow you to detect the return value from the exception handling policy executed by the Exception Handling block (it returns the value of the method or function it executes). In some cases, though perhaps rarely, you may want to detect the return value from the exception handling policy and perform some processing based on this value, and perhaps even capture the exception returned by the Exception Handling block to manipulate it or decide whether or not to throw it in your code.

In this case, you can use the **HandleException** method to pass an exception to the block as an **out** parameter to be populated by the policy, and retrieve the Boolean result that indicates if the policy determined that the exception should be thrown or ignored.

The example *Executing Custom Code Before and After Handling an Exception*, demonstrates this approach. The **SalaryCalculator** class contains two methods in addition to the **GetWeeklySalary** method we've used so far in this chapter. These two methods, named **RaiseDivideByZeroException** and **RaiseArgumentOutOfRangeException**, will cause an exception of the type indicated by the method name when called.

The sample first attempts to execute the **RaiseDivideByZeroException** method, like this.

```
Dim calc As New SalaryCalculator()
Console.WriteLine("Result is: {0}", calc.RaiseDivideByZeroException("jsmith", 0))
```

This exception is caught in the main routine using the exception handling code shown below. This creates a new **Exception** instance and passes it to the Exception Handling block as the **out** parameter, specifying that the block should use the **NotifyingRethrow** policy. This policy specifies that the block should log **DivideByZero** exceptions, and replace the message with a sanitized one. However, it also has the **PostHandlingAction** set to **None**, which means that the **HandleException** method will return false. The sample code simply displays a message and continues.

```
...
Catch ex As Exception
  Dim newException As Exception = Nothing
  Dim rethrow As Boolean = exManager.HandleException(ex, "NotifyingRethrow", _
                                                     newException)

  If rethrow Then
    ' Exception policy setting is "ThrowNewException".
    ' Code here to perform any clean up tasks required.
```

```
  ' Then throw the exception returned by the exception handling policy.
    Throw newException
  Else
    ' Exception policy setting is "None" so exception is not thrown.
    ' Code here to perform any other processing required.
    ' In this example, just ignore the exception and do nothing.
    Console.WriteLine("Detected and ignored Divide By Zero Error " _
                    & "- no value returned.")
  End If
End Try
```

Therefore, when you execute this sample, the following message is displayed.

```
Getting salary for 'jsmith' ... this will raise a DivideByZero exception.
Detected and ignored Divide By Zero Error - no value returned.
```

The sample then continues by executing the **RaiseArgumentOutOfRangeException** method of the **SalaryCalculator** class, like this.

```
Dim calc As New SalaryCalculator()
Console.WriteLine("Result is: {0}", _
                calc.RaiseArgumentOutOfRangeException("jsmith", 0))
```

This section of the sample also contains a **Catch** section, which is—other than the message displayed to the screen—identical to that shown earlier. However, the **Notifying Rethrow** policy specifies that exceptions of type **Exception** (or any exceptions that are not of type **DivideByZeroException**) should simply be wrapped in a new exception that has a sanitized error message. The **PostHandlingAction** for the Exception type is set to **ThrowNewException**, which means that the **HandleException** method will return true. Therefore the code in the Catch block will throw the exception returned from the block, resulting in the output shown here.

```
Getting salary for 'jsmith' ... this will raise an ArgumentOutOfRange exception.

Exception type System.Exception was thrown.
Message: 'An application error has occurred.'
Source: 'ExceptionHandlingExample'

Inner Exception: System.ArgumentOutOfRangeException: startIndex cannot be larger
 than length of string.
Parameter name: startIndex
   at System.String.InternalSubStringWithChecks(Int32 startIndex, Int32 length,
Boolean fAlwaysCopy)
   at System.String.Substring(Int32 startIndex, Int32 length)
   at ExceptionHandlingExample.SalaryCalculator.RaiseArgumentOutOfRangeException
(String employeeId, Int32 weeks) in ...\ExceptionHandling\ExceptionHandling\Sala
ryCalculator.vb:line 56
   at ExceptionHandlingExample.Program.ExecutingCodeAroundException(Int32 positi
onInTitleArray) in ...\ExceptionHandling\ExceptionHandling\Program.vb:line 181
```

Assisting Administrators

Some would say that the Exception Handling block already does plenty to make an administrator's life easy. However, it also contains features that allow you to exert extra control over the way that exception information is made available, and the way that it can be used by administrators and operations staff. If you have ever worked in a technical support role, you'll recognize the scenario. A user calls to tell you that an error has occurred in the application. If you are lucky, the user will be able to tell you exactly what they were doing at the time, and the exact text of the error message. More likely, he or she will tell you that they weren't really doing anything, and that the message said something about contacting the administrator.

To resolve this regularly occurring problem, you can make use of the **Handling InstanceID** value generated by the block to associate logged exception details with specific exceptions, and with related exceptions. The Exception Handling block creates a unique GUID value for the **HandlingInstanceID** of every execution of a policy. The value is available to all of the handlers in the policy while that policy is executing. The **Logging** handler automatically writes the **HandlingInstanceID** value into every log message it creates. The **Wrap** and **Replace** handlers can access the **HandlingInstanceID** value and include it in a message using the special token **{handlingInstanceID}**.

Figure 8 shows how you can configure a **Logging** handler and a **Replace** handler in a policy, and include the **{handlingInstanceID}** token in the **Exception Message** property of the **Replace** handler.

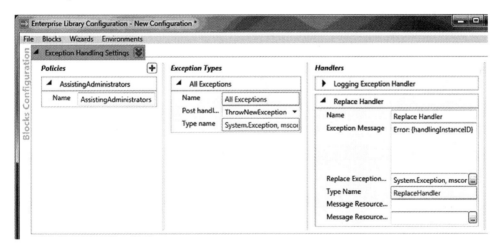

FIGURE 8
Configuring a unique exception handling instance identifier

Now your application can display the unique exception identifier to the user, and they can pass it to the administrator who can use it to identify the matching logged exception information. This logged information will include the information from the original exception, before the **Replace** handler replaced it with the sanitized exception. If you select the option *Providing Assistance to Administrators for Locating Exception Details* in the example application, you can see this in operation. The example displays the following details of the exception returned from the exception handling policy:

```
Exception type System.Exception was thrown.
Message: 'Application error. Please advise your administrator and provide them
with this error code: 22f759d3-8f58-43dc-9adc-93b953a4f733'
Source: 'Microsoft.Practices.EnterpriseLibrary.ExceptionHandling'
No Inner Exception
```

In a production application, you will probably show this message in a dialog of some type. One issue, however, is that users may not copy the GUID correctly from a standard error dialog (such as a message box). If you decide to use the **HandlingInstanceID** value to assist administrators, consider using a form containing a read-only text box or an error page in a Web application to display the GUID value in a way that allows users to copy it to the clipboard and paste into a document or e-mail message. Figure 9 shows a simple Windows Form displayed as a modal dialog. It contains a read-only **TextBox** control that displays the **Message** property of the exception, which contains the **HandlingInstanceID** GUID value.

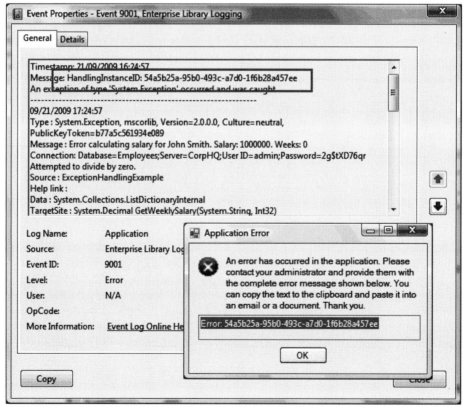

FIGURE 9
Displaying and correlating the handling instance identifier

Extending Your Exception Handling

Like all of the Enterprise Library application blocks, the Exception Handling block is extensible. You can create new exception handlers and exception formatters if you need to perform specific tasks that the block does not implement by default. For example, you could create an exception handler that displays the exception details in a dialog, creates an XML message, or generates a Web page. All that is required is that you implement the **IExceptionHandler** interface defined within the block. This interface contains one method named **HandleException** that the Exception Handling block will execute when you add your handler to a policy chain.

The Exception Handling block uses formatters to create the message sent to the Logging block when you use a **Logging** handler. The two formatters provided are the **TextExceptionFormatter** and the **XmlExceptionFormatter**. The **TextException Formatter** generates a simple text format for the error message, as you have seen in the previous sections of this chapter. The **XmlExceptionFormatter** generates, as you would expect, an XML-formatted document as the error message. You can create custom formatters if you want to control the exact format of this information. You simply create a new class that derives from the **ExceptionFormatter** base class in the Exception Handling block, and override the several methods it contains for formatting the exception information as required.

Summary

In this chapter you have seen why, when, and how you can use the Enterprise Library Exception Handling block to create and implement exception handling strategies. Poor error handling can make your application difficult to manage and maintain, hard to debug and test, and may allow it to expose sensitive information that would be useful to attackers and malicious users.

A good practice for exception management is to implement strategies that provide a controlled and decoupled approach to exception handling through configurable policies. The Exception Handling block makes it easy to implement such strategies for your applications, irrespective of their type and complexity. You can use the Exception Handling block in Web and Windows Forms applications, Web services, console-based applications and utilities, and even in administration scripts and applications hosted in environments such as SharePoint®, Microsoft Office applications, other enterprise systems.

This chapter demonstrated how you can implement common exception handling patterns, such as Exception Shielding, using techniques such as wrapping, replacing, and logging exceptions. It also demonstrated how you can handle different types of exceptions, assist administrators by using unique exception identifiers, and extend the Exception Handling block to perform tasks that are specific to your own requirements.

4   As Easy As Falling Off a Log

Introduction

Just in case you didn't quite grasp it from the title, this chapter is about one of the most useful and popular of the Enterprise Library blocks, the Logging application block, which makes it really easy to perform logging in a myriad of different ways depending on the requirements of your application.

Logging generally fulfills two main requirements: monitoring general application performance, and providing information. In terms of performance, logging allows you to monitor what's happening inside your application and, in some cases, what's happening in the world outside as well. For example, logging can indicate what errors or failures have occurred, when something that should have happened did not, and when things are taking a lot longer than they should. It can also simply provide status information on processes that are working correctly—including those that talk to the outside world. Let's face it, there's nothing more rewarding for an administrator than seeing an event log full of those nice blue information icons.

Secondly, and possibly even more importantly, logging can provide vital information about your application. Often referred to as auditing, this type of logging allows you to track the behavior of users and processes in terms of the tasks they carry out, the information they read and change, and the resources they access. It can provide an audit trail that allows you to follow up and get information about malicious activity (whether it succeeds or not), will allow you to trace events that may indicate future attack vectors or reveal security weaknesses, and even help you to recover when disaster strikes (though this doesn't mean you shouldn't be taking the usual precautions such as backing up systems and data). One other area where audit logging is useful is in managing repudiation. For example, your audit logs may be useful in legal or procedural situations where users or external attackers deny their actions.

The Logging block is a highly flexible and configurable solution that allows you to create and store log messages in a wide variety of locations, categorize and filter messages, and collect contextual information useful for debugging and tracing as well as for auditing and general logging requirements. It abstracts the logging functionality from the log destination so that the application code is consistent, irrespective of the location and type of the target logging store. Changes to almost all of the parameters that control logging are possible simply by changing the configuration after deployment and at run time. This means that administrators and operators can vary the logging behavior as they manage the application, including when using Group Policy.

What Does the Logging Block Do?

The Logging application block allows you to decouple your logging functionality from your application code. The block can route log entries to a Windows® Event Log, a database, or a text (or XML) file. It can also generate an e-mail message containing the logging information, a message you can route through Windows Message Queuing (using a distributor service provided with the block), or a Windows Management Instrumentation (WMI) event. And, if none of these built-in capabilities meets your requirements, you can create a provider that sends the log entry to any other custom location or executes some other action.

In your application, you simply generate a log entry using a suitable logging object, such as the **LogWriter** class, and then call a method to write the information it contains to the logging system. The Logging block routes the log message through any filters you define in your configuration, and on to the listeners that you configure. Each listener defines the target of the log entry, such as Windows Event Log or an e-mail message, and uses a formatter to generate suitably formatted content for that logging target.

You can see from this that there are many objects involved in this multi-step process, and it is important to understand how they interact and how the log message flows through the pipeline of processes. Figure 1 shows the overall process in more detail, and provides an explanation of each stage.

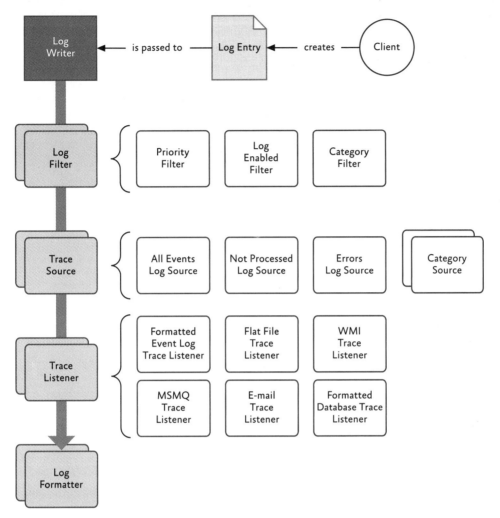

FIGURE 1
An overview of the logging process and the objects in the Logging block

Stage	Description
Creating the Log Entry	The user creates a **LogWriter** instance, uses it to create a new **LogEntry**, and passes it to the Logging block for processing. Alternatively, the user can create a new **LogEntry** explicitly, populate it with the required information, and use a **LogWriter** to pass it to the Logging block for processing.
Filtering the Log Entry	The Logging block filters the **LogEntry** (based on your configuration settings) for message priority, or categories you added to the **LogEntry** when you created it. It also checks to see if logging is enabled. These filters can prevent any further processing of the log entries. This is useful, for example, when you want to allow administrators to enable and disable additional debug information logging without requiring them to restart the application.
Selecting Trace Sources	Trace sources act as the link between the log entries and the log targets. There is a trace source for each category you define in the logging block configuration; plus, there are three built-in trace sources that capture all log entries, unprocessed entries that do not match any category, and entries that cannot be processed due to an error while logging (such as an error while writing to the target log).
Selecting Trace Listeners	Each trace source has one or more trace listeners defined. These listeners are responsible for taking the log entry, passing it through a separate log formatter that translates the content into a suitable format, and passing it to the target log. Several trace listeners are provided with the block, and you can create your own if required.
Formatting the Log Entry	Each trace listener can use a log formatter to format the information contained in the log entry. The block contains log message formatters, and you can create your own formatter if required. The text formatter uses a template containing placeholders that makes it easy to generate the required format for log entries.

LOGGING CATEGORIES

Categories allow you to specify the target(s) for log entries processed by the block. You can define categories that relate to one or more targets. For example, you might create a category named General containing trace listeners that write to text files and XML files, and a category named Auditing for administrative information that is configured to use trace listeners that write to one or more databases. Then you can assign a log entry to one or more categories, effectively mapping it to multiple targets. The three log sources shown in the schematic in Figure 1 (all events log source, not processed log source, and errors log source) are themselves categories for which you can define trace listeners.

> *Logging is an added-value service for applications, and so any failures in the logging process must be handled gracefully without raising an exception to the main business processes. The Logging block achieves this by sending all logging failures to a special category (the errors log source) which is named* **Logging Errors & Warnings**. *By default, these error messages are written to Windows Event Log, though you can configure this category to write to other targets using different trace listeners if you wish.*

LOGGING OVERHEAD AND ADDITIONAL CONTEXT INFORMATION
No matter how you implement logging, it will always have some performance impact. The Logging block provides a flexible and highly configurable logging solution that is carefully designed to minimize performance impact. However, you should be aware of this impact, and consider how your own logging strategy will affect it. For example, a complex configuration that writes log entries to multiple logs and uses multiple filters is likely to have more impact than simple configurations. You must balance your requirements for logging against performance and scalability needs.

To maximize performance, the **LogWriter** class by default exposes properties only for the commonly required information. This includes the event ID, message, priority, and categories you specify in the configuration. The **LogWriter** also automatically collects some context information such as the time, the application domain, the machine name, and the process ID—where possible—using cached values in order to minimize performance impact.

However, collecting additional context information can be expensive in processing terms and, if you are not going to use the information, wastes precious resources and may affect performance. Therefore, the Logging block only collects other less commonly used information from the environment, which you might require only occasionally, if you specify that you want this information when you create the **LogEntry** instance. Four classes within the Logging block can collect specific sets of context information that you can add to your log entry. This includes COM+ diagnostic information, the current stack trace, the security-related information from the managed runtime, and security-related information from the operating system. There is also a dictionary property for the log entry where you can add any additional custom information you require, and which must appear in your logs.

How Do I Use the Logging Block?

It's time to see some examples of the Logging block use, including how to create log entries and write them to various targets such as the Windows Event Log, disk files, and a database. Later you'll see how you can use some of the advanced features of the block, such as checking filter status and adding context information to a log entry. However, before you can start using the Logging block, you must configure it.

CONFIGURING THE LOGGING BLOCK
You can configure the Logging block using the configuration tool described in Chapter 1, "Introduction." The logging settings section of the configuration tool contains three columns where you configure filters (trace sources), logging target listeners (trace listeners), and log message formatters. The first column contains three types of filter: categories (category sources), special categories, and logging filters. All of these items were described in the schematic shown in Figure 1 and the accompanying table.

Figure 2 shows the configuration tool loaded with the configuration for the examples used in this chapter. You can see that we have configured several types of filters, listeners, and formatters. As the configuration contains the Database trace listener, the configuration tool has automatically added the Database Settings section as well.

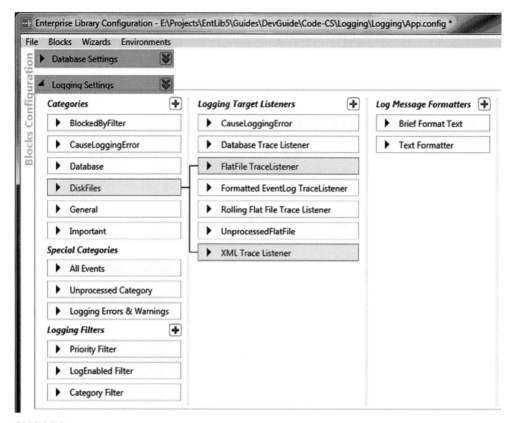

FIGURE 2
The configuration settings for the sample application

The easiest way to learn about how the Logging block configuration works is to run the configuration tool yourself and open the App.config file from the example application. You can expand each of the sections to see the property settings, and to relate each item to the others.

INITIALIZING THE LOGGING BLOCK

Now you must edit your code to use the Logging block. You'll need to add references to the appropriate Enterprise Library assemblies and namespaces. The assemblies you must add to your project (in addition to the assemblies required for all Enterprise Library projects) are:

- Microsoft.Practices.EnterpriseLibrary.Logging.dll
- Microsoft.Practices.EnterpriseLibrary.Logging.Database.dll
- Microsoft.Practices.EnterpriseLibrary.Data.dll

However, if you do not intend to send log entries to a database, you will not require the last two assemblies on this list.

Now you are ready to write some code.

DIVING IN WITH AN EXAMPLE

To demonstrate the features of the Logging block, we provide a sample application that you can download and run on your own computer. You can run the executable directly from the bin\Debug folder, or you can open the solution named **Logging** in Microsoft® Visual Studio® to see the code and run it under Visual Studio. The application includes a preconfigured database for storing log entries, as well as scripts you can use to create the Logging database within a different database server if you prefer.

> *You do not need to run the scripts if you have Microsoft SQL Server® Express installed locally. If you want to specify a different database for logging, edit the script named CreateLoggingDb.cmd to specify the location of the database and execute it. After you do that, you must change the connection string named* **ExampleDatabase** *to point to your new database.*
>
> *In addition, depending on the version of the operating system you are using, you may need to execute the application under the context of an account with administrative privileges. If you are running the sample from within Visual Studio, start Visual Studio by right-clicking the entry in your Start menu and selecting* **Run as administrator***.*

One other point to note about the sample application is that it creates a folder named **Temp** in the root of your C: drive if one does not already exist, and writes the text log files there so that you can easily find and view them.

CREATING AND WRITING LOG ENTRIES WITH A LOGWRITER

The first of the examples, *Simple logging with the Write method of a LogWriter*, demonstrates how you can use a **LogWriter** directly to create log entries. The first stage is to obtain a **LogWriter**, and the example uses the simplest approach—the **GetInstance** method of the current Enterprise Library container. See the following code.

```
' Resolve the default LogWriter object from the container.
Dim defaultWriter As LogWriter _
        = EnterpriseLibraryContainer.Current.GetInstance(Of LogWriter)()
```

Now you can call the **Write** method and pass in any parameter values you require. There are many overloads of the **Write** method. They allow you to specify the message text, the category, the priority (a numeric value), the event ID, the severity (a value from the **TraceEventType** enumeration), and a title for the event. There is also an overload that allows you to add custom values to the log entry by populating a **Dictionary** with name and value pairs (you will see this used in a later example). Our example code uses several of these overloads. We've removed some of the **Console.WriteLine** statements from the code listed here to make it easier to see what it actually does.

```
' Check if logging is enabled before creating log entries.
If defaultWriter.IsLoggingEnabled() Then

    defaultWriter.Write("Log entry created using the simplest overload.")
    defaultWriter.Write("Log entry with a single category.", "General")
```

```
   defaultWriter.Write("Log entry with a category, priority, and event ID.", _
                       "General", 6, 9001)
   defaultWriter.Write("Log entry with a category, priority, event ID, " _
                       & "and severity.", "General", 5, 9002, _
                       TraceEventType.Warning)
   defaultWriter.Write("Log entry with a category, priority, event ID, " _
                       & "severity, and title.", "General", 8, 9003, _
                       TraceEventType.Warning, "Logging Block Examples")
Else
   Console.WriteLine("Logging is disabled in the configuration.")
End If
```

Notice how the code first checks to see if logging is enabled. There is no point using valuable processor cycles and memory generating log entries if they aren't going anywhere. The **Filters** section of the Logging block configuration can contain a special filter named the **Log Enabled Filter** (we have configured one in our example application). This filter has the single property, **Enabled,** that allows administrators to enable and disable all logging for the block. When it is set to **False**, the **IsLoggingEnabled** property of the **LogWriter** will return **False** as well.

The example produces the following result. All of the events are sent to the **General** category, which is configured to write events to the Windows Application Event Log (this is the default configuration for the block).

```
Created a Log Entry using the simplest overload.
Created a Log Entry with a single category.
Created a Log Entry with a category, priority, and event ID.
Created a Log Entry with a category, priority, event ID, and severity.
Created a Log Entry with a category, priority, event ID, severity, and title.
Open Windows Event Viewer 'Application' Log to see the results.
```

You can open Windows Event Viewer to see the results. Figure 3 shows the event generated by the last of the **Write** statements in this example.

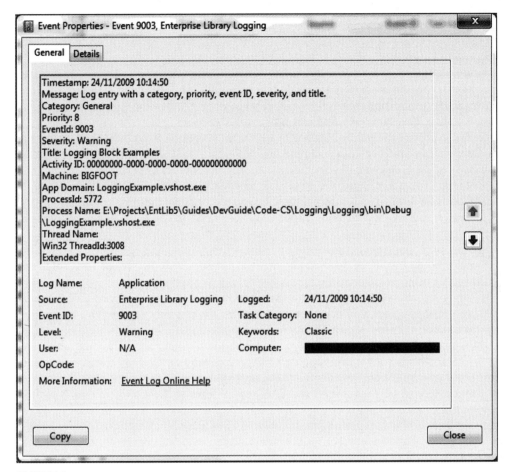

FIGURE 3
The logged event

If you do not specify a value for one of the parameters of the **Write** *method, the Logging block uses the default value for that parameter. The defaults are Category = General, Priority = -1, Event ID = 1, Severity = Information, and an empty string for Title.*

About Logging Categories

Categories are the way that Enterprise Library routes events sent to the block to the appropriate target, such as a database, the event log, an e-mail message, and more. The previous example makes use of the default configuration for the Logging block. When you add the Logging block to your application configuration using the Enterprise Library configuration tools, it contains the single category named **General** that is configured to write events to the Windows Application Event Log.

You can change the behavior of logging for any category. For example, you can change the behavior of the previous example by reconfiguring the event log trace listener specified for the **General** category, or by reconfiguring the text formatter that this trace listener uses. You can change the event log to which the event log trace listener sends events; edit the template used by the text formatter; or add other trace listeners.

However, it's likely that your application will need to perform different types of logging for different tasks. The typical way to achieve this is to define additional categories, and then specify the type of trace listener you need for each category. For example, you may want to send audit information to a text file or an XML file, to a database, or both; instead of to Windows Event Log. Or you may want to send indications of catastrophic failures to administrators as e-mail messages. If you are using an enterprise-level monitoring system, you may instead prefer to write events to the WMI subsystem, or send them to another system through Windows Message Queuing.

You can easily add categories to your application configuration. The approach is to add the trace listeners for the logging targets you require, such as the flat file trace listener or database trace listener to the **Logging Target Listeners** section, and then add the categories you require to the **Category Filters** section. Finally, you link them together in any combination by adding each of the required trace listener(s) to the category filter in the **Category Filters** section. Figure 4 shows this type of configuration, were the General category will output log messages to an event log listener and a database trace listener.

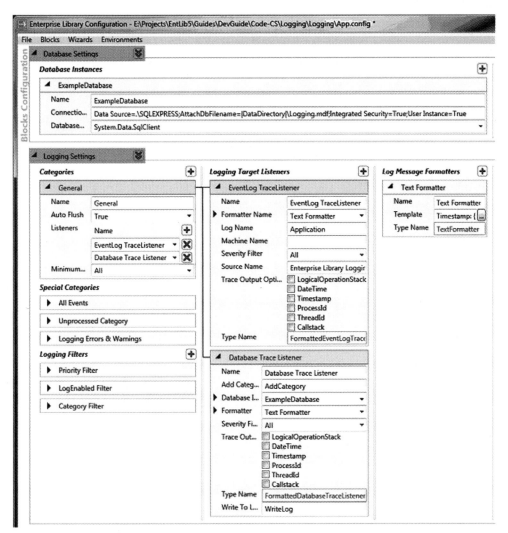

FIGURE 4
Configuring trace listeners for different categories

You can specify two properties for each category (source) you add, and for the default **General** category. You can set the **Auto Flush** property to specify that the block should flush log entries to their configured target trace listeners each time as soon as they are written to the block, or only when you call the **FlushContextItems** method of the **LogWriter**. If you set the **Auto Flush** property to **False**, ensure that your code calls this method when an exception or failure occurs to avoid losing any cached logging information.

The other property you can set for each category is the **Minimum Severity** (which sets the **Source Levels** property of each listener). This specifies the minimum severity (such as Warning or Critical) for the log entries that the category filter will pass to its configured trace listeners. Any log entries with a lower severity will be blocked. The default severity is **All**, and so no log entries will be blocked unless you change this value. You can also configure a **Severity Filter** (which sets the **Filter** property) for each individual trace listener, and these values can be different for trace listeners in the same category. You will see how to use the **Filter** property of a trace listener in the next example in this chapter.

Filtering by Category

The **Logging Filters** section of the Logging block configuration can contain a filter that you can use to filter log entries sent to the block based on their membership in specified categories. You can add multiple categories to your configuration to manage filtering, though overuse of this capability can make it difficult to manage logging.

To help you define filters, the configuration tool contains a filter editor dialog that allows you to specify the filter mode (Allow all except..., or Deny all except...) and then build a list of categories to which this filter will apply. The example application contains only a single filter that is configured to allow logging to all categories except for the category named (rather appropriately) **BlockedByFilter**. You will see the **BlockedByFilter** category used in the section "Capturing Unprocessed Events and Logging Errors" later in this chapter.

Writing Log Entries to Multiple Categories

In addition to being able to define multiple categories, you can send a log entry to more than one category in a single operation. This approach often means you can define fewer categories, and it simplifies the configuration because each category can focus on a specific task. You don't need to have multiple categories with similar sets of trace listeners.

The second example, *Logging to multiple categories with the Write method of a LogWriter*, shows how to write to multiple categories. The example has two categories, named **DiskFiles** and **Important**, defined in the configuration. The **DiskFiles** category contains references to a flat file trace listener and an XML trace listener. The **Important** category contains references to an event log trace listener and a rolling flat file trace listener.

The example uses the following code to create an array of the two category names, **DiskFiles** and **Important**, and then it writes three log messages to these two categories using the **Write** method of the **LogWriter** in the same way as in the previous example. Again, we've removed some of the **Console.WriteLine** statements to make it easier to see what the code actually does.

```
' Check if logging is enabled before creating log entries.
If defaultWriter.IsLoggingEnabled() Then

  ' Create a string array (or List<>) containing the categories.
  Dim logCategories As String() = New String() {"DiskFiles", "Important"}

  ' Write the log entries using these categories.
  defaultWriter.Write("Log entry with multiple categories.", logCategories)
```

```
defaultWriter.Write("Log entry with multiple categories, a priority, " _
                & "and an event ID.", logCategories, 7, 9004)
defaultWriter.Write("Log entry with multiple categories, a priority, " _
                & "event ID, severity, and title.", logCategories, 10, _
                9005, TraceEventType.Critical, "Logging Block Examples")
Else
  Console.WriteLine("Logging is disabled in the configuration.")
End If
```

Controlling Output Formatting

If you run the example above and then open Windows Event Log, you will see the three events generated by this example. Also, in the C:\Temp folder, you will see three files. RollingFlatFile.log is generated by the rolling flat file trace listener, and contains the same information as the event log event generated by the event log trace listener. If you explore the configuration, you will see that they both use the same text formatter to format the output.

The FlatFile.log file, which is generated by the flat file trace listener, contains only a simplified set of values for each event. For example, this is the output generated for the last of the three log entries.

```
----------------------------------------
Timestamp: 24/11/2009 10:49:26
Message: Log entry with multiple categories, a priority, event ID, severity,
  and title.
Category: DiskFiles, Important
Priority: 10
EventId: 9005
ActivityId: 00000000-0000-0000-0000-000000000000
Severity: Critical
Title:Logging Block Examples
----------------------------------------
```

The reason is that the flat file trace listener is configured to use a different text formatter—in this case one named Brief Format Text (listed in the **Formatters** section of the configuration tool). All trace listeners use a formatter to translate the contents of the log entry properties into the appropriate format for the target of that trace listener. Trace listeners that create text output, such as a text file or an e-mail message, use a text formatter defined within the configuration of the block.

If you examine the configured text formatter, you will see that it has a **Template** property. You can use the Template Editor dialog available for editing this property to change the format of the output by adding tokens (using the drop-down list of available tokens) and text, or by removing tokens and text. Figure 5 shows the default template for a text formatter, and how you can edit this template. A full list of tokens and their meaning is available in the online documentation for Enterprise Library, although most are fairly self-explanatory.

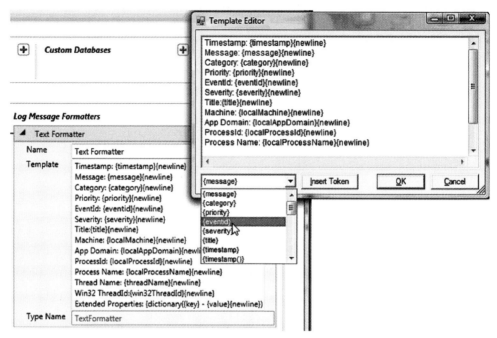

FIGURE 5
Editing the template for a text formatter

The template we used in the Brief Format text formatter is shown here.

```
Timestamp: {timestamp(local)}{newline}Message: {message}{newline}Category:
{category}{newline}Priority: {priority}{newline}EventId:
{eventid}{newline}ActivityId: {property(ActivityId)}{newline}Severity:
{severity}{newline}Title:{title}{newline}
```

Non-Formatted Trace Listeners

While we are discussing output formatting, there is one other factor to consider. Some trace listeners do not use a text formatter to format the output they generate. This is generally because the output is in a binary or specific format. The WMI trace listener is a typical example that does not use a text formatter.

For such trace listeners, you can set the **TraceOutputOptions** property to one of a range of values to specify the values you want to include in the output. The **Trace OutputOptions** property accepts a value from the **System.Diagnostics.TraceOptions** enumeration. Valid values include **CallStack**, **DateTime**, **ProcessId**, **LogicalOperation Stack**, **Timestamp**, and **ThreadId**. The documentation installed with Enterprise Library, and the documentation for the System.Diagnostics namespace on MSDN®, provide more information.

Filtering by Severity in a Trace Listener

The previous example generates a third disk file that we haven't looked at yet. We didn't forget this, but saved if for this section because it demonstrates another feature of the trace listeners that you will often find extremely useful. To see this, you need to view the file XmlLogFile.xml that was generated in the C:\Temp folder by the XML trace listener we used in the previous example. You should open it in Microsoft Internet Explorer® (or another Web browser or text editor) to see the structure.

You will see that the file contains only one event from the previous example, not the three that the code in the example generated. This is because the XML trace listener has the **Filter** property in its configuration set to **Error**. Therefore, it will log only events with a severity of **Error** or higher. If you look back at the example code, you will see that only the last of the three calls to the **Write** method specified a value for the severity (**TraceEventType.Critical** in this case), and so the default value **Information** was used for the other two events.

> *If you get an error indicating that the XML document created by the XML trace listener is invalid, it's probably because you have more than one log entry in the file. This means that it is not a valid XML document—it contains separate event log entries added to the file each time you ran this example. To view it as XML, you must open the file in a text editor and add an opening and closing element (such as* **<root>** *and* **</root>**) *around the content. Or, just delete it and run the example once more.*

All of the trace listeners provided with Enterprise Library expose the **Filter** property, and you can use this to limit the log entries written to the logging target to only those that are important to you. If your code generates many information events that you use for monitoring and debugging only under specific circumstances, you can filter these to reduce the growth and size of the log when they are not required.

Alternatively, (as in the example) you can use the **Filter** property to differentiate the granularity of logging for different listeners in the same category. It may be that a flat file trace listener will log all entries to an audit log file for some particular event, but an Email trace listener in the same category will send e-mail messages to administrators only when an Error or Critical event occurs.

Filtering All Log Entries by Priority

As well as being able to filter log entries in individual trace listeners based on their severity, you can set the Logging block to filter all log entries sent to it based on their priority. Alongside the log-enabled filter and category filter in the **Filters** section of the configuration (which we discussed earlier in this chapter), you can add a filter named Priority Filter.

This filter has two properties that you can set: **Minimum Priority** and **Maximum Priority**. The default setting for the priority of a log entry is **-1**, which is the same as the default setting of the **Minimum Priority** property of the filter, and there is no maximum priority set. Therefore, this filter will not block any log entries. However, if you change the defaults for these properties, only log entries with a priority between the configured values (including the specified maximum and minimum values) will be logged. The exception is log entries that have the default priority of **-1**. These are never filtered.

CREATING AND USING LOGENTRY OBJECTS

So far we have used the **Write** method of the **LogWriter** class to generate log entries. An alternative approach that may be useful if you want to create log entries individually, perhaps to return them from methods or to pass them between processes, is to generate instances of the **LogEntry** class and then write them to the configured targets afterwards.

The example, *Creating and writing log entries with a LogEntry object,* demonstrates this approach. It creates two **LogEntry** instances. The code first calls the most complex constructor of the **LogEntry** class that accepts all of the possible values. This includes a **Dictionary** of objects with a string key (in this example, the single item **Extra Information**) that will be included in the output of the trace listener and formatter. Then it writes this log entry using an overload of the **Write** method of the **LogWriter** that accepts a **LogEntry** instance.

Next, the code creates a new empty **LogEntry** using the default constructor and populates this by setting individual properties, before writing it using the same **Write** method of the **LogWriter**.

```
' Check if logging is enabled before creating log entries.
If defaultWriter.IsLoggingEnabled() Then

  ' Create a Dictionary of extended properties
  Dim exProperties As New Dictionary(Of String, Object)()
  exProperties.Add("Extra Information", "Some Special Value")

  ' Create a LogEntry using the constructor parameters.
  Dim entry1 As New LogEntry("LogEntry with category, priority, event ID, " _
                     & "severity, and title.", "General", 8, 9006, _
                     TraceEventType.[Error], "Logging Block Examples", _
                     exProperties)
  defaultWriter.Write(entry1)

  ' Create a LogEntry and populate the individual properties.
  Dim entry2 As New LogEntry()
  entry2.Categories = New String() {"General"}
  entry2.EventId = 9007
  entry2.Message = "LogEntry with individual properties specified."
  entry2.Priority = 9
  entry2.Severity = TraceEventType.Warning
  entry2.Title = "Logging Block Examples"
  entry2.ExtendedProperties = exProperties
  defaultWriter.Write(entry2)

Else
  Console.WriteLine("Logging is disabled in the configuration.")
End If
```

This example writes the log entries to the Windows Application Event Log by using the **General** category. If you view the events this example generates, you will see the values set in the code above including (at the end of the list) the extended property we specified using a **Dictionary**. You can see this in Figure 6.

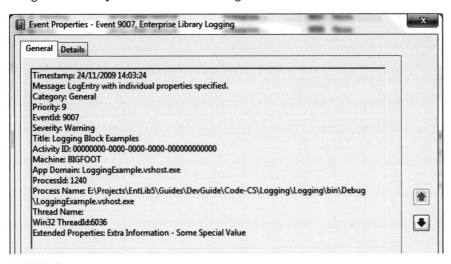

FIGURE 6
A log entry written to the General category

CAPTURING UNPROCESSED EVENTS AND LOGGING ERRORS

The capability to route log entries through different categories to a configured set of trace listener targets provides a very powerful mechanism for performing a wide range of logging activities. However, it prompts some questions. In particular, what happens if the categories specified in a log entry don't match any in the configuration? And what happens if there is an error when the trace listener attempts to write the log entry to the target?

About Special Sources

In fact, the Logging block includes three special sources that handle these situations. Each is effectively a category, and you can add references to configured trace listeners to each one so that events arriving in that category will be written to the target(s) you specify.

The **All Events** special source receives all events, irrespective of all other settings within the configuration of the block. You can use this to provide an audit trail of all events, if required. By default, it has no trace listeners configured.

The **Unprocessed Category** special source receives any log entry that has a category that does not match any configured categories. By default, this category has no trace listeners configured.

The **Logging Errors & Warnings** special source receives any log entry that causes an error in the logging process. By default, this category contains a reference to a trace listener that writes details of the error to the Windows Application Event Log, though you can reconfigure this if you wish.

An Example of Using Special Sources

The example, *Using Special Sources to capture unprocessed events or errors,* demonstrates how the Logging block reacts under these two circumstances. The code first writes a log entry to a category named **InvalidCategory**, which does not exist in the configuration. Next, it writes another log entry to a category named **CauseLoggingError** that is configured to use a Database trace listener. However, this trace listener specifies a connection string that is invalid; it points to a database that does not exist.

```
' Check if logging is enabled before creating log entries.
If defaultWriter.IsLoggingEnabled() Then

    ' Create a log entry to be processed by the "Unprocessed" special source.
    defaultWriter.Write("Entry with category not defined in configuration.", _
                    "InvalidCategory")

    ' Create log entry to be processed by the "Errors & Warnings" special source.
    defaultWriter.Write("Entry that causes a logging error.", "CauseLoggingError")

Else
    Console.WriteLine("Logging is disabled in the configuration.")
End If
```

You might expect that neither of these log entries would actually make it to their target. However, the example generates the following messages that indicate where to look for the log entries that are generated.

```
Created a Log Entry with a category name not defined in the configuration.
The Log Entry will appear in the Unprocessed.log file in the C:\Temp folder.

Created a Log Entry that causes a logging error.
The Log Entry will appear in the Windows Application Event Log.
```

This occurs because we configured the Unprocessed Category in the **Special Sources** section with a reference to a flat file trace listener that writes log entries to a file named Unprocessed.log. If you open this file, you will see the log entry that was sent to the **InvalidCategory** category.

The example uses the default configuration for the **Logging Errors & Warnings** special source. This means that the log entry that caused a logging error will be sent to the formatted event log trace listener referenced in this category. If you open the application event log, you will see this log entry. The listing below shows some of the content.

```
Timestamp: 24/11/2009 15:14:30
Message: Tracing to LogSource 'CauseLoggingError' failed. Processing for other
sources will continue. See summary information below for more information. Should
this problem persist, stop the service and check the configuration file(s) for
possible error(s) in the configuration of the categories and sinks.
```

```
Summary for Enterprise Library Distributor Service:
=======================================
-->
Message:
Timestamp: 24/11/2009 15:14:30
Message: Entry that causes a logging error.
Category: CauseLoggingError
...
...
Exception Information Details:
=======================================
Exception Type: System.Data.SqlClient.SqlException
Errors: System.Data.SqlClient.SqlErrorCollection
Class: 11
LineNumber: 65536
Number: 4060
Procedure:
Server: (local)\SQLEXPRESS
State: 1
Source: .Net SqlClient Data Provider
ErrorCode: -2146232060
Message: Cannot open database "DoesNotExist" requested by the login.
The login failed.
Login failed for user 'xxxxxxx\xxx'.
...
...
StackTrace Information Details:
=======================================
...
...
```

In addition to the log entry itself, you can see that the event contains a wealth of information to help you to debug the error. It contains a message indicating that a logging error occurred, followed by the log entry itself. However, after that is a section containing details of the exception raised by the logging mechanism (you can see the error message generated by the **SqlClient** data access code), and after this is the full stack trace.

> One point to be aware of is that logging database and security exceptions should always be done in such a way as to protect sensitive information that may be contained in the logs. You must ensure that you appropriately restrict access to the logs, and only expose non-sensitive information to other users. You may want to consider applying exception shielding, as described in Chapter 3, "Error Management Made Exceptionally Easy."

LOGGING TO A DATABASE

One of the most common requirements for logging, after Windows Event Log and text files, is to store log entries in a database. The Logging block contains the database trace listener that makes this easy. You configure the database using a script provided with Enterprise Library, located in the \Blocks\Logging\Src\DatabaseTraceListener\Scripts folder of the source code. We also include these scripts with the example for this chapter.

The scripts assume that you will use the locally installed SQL Server Express database, but you can edit the **CreateLoggingDb.cmd** file to change the target to a different database server. The SQL script that the command file executes creates a database named **Logging**, and adds the required tables and stored procedures to it.

However, if you only want to run the example application we provide for this chapter, you do not need to create a database. The project contains a preconfigured database file named Logging.mdf (located in the bin\Debug folder) that is auto-attached to your local SQL Server Express instance. You can connect to this database using Visual Studio Server Explorer to see the contents. The configuration of the database trace listener contains the **Database Instance** property, which is a reference to this database as configured in the settings section for the Data Access application block (see Figure 7).

FIGURE 7
Configuration of the Database trace listener

The database trace listener uses a text formatter to format the output, and so you can edit the template used to generate the log message to suit your requirements. You can also add extended properties to the log entry if you wish. In addition, as with all trace listeners, you can filter log entries based on their severity if you like.

The **Log** table in the database contains columns for only the commonly required values, such as the message, event ID, priority, severity, title, timestamp, machine and process details, and more. It also contains a column named **FormattedMessage** that contains the message generated by the text formatter.

Using the Database Trace Listener

The example, *Sending log entries to a database,* demonstrates the use of the database trace listener. The code is relatively simple, following the same style as the earlier example of creating a **Dictionary** of extended properties, and then using the **Write** method of the **LogWriter** to write two log entries. The first log entry is created by the **LogWriter** from the parameter values provided to the **Write** method. The second is generated in code as a new **LogEntry** instance by specifying the values for the constructor parameters. Also notice how easy it is to add additional information to a log entry using a simple Dictionary as the **ExtendedProperties** of the log entry.

```
' Check if logging is enabled before creating log entries.
If defaultWriter.IsLoggingEnabled() Then

  ' Create a Dictionary of extended properties
  Dim exProperties As New Dictionary(Of String, Object)()
  exProperties.Add("Extra Information", "Some Special Value")

  ' Create a LogEntry using the constructor parameters.
  defaultWriter.Write("Log entry with category, priority, event ID, severity, " _
                  & "title, and extended properties.", "Database", _
                  5, 9008, TraceEventType.Warning, _
                  "Logging Block Examples", exProperties)

  ' Create a LogEntry using the constructor parameters.
  Dim entry As New LogEntry("LogEntry with category, priority, event ID, " _
                  & "severity, title, and extended properties.", _
                  "Database", 8, 9009, TraceEventType.Error, _
                  "Logging Block Examples", exProperties)
  defaultWriter.Write(entry)

Else
  Console.WriteLine("Logging is disabled in the configuration.")
End If
```

To see the two log messages created by this example, you can open the **Logging.mdf** database from the bin\Debug folder using Visual Studio Server Explorer. You will find that the **FormattedMessage** column of the second message contains the following. You can see the extended property information we added using a **Dictionary** at the end of the message.

```
Timestamp: 03/12/2009 17:14:02
Message: LogEntry with category, priority, event ID, severity, title, and extended
properties.
Category: Database
Priority: 8
EventId: 9009
Severity: Error
Title: Logging Block Examples
Activity ID: 00000000-0000-0000-0000-000000000000
Machine: BIGFOOT
App Domain: LoggingExample.vshost.exe
ProcessId: 5860
Process Name: E:\Logging\Logging\bin\Debug\LoggingExample.vshost.exe
Thread Name:
Win32 ThreadId:3208
Extended Properties: Extra Information - Some Special Value
```

Note that you cannot simply delete logged information due to the references between the **Log** and **CategoryLog** tables. However, the database contains a stored procedure named **ClearLogs** that you can execute to remove all log entries.

> *The connection string for the database we provide with this example is:*
> *Data Source=.\SQLEXPRESS;AttachDbFilename=|DataDirectory|\Logging. mdf;Integrated Security=True;User Instance=True*
> *If you have configured a different database using the scripts provided with Enterprise Library, you may find that you get an error when you run this example. It is likely to be that you have an invalid connection string in your App.config file for your database. In addition, use the Services applet in your Administrative Tools folder to check that the SQL Server (SQLEXPRESS) database service (the service is named* **MSSQL$SQLEXPRESS***) is running.*

TESTING LOGGING FILTER STATUS

As you've seen in earlier examples, the Logging block allows you to check if logging is enabled before you create and write a log entry. You can avoid the additional load that this places on your application if logging is not enabled. However, even when logging is enabled, there is no guarantee that a specific log entry will be written to the target log store. For example, it may be blocked by a priority filter if the message priority is below a specified level, or it may belong only to one or more categories where the relevant category filter(s) have logging disabled (a common scenario in the case of logging code specifically designed only for debugging use).

The example, *Checking filter status and adding context information to the log entry,* demonstrates how you can check if a specific log entry will be written to its target before you actually call the **Write** method. After checking that logging is not globally disabled, the example creates two **LogEntry** instances with different categories and priorities. It passes each in turn to another method named **ShowDetailsAndAddExtraInfo**. The following is the code that creates the **LogEntry** instances.

```
' Check if logging is enabled before creating log entries.
If defaultWriter.IsLoggingEnabled() Then

    ' Create a new LogEntry with two categories and priority 3.
    Dim logCategories As String() = New String() {"General", "DiskFiles"}
    Dim entry1 As New LogEntry("LogEntry with categories 'General' and " _
                        & "'DiskFiles' and Priority 3.", logCategories, _
                        3, 9009, TraceEventType.Error, _
                        "Logging Block Examples", Nothing)
    ShowDetailsAndAddExtraInfo(entry1)

    ' Create a new LogEntry with one category and priority 1.
    logCategories = New String() {"BlockedByFilter"}
    Dim entry2 As New LogEntry("LogEntry with category 'BlockedByFilter' and " _
                        & "Priority 1.", logCategories, 1, 9010, _
                        TraceEventType.Information, _
                        "Logging Block Examples", Nothing)
    ShowDetailsAndAddExtraInfo(entry2)

Else
    Console.WriteLine("Logging is disabled in the configuration.")
End If
```

The **ShowDetailsAndAddExtraInfo** method takes a **LogEntry** instance and does two different things. Firstly, it shows how you can obtain information about the way that the Logging block will handle the log entry. This may be useful in advanced scenarios where you need to be able to programmatically determine if a specific log entry was detected by a specific trace source, or will be written to a specific target. Secondly, it demonstrates how you can check if specific filters, or all filters, will block a log entry from being written to its target.

Obtaining Information about Trace Sources and Trace Listeners

The first section of the **ShowDetailsAndAddExtraInfo** method iterates through the collection of trace sources (**LogSource** instances) exposed by the **GetMatchingTrace Sources** method of the **LogWriter** class. Each **LogSource** instance exposes a **Listeners** collection that contains information about the listeners (which specify the targets to which the log entry will be sent).

```
Sub ShowDetailsAndAddExtraInfo(ByVal entry As LogEntry)

  ' Display information about the Trace Sources and Listeners for this LogEntry.
  Dim sources As IEnumerable(Of LogSource) _
                  = defaultWriter.GetMatchingTraceSources(entry)
  For Each source As LogSource In sources
    Console.WriteLine("Log Source name: '{0}'", source.Name)
    For Each listener As TraceListener In source.Listeners
      Console.WriteLine(" - Listener name: '{0}'", listener.Name)
    Next
  Next
  ...
```

Checking if Filters Will Block a Log Entry

Next, the **ShowDetailsAndAddExtraInfo** method checks if any filters will block the current log entry. There are two ways you can do this. You can query each filter type in turn, or just a specific filter type, by using the **GetFilter** method of the **LogWriter** class to get a reference to that type of filter. Then you can check if this filter is enabled, and also use the **ShouldLog** method (to which you pass the list of categories for the log entry) to see if logging will succeed.

The following code shows this approach. It also shows the simpler approach that you can use if you are not interested in the result for a specific filter type. The **LogWriter** class also exposes the **ShouldLog** method, which indicates if any filters will block this entry.

```
...
  ' Check if any filters will block this LogEntry.
  ' This approach allows you to check for specific types of filter.
  ' If there are no filters of the specified type configured, the GetFilter
  ' method returns null, so check this before calling the ShouldLog method.
  Dim catFilter As CategoryFilter = defaultWriter.GetFilter(Of CategoryFilter)()
  If catFilter Is Nothing OrElse catFilter.ShouldLog(entry.Categories) Then
    Console.WriteLine("Category Filter(s) will not block this LogEntry.")
  Else
    Console.WriteLine("A Category Filter will block this LogEntry.")
  End If

  Dim priFilter As PriorityFilter = defaultWriter.GetFilter(Of PriorityFilter)()
  If priFilter Is Nothing OrElse priFilter.ShouldLog(entry.Priority) Then
    Console.WriteLine("Priority Filter(s) will not block this LogEntry.")
  Else
    Console.WriteLine("A Priority Filter will block this LogEntry.")
  End If

  ' Alternatively, a simple approach can be used to check for any type of filter
  If defaultWriter.ShouldLog(entry) Then
```

```
      Console.WriteLine("This LogEntry will not be blocked by config settings.")
      ....
      ' Add context information to log entries after checking that the log entry
      ' will not be blocked due to configuration settings. See the following
      ' section 'Adding Additional Context Information' for details.
      ....
    Else
      Console.WriteLine("This LogEntry will be blocked by configuration settings.")
    End If

  End Sub
```

After you determine that logging will succeed, you can add extra context information and write the log entry. You'll see the code to achieve this shortly. In the meantime, this is the output generated by the example. You can see that it contains details of the log (trace) sources and listeners for each of the two log entries created by the earlier code, and the result of checking if any category filters will block each log entry.

```
Created a LogEnCreated a LogEntry with categories 'General' and 'DiskFiles'.
Log Source name: 'General'
 - Listener name: 'Formatted EventLog TraceListener'
Log Source name: 'DiskFiles'
 - Listener name: 'FlatFile TraceListener'
 - Listener name: 'XML Trace Listener'
Category Filter(s) will not block this LogEntry.
Priority Filter(s) will not block this LogEntry.
...
This LogEntry will not be blocked due to configuration settings.
Created a LogEntry with category 'BlockedByFilter', and Priority 1.
Log Source name: 'BlockedByFilter'
 - Listener name: 'Formatted EventLog TraceListener'
A Category Filter will block this LogEntry.
A Priority Filter will block this LogEntry.
This LogEntry will be blocked due to configuration settings.
```

ADDING ADDITIONAL CONTEXT INFORMATION

While it's useful to have every conceivable item of information included in your log messages, it's not always the best approach. Collecting information from the environment absorbs processing cycles and increases the load that logging places on your application. The Logging block is highly optimized to minimize the load that logging incurs. As an example, some of the less useful information is not included in the log messages by default—particularly information that does require additional resources to collect.

However, you can collect this information if you wish. You may decide to do so in special debugging instrumentation that you only turn on when investigating problems, or for specific areas of your code where you need the additional information, such as security context details for a particularly sensitive process.

After checking that a log entry will not be blocked by filters, the **ShowDetails AndAddExtraInfo** method (shown in the previous section) adds a range of additional context and custom information to the log entry. It uses the four standard Logging block helper classes that can generate additional context information and add it to a **Dictionary**. These helper classes are:

- The **DebugInformationProvider**, which adds the current stack trace to the **Dictionary**.
- The **ManagedSecurityContextInformationProvider**, which adds the current identity name, authorization type, and authorization status to the **Dictionary**.
- The **UnmanagedSecurityContextInformationProvider**, which adds the current user name and process account name to the **Dictionary**.
- The **ComPlusInformationProvider**, which adds the current activity ID, application ID, transaction ID (if any), direct caller account name, and original caller account name to the **Dictionary**.

The following code shows how you can use these helper classes to create additional information for a log entry. It also demonstrates how you can add custom information to the log entry—in this case by reading the contents of the application configuration file into the **Dictionary**. After populating the **Dictionary**, you simply set it as the value of the **ExtendedProperties** property of the log entry before writing that log entry.

```
...
' Create the additional context information to add to the LogEntry.
Dim dict As New Dictionary(Of String, Object)()
' Use the information helper classes to get information about
' the environment and add it to the dictionary.
Dim debugHelper As New DebugInformationProvider()
debugHelper.PopulateDictionary(dict)

Dim infoHelper As New ManagedSecurityContextInformationProvider()
infoHelper.PopulateDictionary(dict)

Dim secHelper As New UnmanagedSecurityContextInformationProvider()
secHelper.PopulateDictionary(dict)

Dim comHelper As New ComPlusInformationProvider()
comHelper.PopulateDictionary(dict)

' Get any other information you require and add it to the dictionary.
Dim configInfo As String = File.ReadAllText("..\..\App.config")
dict.Add("Config information", configInfo)

' Set the dictionary in the LogEntry and write it using the default LogWriter.
```

```
entry.ExtendedProperties = dict
defaultWriter.Write(entry)
...
```

The example produces the following output on screen.

```
Added the current stack trace to the Log Entry.
Added current identity name, authentication type, and status to the Log Entry.
Added the current user name and process account name to the Log Entry.
Added COM+ IDs and caller account information to the Log Entry.
Added information about the configuration of the application to the Log Entry.
LogEntry written to configured trace listeners.
```

To see the additional information added to the log entry, open Windows Event Viewer and locate the new log entry. We haven't shown the contents of this log entry here as it runs to more than 350 lines and contains just about all of the information about an event occurring in your application that you could possibly require!

TRACING AND CORRELATING ACTIVITIES

The final topic for this chapter demonstrates another feature of the Logging block that makes it easier to correlate multiple log entries when you are trying to trace or debug some recalcitrant code in your application. One of the problems with logging is that relying simply on the event ID to correlate multiple events that are related to a specific process or section of code is difficult and error prone. Event IDs are often not unique, and there can be many events with the same event ID generated from different instances of the components in your application that are intermixed in the logs.

The Logging block makes it easy to add an additional unique identifier to specific log entries that you can later use to filter the log and locate only entries related to a specific process or task. The Logging block tracing feature makes use of the .NET Correlation Manager class, which maintains an Activity ID that is a GUID. By default, this is not set, but the Logging block allows you to use a **TraceManager** to generate **Tracer** instances. Each of these sets the Activity ID to a randomly generated GUID value that is maintained only during the context of the tracer. The Activity ID returns to its previous value when the tracer is disposed or goes out of scope.

You specify an operation name when you create the tracer. This is effectively the name of a category defined in the configuration of the block. All log entries created within the context of the tracer will be assigned to that category in addition to any categories you specify when you create the log entry.

You can specify a GUID value when you create and start a tracer, and all subsequent log entries within the scope of that tracer and all nested tracers that do not specify a different GUID will have the specified activity ID. If you start a new nested tracer instance within the scope of a previous one, it will have the same activity ID as the parent tracer unless you specify a different one when you create and start the nested tracer; in that case, this new activity ID will be used in subsequent log entries within the scope of this tracer.

Although the Logging block automatically adds the activity ID to each log entry, this does not appear in the resulting message when you use the text formatter with the default template. To include the activity ID in the logged message that uses a text formatter, you must edit the template property in the configuration tools to include the token **{property(ActivityId)}**. *Note that property names are case-sensitive in the template definition.*

An Example of Tracing Activities

The example, *Tracing activities and publishing activity information to categories,* should help to make this clear. At the start of the application, the code resolves a **TraceManager** instance from the Enterprise Library container in the same way as we resolved the **LogWriter** we've been using so far.

```
' Resolve a TraceManager object from the container.
Dim traceMgr As TraceManager _
    = EnterpriseLibraryContainer.Current.GetInstance(Of TraceManager)()
```

Next, the code creates and starts a new **Tracer** instance using the **StartTrace** method of the **TraceManager**, specifying the category named **General**. As it does not specify an Activity ID value, the **TraceManager** creates one automatically. This is the preferred approach, because each separate process running an instance of this code will generate a different GUID value. This means you can isolate individual events for each process.

The code then creates and writes a log entry within the context of this tracer, specifying that it belongs to the **DiskFiles** category in addition to the **General** category defined by the tracer. Next, it creates a nested **Tracer** instance that specifies the category named **Database**, and writes another log entry that itself specifies the category named **Important**. This log entry will therefore belong to the **General**, **Database**, and **Important** categories. Then, after the **Database** tracer goes out of scope, the code creates a new **Tracer** that again specifies the **Database** category, but this time it also specifies the Activity ID to use in the context of this new tracer. Finally, it writes another log entry within the context of the new **Database** tracer scope.

```
' Start tracing for category 'General'. All log entries within trace context
' will be included in this category and use any specified Activity ID (GUID).
' If you do not specify an Activity ID, the TraceManager will create a new one.
Using traceMgr.StartTrace("General")

  ' Write a log entry with another category, will be assigned to both.
  defaultWriter.Write("LogEntry with category 'DiskFiles' created within " _
                  & "context of 'General' category tracer.", "DiskFiles")

  ' Start tracing for category 'Database' within context of 'General' tracer.
  ' Do not specify a GUID to use so that the existing one is used.
  Using traceMgr.StartTrace("Database")
```

```
  ' Write a log entry with another category, will be assigned to all three.
  defaultWriter.Write("LogEntry with category 'Important' created within " _
      & "context of first nested 'Database' category tracer.", "Important")
End Using

' Back in context of 'General' tracer here.
' Start tracing for category 'Database' within context of 'General' tracer
' as above, but this time specify a GUID to use.
Using traceMgr.StartTrace("Database", _
            New Guid("{12345678-1234-1234-1234-123456789ABC}"))

  ' Write a log entry with another category, will be assigned to all three.
  defaultWriter.Write("LogEntry with category 'Important' created within " _
          & "context of nested 'Database' category tracer.", "Important")
  End Using

  ' Back in context of 'General' tracer here.
End Using
```

Not shown above are the lines of code that, at each stage, write the current Activity ID to the screen. The output generated by the example is shown here. You can see that, initially, there is no Activity ID. The first tracer instance then sets the Activity ID to a random value (you will get a different value if you run the example yourself), which is also applied to the nested tracer.

However, the second tracer for the **Database** category changes the Activity ID to the value we specified in the **StartTrace** method. When this tracer goes out of scope, the Activity ID is reset to that for the parent tracer. When all tracers go out of scope, the Activity ID is reset to the original (empty) value.

```
- Current Activity ID is: 00000000-0000-0000-0000-000000000000

Written LogEntry with category 'DiskFiles' created within context of 'General'
  category tracer.

- Current Activity ID is: a246ada3-e4d5-404a-bc28-4146a190731d

Written LogEntry with category 'Important' created within context of first
  'Database' category tracer nested within 'DiskFiles' category TraceManager.

- Current Activity ID is: a246ada3-e4d5-404a-bc28-4146a190731d

Leaving the context of the first Database tracer

- Current Activity ID is: a246ada3-e4d5-404a-bc28-4146a190731d
```

```
Written LogEntry with category 'Important' created within context of second
 'Database' category tracer nested within 'DiskFiles' category TraceManager.

- Current Activity ID is: 12345678-1234-1234-1234-123456789abc

Leaving the context of the second Database tracer

- Current Activity ID is: a246ada3-e4d5-404a-bc28-4146a190731d

Leaving the context of the General tracer

- Current Activity ID is: 00000000-0000-0000-0000-000000000000

Open the log files in the folder C:\Temp to see the results.
```

If you open the RollingFlatFile.log file you will see the two log entries generated within the context of the nested tracers. These belong to the categories Important, Database, and General. You will also see the Activity ID for each one, and can confirm that it is different for these two entries. For example, this is the first part of the log message for the second nested tracer, which specifies the Activity ID GUID in the **StartTrace** method.

```
Timestamp: 01/12/2009 12:12:00
Message: LogEntry with category 'Important' created within context of second
nested 'Database' category tracer.
Category: Important, Database, General
Priority: -1
EventId: 1
Severity: Information
Title:
Activity ID: 12345678-1234-1234-1234-123456789abc
```

> *Be aware that other software and services may use the Activity ID of the Correlation Manager to provide information and monitoring facilities. An example is Windows Communication Foundation (WCF), which uses the Activity ID to implement tracing.*
>
> *You must also ensure that you correctly dispose **Tracer** instances. If you do not take advantage of the **Using** construct to automatically dispose instances, you **must** ensure that you dispose nested instances in the reverse order you created them—by disposing the child instance before you dispose the parent instance. You must also ensure that you dispose **Tracer** instances on the same thread that created them.*

✳ Creating Custom Trace Listeners, Filters, and Formatters

You can extend the capabilities of the Logging block if you need to add specific functionality to it. In general, you will only need to implement custom log filters, trace listeners, or log formatters. The design of the block makes it easy to add these and make them available through configuration.

To create a new log filter, you can either implement the **ILogFilter** interface, which specifies the single method **Filter** that must accept an instance of a **LogEntry** and return true or false, or you can inherit the base class **LogFilter** and implement the **Filter** method.

To create a custom trace listener, you can inherit from the abstract base class **CustomTraceListener** and implement the methods required to send your log entry to the appropriate location or execute the relevant actions to log the message. You can expose a property for the relevant log formatter if you want to allow users to select a specific formatter for the message.

To create a custom log formatter, you can either implement the **ILogFormatter** interface, which specifies the single method, **Format**, that must accept an instance of a **Log Entry** and return the formatted message, or you can inherit the base class, **LogFormatter**, and implement the **Format** method.

For more information about extending the Logging block, see the online documentation at http://go.microsoft.com/fwlink/?LinkId=188874 or consult the installed help files.

Summary

This chapter described the Enterprise Library Logging Application Block. This block is extremely useful for logging activities, events, messages, and other information that your application must persist or expose—both to monitor performance and to generate auditing information. The Logging block is, like all of the other Enterprise Library blocks, highly customizable and driven through configuration so that you (or administrators and operations staff) can modify the behavior to suit your requirements exactly.

You can use the Logging block to categorize, filter, and write logging information to a wide variety of targets, including Windows event logs, e-mail messages, disk files, Windows Message Queuing, and a database. You can even collect additional context information and add it to the log entries automatically, and add activity IDs to help you correlate related messages and activities. And, if none of the built-in features meets your requirements, you can create and integrate custom listeners, filters, and formatters.

This chapter explained why you should consider decoupling your logging features from your application code, what the Logging block can do to help you implement flexible and configurable logging, and how you actually perform the common tasks related to logging. For more information about using the Logging block, see the online documentation at http://go.microsoft.com/fwlink/?LinkId=188874 or consult the installed help files.

5   A Cache Advance for your Applications

Introduction

How do you make your applications perform faster? You could simply throw hardware at the problem, but with the increasing move towards green data centers, soaking up more electricity and generating more heat that you have to get rid of is not exactly a great way to showcase your environmental awareness. Of course, you should always endeavor to write efficient code and take full advantage of the capabilities of the platform and operating system, but what does that entail?

One of the ways that you may be able to make your application more efficient is to ensure you employ an appropriate level of caching for data that you reuse, and which is expensive to create. However, caching every scrap of data that you use may be counterproductive. For example, I once installed a photo screensaver that used caching to store the transformed versions of the original images and reduce processing requirements as it repeatedly cycled through the collection of photos. It probably works fine if you only have a few dozen images, but with my vast collection of high-resolution photos it very quickly soaked up three gigabytes of memory, bringing my machine (with only one gig of memory installed) to its knees.

So, before you blindly implement caching across your whole application, think about what, how, where, and when you should implement caching. Table 1 contains some pointers.

TABLE 1 **Defining a caching strategy**

What?	Data that applies to all users of the application and does not change frequently, or data that you can use to optimize reference data lookups, avoid network round-trips, and avoid unnecessary and duplicate processing. Examples are data such as product lists, constant values, and values read from configuration or a database. Where possible, cache data in a ready-to-use format. Do not cache volatile data, and do not cache sensitive data unless you encrypt it.
When?	You can cache data when the application starts if you know it will be required and it is unlikely to change. However, you should cache data that may or may not be used, or data that is relatively volatile, only when your application first accesses it.
Where?	Ideally, you should cache data as near as possible to the code that will use it, especially in a layered application that is distributed across physical tiers. For example, cache data you use for controls in your user interface in the presentation layer, cache business data in the business layer, and cache parameters for stored procedures in your data layer. If your application runs on multiple servers and the data may change as the application runs, you will usually need to use a distributed cache accessible from all servers. If you are caching data for a user interface, you can usually cache the data on the client.
How ?	Caching is a crosscutting concern—you are likely to implement caching in several places, and in many of your applications. Therefore, a reusable and configurable caching mechanism that you can install in the appropriate locations is the obvious choice. The Caching Application Block is an ideal solution for non-distributed caching. It supports both an in-memory cache and, optionally, a backing store that can be either a database or isolated storage. The block provides all the functionality needed to retrieve, add, and remove cached data, and supports configurable expiration and scavenging policies.

This chapter concentrates (obviously) on the patterns & practices Caching Application Block, which is designed for use as a non-distributed cache on a client machine. It is ideal for caching data in Windows® Forms, Windows Presentation Foundation (WPF), and console-based applications. You can use it in server-based roles such as ASP.NET applications, services, business layer code, or data layer code; but only where you have a single instance of the code running.

Out of the box, the Caching Application Block does not provide the features required for distributed caching across multiple servers. Other solutions you may consider for caching are the ASP.NET cache mechanism, which can be used on a single server (in-process) and on multiple servers (using a state server or a SQL Server® database), or a third party solution that uses the Caching Application Block extension points.

Also keep in mind that version 4.0 of the .NET Framework includes the System. Runtime.Caching namespace, which provides features to support in-memory caching. The current version of the Caching block is likely to be deprecated after this release, and Enterprise Library will instead make use of the caching features of the .NET Framework.

What Does the Caching Block Do?

The Caching Application Block provides high-performance and scalable caching capabilities, and is both thread safe and exception safe. It caches data in memory, and optionally maintains a synchronized backing store that, by default, can be isolated storage or a database. It also provides a wide range of expiration features, including the use of multiple expiration settings for cached items (including both time-based and notification-based policies).

Even better, if the cache locations are not suitable for your requirements, or the caching mechanism doesn't do quite what you want in terms of storing or retrieving cache items, you can modify or extend it. For example, you can create your own custom expiration policies and backing store providers, and plug them in using the built-in extension points. This means that you can implement caching operations throughout your applications that you access from code using a single simple API.

On top of all that, the caches you implement are configurable at design time and run time, so that administrators can change the caching behavior as required both before and after deployment. Administrators can change the backing store that the caching mechanism uses, configure encryption of the cached contents, and change the scavenging behavior—all through configuration settings.

FLUSHED OR EXPIRED?

One of the main factors that can affect application performance is memory availability. While caching data can improve performance, caching too much data can (as you saw earlier) reduce performance if the cache uses too much of the available memory. To counter this, the Caching block performs scavenging on a fixed cycle in order remove items when memory is in short supply. Items may be removed from the cache in two ways:

- **When they expire**. If you specify an expiration setting, the item is removed from the cache during the next scavenging cycle if they have expired. You can specify a combination of settings based on the absolute time, sliding time, extended time format (for example, every evening at midnight), file dependency, or never. You can also specify a priority, so that lower priority items are scavenged first. The scavenging interval and the maximum number of items to scavenge on each pass are configurable.
- **When they are flushed**. You can explicitly expire (mark for removal) individual items in the cache, or explicitly expire all items, using methods exposed by the Caching block. This allows you to control which items are available from the cache. The scavenging mechanism removes items that it detects have expired and are no longer valid. However, until the scavenging cycle occurs, the items remain in the cache but are marked as expired, and you cannot retrieve them.

The difference is that flushing might remove valid cache items to make space for more frequently used items, whereas expiration removes invalid and expired items. Remember that items may have been removed from the cache by the scavenging mechanism even if they haven't expired, and you should always check that the cached item exists when you try to retrieve and use it. You may choose to recreate the item and re-cache it at this point.

WHICH EXPIRATION POLICY?

If you have data that is relatively volatile, is updated regularly, or is valid for only a specific time or interval, you can use a time-based expiration policy to ensure that items do not remain in the cache beyond their useful valid lifetime. You can specify how long an item should remain in the cache if not accessed (effectively the timer starts at zero again each time it is accessed), or specify the absolute time that it should be removed irrespective of whether it has been accessed in the meantime.

If the data you cache depends on changes to another resource, such as a disk file, you can improve caching efficiency by using a notification-based expiration policy. The Caching block contains an expiration provider that detects changes to disk files. You can create your own custom expiration policy providers that detect, for example, WMI events, database events, or business logic operations and invalidate the cached item when they occur.

How Do I Configure the Caching Block?

Like all of the Enterprise Library application blocks, you start by configuring your application to use the block. Chapter 1, "Introduction," demonstrates the basic principles for using the configuration tool. To configure the Caching block, you add the Caching Settings section to the tool, which adds a default cache manager. The cache manager exposes the caching API and is responsible for manipulating the cached items. You can add more than one cache manager to the configuration if you want to implement multiple caches, or change the default cache manager for a custom one that you create. For example, you may decide to replace it with a custom or third party cache manager that supports distributed caching for a Web farm or application farm containing multiple servers.

Figure 1 shows the configuration for the examples in this chapter of the guide. You can see the four cache managers we use, with the section for the **EncryptedCache Manager** expanded to show its property settings.

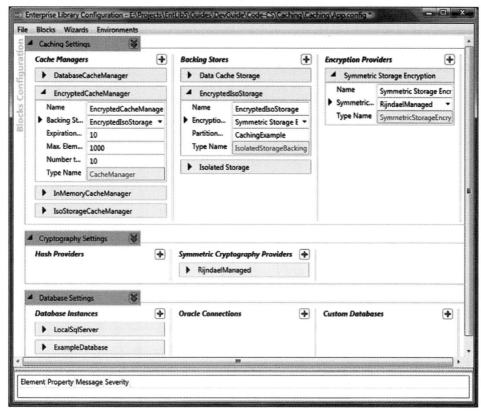

FIGURE 1
Configuring caching in Enterprise Library

For each cache manager, you can specify the expiration poll frequency (the interval in seconds at which the block will check for expired items and remove them), the maximum number of items in the cache before scavenging will occur irrespective of the polling frequency, and the number of items to remove when scavenging the cache.

You can also specify, in the configuration properties of the Caching Application Block root node, which of the cache managers you configure should be the default. The Caching block will use the one you specify if you instantiate a cache manager without providing the name of that cache manager.

PERSISTENT CACHING

The cache manager caches items in memory only. If you want to persist cached items across application and system restarts, you can add a persistent backing store to your configuration. You can specify only a single backing store for each cache manager (obviously, or it would get extremely confused), and the Caching block contains providers for caching in both a database and isolated storage. You can specify a partition name for each persistent backing store, which allows you to target multiple cache storage providers at isolated storage or at the same database.

If you add a data cache store to your configuration, the configuration tool automatically adds the Data Access Application Block to the configuration. You configure a database connection in the Data Access block configuration section, and then select this connection in the properties of the data cache store provider. For details of how you configure the Data Access Application Block, see Chapter 2 "Much ADO about Data Access."

ENCRYPTING CACHED ITEMS

You can add a provider that implements symmetric storage encryption to each persistent backing store you configure if you want to encrypt the stored items. This is a really good plan if you must store sensitive information. When you add a symmetric storage encryption provider to your configuration, the configuration tool automatically adds the Cryptography Application Block to the configuration.

You configure a symmetric cryptography provider in the Cryptography block configuration section. You can use the Windows Data Protection API (DPAPI) symmetric provider, or select from other providers such as AES, Triple DES, and Rijndael. For details of how you configure the Cryptography Application Block, see Chapter 7, "Relieving Cryptography Complexity." Then in the properties of the symmetric storage encryption provider in the Caching block section, select the provider you just configured.

> Note that the Caching Application Block does not encrypt data in the in-memory cache, even if you configure encryption for the associated backing store. If it is possible that a malicious user could access the application process's memory, do not store sensitive information, such as credit card numbers or passwords, in the cache.

And now, at last, you are ready to write code that uses the Caching block. You'll see the ways that you can use it demonstrated in the examples in this chapter.

INITIALIZING THE CACHING BLOCK

When you create a project that uses the Caching block, you must edit the project and code to add references to the appropriate Enterprise Library assemblies and namespaces. The examples in this chapter demonstrate caching to a database and encrypting cached data, as well as writing to the isolated storage backing store.

The assemblies you must add to your project (in addition to the assemblies listed in Chapter 1, "Introduction," that are required for all Enterprise Library projects) are:

- Microsoft.Practices.EnterpriseLibrary.Caching.dll
- Microsoft.Practices.EnterpriseLibrary.Caching.Cryptography.dll
- Microsoft.Practices.EnterpriseLibrary.Caching.Database.dll
- Microsoft.Practices.EnterpriseLibrary.Data.dll
- Microsoft.Practices.EnterpriseLibrary.Security.Cryptography.dll

> If you do not wish to cache items in a database, you don't need to add the Database and Data assemblies. If you do not wish to encrypt cached items, you don't need to add the two Cryptography assemblies.

To make it easier to use the objects in the Caching block, you can add references to the relevant namespaces to your project. Then you are ready to write some code.

How Do I Use the Caching Block?

You manipulate your caches using the interface of the Cache Manager. It is a relatively simple interface. There are two overloads of the **Add** method for adding items to the cache; plus methods to retrieve a cached item, remove a single item, flush all items, and check if the cache contains a specified item. The single property, **Count**, returns the number of items currently in the cache.

ABOUT THE EXAMPLE APPLICATION

The code you can download for this guide contains a sample application named *Caching* that demonstrates the techniques described in this chapter. The sample provides a number of different examples that you can run.

> *Before you attempt to run the example, you must create a new encryption key for the Caching block to use to encrypt the data in one of the examples that uses a symmetric encryption provider. This is because the key is tied to either the user or the machine, and so the key included in the sample files will not work on your machine. In the configuration console, navigate to the Symmetric Cryptography Providers section of the Cryptography Application Block Settings and select the* **RijndaelManaged** *provider. Click the "..." button next to the* **Key** *property to start the Cryptographic Key Wizard. Use this wizard to generate a new key, save the key file, and automatically update the contents of App.config.*

The first of the examples, *Cache data in memory using the null backing store*, demonstrates some of the options you have when adding items to the cache.

ADDING ITEMS TO AND RETRIEVING ITEMS FROM THE CACHE

To add an item to the cache, you can use the simple approach of specifying just the key for the item and the value to cache as parameters to the **Add** method. The item is cached with a never expired lifetime, and normal priority. If you want more control over the way an item is cached, you can use the other overload of the **Add** method, which additionally accepts a value for the priority, a reference to a callback that will execute when the cached item expires, and an array of expirations that specify when the item should expire.

Possible values for the priority, as defined in the **CacheItemPriority** enumeration, are **None**, **Low**, **Normal**, **High**, and **NotRemovable**. In addition to the **NeverExpired** value for the expirations, you can use **AbsoluteTime**, **SlidingTime**, **FileDependency**, and **ExtendedFormatTime** expirations. If you create an array containing more than one expiration instance, the block will expire the item when any one of these indicates that it has expired.

The example starts by obtaining a reference to an instance of a **CacheManager**—in this case one that has no backing store defined in its configuration (or, to be more precise, it has the **NullBackingStore** class defined) and so uses only the in-memory cache. It stores this reference as the interface type **ICacheManager**.

Next, it calls a separate routine that adds items to the cache and then displays the contents of the cache. This routine is reused in many of the examples in this chapter.

```
' Resolve the default CacheManager object from the container.
' The actual concrete type is determined by the configuration settings.
' In this example, the default is the InMemoryCacheManager instance.
Dim defaultCache As ICacheManager _
    = EnterpriseLibraryContainer.Current.GetInstance(Of ICacheManager)()


' Store some items in the cache and show the contents using a separate routine.
CacheItemsAndShowCacheContents(defaultCache)
```

The **CacheItemsAndShowCacheContents** routine uses the cache manager passed to it; in this first example, this is the *in-memory only* cache manager. However, the code to add items to the cache and manipulate the cache is (as you would expect) identical for all configurations of cache managers. Notice that the code defines a set of string values that it uses as the cache keys. This makes it easier for the code later on to examine the contents of the cache. This is the declaration of the cache keys array and the first part of the code in the **CacheItemsAndShowCacheContents** routine.

```
Dim DemoCacheKeys As String() _
    = {"ItemOne", "ItemTwo", "ItemThree", "ItemFour", "ItemFive"}


Sub CacheItemsAndShowCacheContents(ByVal theCache As ICacheManager)
  ' Add some items to the cache using the key names in the DemoCacheKeys array.
  theCache.Add(DemoCacheKeys(0), "Some Text")
  theCache.Add(DemoCacheKeys(1), _
            New StringBuilder("Some text in a StringBuilder"))
  theCache.Add(DemoCacheKeys(2), 42, CacheItemPriority.High, Nothing, _
            New NeverExpired())
  theCache.Add(DemoCacheKeys(3), New DataSet(), CacheItemPriority.Normal, _
            Nothing, New AbsoluteTime(New DateTime(2099, 12, 31)))


  ' Note that the next item will expire after three seconds
  theCache.Add(DemoCacheKeys(4), _
            New Product(10, "Exciting Thing", "Useful for everything"), _
            CacheItemPriority.Low, Nothing, _
            New SlidingTime(New TimeSpan(0, 0, 3)))


  ' Display the contents of the cache.
  ShowCacheContents(theCache)
  ...
```

In the code shown above, you can see that the **CacheItemsAndShowCacheContents** routine uses the simplest overload to cache the first two items; a **String** value and an instance of the **StringBuilder** class. For the third item, the code specifies the item to cache as the Integer value 42 and indicates that it should have high priority (it will remain in the cache after lower priority items when the cache has to be minimized due to memory or other constraints). There is no callback required, and the item will never expire.

The fourth item cached by the code is a new instance of the DataSet class, with normal priority and no callback. However, the expiry of the cached item is set to an absolute date and time (which should be well after the time that you run the example).

The final item added to the cache is a new instance of a custom class defined within the application. The **Product** class is a simple class with just three properties: **ID**, **Name**, and **Description**. The class has a constructor that accepts these three values and sets the properties in the usual way. It is cached with low priority, and a sliding time expiration set to three seconds.

The final line of code above calls another routine named **ShowCacheContents** that displays the contents of the cache. Not shown here is code that forces execution of the main application to halt for five seconds, redisplay the contents of the cache, and repeat this process again. This is the output you see when you run this example.

```
The cache contains the following 5 item(s):
Item key 'ItemOne' (System.String) = Some Text
Item key 'ItemTwo' (System.Text.StringBuilder) = Some text in a StringBuilder
Item key 'ItemThree' (System.Int32) = 42
Item key 'ItemFour' (System.Data.DataSet) = System.Data.DataSet
Item key 'ItemFive' (CachingExample.Product) = CachingExample.Product

Waiting for last item to expire...
Waiting... Waiting... Waiting... Waiting... Waiting...

The cache contains the following 5 item(s):
Item key 'ItemOne' (System.String) = Some Text
Item key 'ItemTwo' (System.Text.StringBuilder) = Some text in a StringBuilder
Item key 'ItemThree' (System.Int32) = 42
Item key 'ItemFour' (System.Data.DataSet) = System.Data.DataSet
Item with key 'ItemFive' has expired.

Waiting for the cache to be scavenged...
Waiting... Waiting... Waiting... Waiting... Waiting...

The cache contains the following 4 item(s):
Item key 'ItemOne' (System.String) = Some Text
Item key 'ItemTwo' (System.Text.StringBuilder) = Some text in a StringBuilder
Item key 'ItemThree' (System.Int32) = 42
Item key 'ItemFour' (System.Data.DataSet) = System.Data.DataSet
```

You can see in this output that the cache initially contains the five items we added to it. However, after a few seconds, the last one expires. When the code examines the contents of the cache again, the last item (with key **ItemFive**) has expired but is still in the cache. However, the code detects this and shows it as invalidated. After a further five seconds, the code checks the contents of the cache again, and you can see that the invalidated item has been removed.

Depending on the performance of your machine, you may need to change the value configured for the expiration poll frequency of the cache manager in order to see the invalidated item in the cache and the contents after the scavenging cycle completes.

What's In My Cache?

The example you've just seen displays the contents of the cache, indicating which items are still available in the cache, and which (if any) are in the cache but not available because they are waiting to be scavenged. So how can you tell what is actually in the cache and available for use? In the time-honored way, you might like to answer "Yes" or "No" to the following questions:

- Can I use the **Contains** method to check if an item with the key I specify is available in the cache?
- Can I query the **Count** property and retrieve each item using its index?
- Can I iterate over the collection of cached items, reading each one in turn?

If you answered "Yes" to any of these, the bad news is that you are wrong. All of these are false. Why? Because the cache is managed by more than one process. The cache manager you are using is responsible for adding items to the cache and retrieving them through the public methods available to your code. However, a background process also manages the cache, checking for any items that have expired and removing (scavenging) those that are no longer valid. Cached items may be removed when memory is scarce, or in response to dependencies on other items, as well as when the expiry date and time you specified when you added an item to the cache has passed.

So, even if the **Contains** method returns **True** for a specified cache key, that item might have been invalidated and is only in the cache until the next scavenging operation. You can see this in the output for the previous example, where the two waits force the code to halt until the item has been flagged as expired, and then halt again until it is scavenged. The actual delay before scavenging takes place is determined by the expiration poll frequency configuration setting of the cache manager. In the previous example, this is 10 seconds.

The correct approach to extracting cached items is to simply call the **GetData** method and check that it did not return **Nothing**. However, you can use the **Contains** method to see if an item was previously cached and will (in most cases) still be available in the cache. This is efficient, but you must still (and always) check that the returned item is not null after you attempt to retrieve it from the cache.

The code used in the examples to read the cached items depends on the fact that we use an array of cache keys throughout the examples, and we can therefore check if any of these items are in the cache. The code we use is shown here.

```vbnet
Sub ShowCacheContents(ByVal theCache As ICacheManager)
  If theCache.Count > 0 Then
    Console.WriteLine("The cache contains the following {0} item(s):", _
                      theCache.Count)
    ' Cannot iterate the cache, so use the five known keys
    For Each key As String In DemoCacheKeys
      If theCache.Contains(key) Then

        ' Try and get the item from the cache
        Dim theData As Object = theCache.GetData(key)

        ' If item has expired but not yet been scavenged, it will still show
        ' in the count of the number of cached items, but the GetData method
        ' will return null.
        If theData Is Nothing Then
          Console.WriteLine("Item with key '{0}' has expired", key)
        Else
          Console.WriteLine("Item key '{0}' ({1}) = {2}", key, _
                            theData.[GetType]().ToString(), theData.ToString())
        End If
      End If
    Next

  Else
    Console.WriteLine("The cache is empty.")
  End If
End Sub
```

USING THE ISOLATED STORAGE BACKING STORE

The previous example showed how you can use the Caching Block as a powerful in-memory caching mechanism. However, often you will want to store the items in the cache in some type of persistent backing store. The Caching block contains a provider that uses Windows Isolated Storage on the local machine. This stores data in a separate area for each user, which means that different users will be able to see and retrieve only their own cached data.

One point to note is that objects to be cached in any of the physical backing stores must be serializable. The only case where this does not apply is when you use the in-memory only (null backing store) approach. The **Product** class used in these examples contains only standard value types as its properties, and carries the **Serializable** attribute. For more information about serialization, see "Object Serialization in the .NET Framework" at http://msdn.microsoft.com/en-us/library/ms973893.aspx.

To use isolated storage as your backing store, you simply add the isolated storage backing store provider to your cache manager using the configuration tools, as shown in Figure 2.

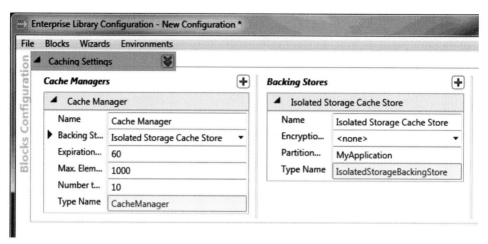

FIGURE 2
Adding the isolated storage backing store

Notice that you can specify a partition name for your cache. This allows you to separate the cached data for different applications (or different cache managers) for the same user by effectively segregating each one in a different partition within that user's isolated storage area.

Other than the configuration of the cache manager to use the isolated storage backing store, the code you use to cache and retrieve data is identical. The example, *Cache data locally in the isolated storage backing store,* uses a cache manager named **IsoStorageCache Manager** that is configured with an isolated storage backing store. It retrieves a reference to this cache manager by specifying the name when calling the **GetInstance** method of the current Enterprise Library container.

```
' Resolve a named CacheManager object from the container.
' In this example, this one uses the Isolated Storage Backing Store.
Dim isoStorageCache As ICacheManager _
    = EnterpriseLibraryContainer.Current.GetInstance(Of _
                          ICacheManager)("IsoStorageCacheManager")
...
CacheItemsAndShowCacheContents(isoStorageCache)
```

The code then executes the same **CacheItemsAndShowCacheContents** routine you saw in the first example, and passes to it the reference to the **isoStorageCache** cache manager. The result you see when you run this example is the same as you saw in the first example in this chapter.

> *If you find that you get an error when you re-run this example, it may be because the backing store provider cannot correctly access your local isolated storage store. In most cases, you can resolve this by deleting the previously cached contents. Open the folder* **Users**<*your-user-name*>**\AppData\Local\IsolatedStorage**, *and expand each of the*

subfolders until you find the **Files\CachingExample** *subfolder. Then delete this entire folder tree. You should avoid deleting all of the folders in your* **IsolatedStorage** *folder as these may contain data used by other applications.*

ENCRYPTING THE CACHED DATA

By default, the Caching block does not encrypt the data that it stores in memory or in a persistent backing store. However, you can configure the block to use an encryption provider that will encrypt the data that the cache manager stores in the backing store—but be aware that data in the in-memory cache is never encrypted.

To use encryption, you simple add an encryption provider to the configuration of the backing store. When you first add an encryption provider, the configuration tool automatically adds the Cryptography block to your configuration. Therefore, you must ensure that the relevant assembly, **Microsoft.Practices.EnterpriseLibrary.Security. Cryptography.dll**, is referenced in your project.

After you add the encryption provider to the configuration of the backing store, configure the Cryptography section by adding a new symmetric provider, and use the Key wizard to generate a new encryption key file or import an existing key. Then, back in the configuration for the Caching block, select the new symmetric provider you added for the symmetric encryption property of the backing store. For more information about configuring the Cryptography block, see Chapter 7, "Relieving Cryptography Complexity."

The examples provided for this chapter include one named *Encrypt cached data in a backing store,* which demonstrates how you can encrypt the persisted data. It instantiates the cache manager defined in the configuration of the application with the name **EncryptedCacheManager**:

```
' Resolve a CacheManager instance that encrypts the cached data.
Dim encryptedCache As ICacheManager _
    = EnterpriseLibraryContainer.Current.GetInstance(Of _
                                ICacheManager)("EncryptedCacheManager")
...
CacheItemsAndShowCacheContents(encryptedCache)
```

The code then executes the same **CacheItemsAndShowCacheContents** routine you saw in the first example, and passes to it the reference to the **encryptedCache** cache manager. And, again, the result you see when you run this example is the same as you saw in the first example in this chapter.

> *If you find that you get an error when you run this example, it is likely to be that you have not created a suitable encryption key that the Cryptography block can use, or the absolute path to the key file in the App.config file is not correct. To resolve this, open the configuration console, navigate to the Symmetric Providers section of the Cryptography Application Block Settings, and select the* **RijndaelManaged** *provider. Click the "..." button in the* **Key** *property to start the Cryptographic Key Wizard. Use this wizard to generate a new key, save the key file, and automatically update the contents of App.config.*

USING THE DATABASE BACKING STORE

You can easily and quickly configure the Caching block to use a database as your persistent backing store for cached data if you wish. Enterprise Library contains a script and a command file that you can run to create the database (located in the \Blocks\Caching\Src\Database\Scripts folder of the Enterprise Library source code). We also include these scripts with the example for this chapter.

The scripts assume that you will use the locally installed SQL Server Express database, but you can edit the **CreateCachingDb.cmd** file to change the target to a different database server. The SQL script that the command file executes creates a database named **Caching**, and adds the required tables and stored procedures to it.

However, if you only want to run the example application we provide for this chapter, you do not need to create a database. The project contains a preconfigured database file (located in the bin\Debug folder) that is auto-attached to your local SQL Server Express instance. You can connect to this database using the Microsoft® Visual Studio® Server Explorer to see the contents, as shown in Figure 3.

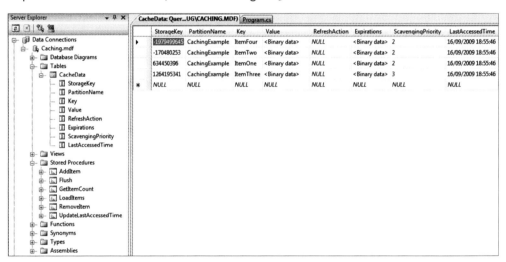

FIGURE 3
Viewing the contents of the cache in the database table

To configure caching to a database, you simply add the database cache storage provider to the cache manager using the configuration console, and specify the connection string and ADO.NET data provider type (the default is **System.Data.SqlClient**, though you can change this if you are using a different database system).

You can also specify a partition name for your cache, in the same way as you can for the isolated storage backing store provider. This allows you to separate the cached data for different applications (or different cache managers) for the same user by effectively segregating each one in a different partition within the database table.

Other than the configuration of the cache manager to use the database backing store, the code you use to cache and retrieve data is identical. The example, *Cache data in a database backing store,* uses a cache manager named **DatabaseCacheManager** that is configured with a data cache storage backing store. As with the earlier example, the code retrieves a reference to this cache manager by specifying the name when calling the **GetInstance** method of the current Enterprise Library container.

```
' Resolve a CacheManager instance that uses a Database Backing Store.
Dim databaseCache As ICacheManager _
    = EnterpriseLibraryContainer.Current.GetInstance(Of _
                                ICacheManager)("DatabaseCacheManager")
...
CacheItemsAndShowCacheContents(databaseCache)
```

The code then executes the same **CacheItemsAndShowCacheContents** routine you saw in the first example, and passes to it the reference to the **databaseCache** cache manager. As you will be expecting by now, the result you see when you run this example is the same as you saw in the first example in this chapter.

> *The connection string for the database we provide with this example is:*
> *Data Source=.\SQLEXPRESS; AttachDbFilename=|DataDirectory|\Caching.mdf;*
> *Integrated Security=True; User Instance=True*
> *If you have configured a different database using the scripts provided with the example, you may find that you get an error when you run this example. It is likely to be that you have an invalid connection string in your App.config file for your database. In addition, use the Services applet in your Administrative Tools folder to check that the SQL Server (SQLEXPRESS) database service (the service is named* **MSSQL$SQLEXPRESS***) is running.*

REMOVING ITEMS FROM AND FLUSHING THE CACHE

Having seen how you can add items to your cache, and use a variety of backing store options and encryption, it's time now to see how you can manipulate the cache to remove items, or clear it completely by flushing it. Items are removed from the cache automatically based on their expiration or dependencies, but you can also remove individual items or remove all items.

The example, *Remove and flush cached items,* actually demonstrates more than just removing and flushing items—it shows how you can use a dependency to remove related items from your cache, how to create extended time expirations, and how to use an array of expirations. There is quite a lot of code in this example, so we'll step through it and explain each part in turn.

Using a File Dependency and Extended Time Expiration

The example starts by creating a **NeverExpired** expiration instance, followed by writing a text file to the current execution folder. It then creates a **FileDependency** on that file. This is a typical scenario where you read data from a file, such as a text file or an XML document, which you will access frequently in your code. However, if the original file is changed or deleted, you want the equivalent cached item to be removed from the cache.

```
' Create an expiration that never expires
Dim never As New NeverExpired()

' Create a text file to use in a FileDependency
File.AppendAllText("ATextFile.txt", "Some contents for the file")

' Create an expiration dependency on the new text file
Dim fileDep As New FileDependency("ATextFile.txt")
```

Next, the code creates an instance of the **ExtendedFormatTime** class. This class allows you to specify expiration times for the cached item based on a repeating schedule. It provides additional opportunities compared to the more common **SlidingTime** and **AbsoluteTime** expiration types you have seen so far.

The constructor of the **ExtendedFormatTime** class accepts a string value that it parses into individual values for the minute, hour, day, month, and weekday (where zero is Sunday) that together specify the frequency with which the cached item will expire. Each value is delimited by a space. An asterisk indicates that there is no value for that part of the format string, and effectively means that expiration will occur for every occurrence of that item. It all sounds very complicated, so some examples will no doubt be useful (see Table 2).

TABLE 2 Expiration

Extended Format String	Meaning
* * * * *	Expires every minute.
5 * * * *	Expires at the 5th minute of every hour.
* 21 * * *	Expires every minute of the 21st hour of every day.
31 15 * * *	Expires at 3:31 PM every day.
7 4 * * 6	Expires every Saturday 4:07 AM.
15 21 4 7 *	Expires at 9:15 PM on every 4th of July.

The example generates an **ExtendedFormatTime** that expires at 30 minutes past every hour. Then it creates an array of type **ICacheItemExpiration** that contains the **File Dependency** created earlier and the new **ExtendedFormatTime** instance.

```
' Create an extended expiration for 30 minutes past every hour
Dim extTime As New ExtendedFormatTime("30 * * * *")

' Create array of expirations containing the file dependency and extended format
Dim expirations As ICacheItemExpiration() _
    = New ICacheItemExpiration() {fileDep, extTime}
```

Adding the Items to the Cache

Now (at last) the code can add some items to the cache. It adds four items: the first uses the **NeverExpired** expiration, the second uses the array that contains the file dependency and extended format time expiration, and the other two just use the simple approach to caching items that you saw in the first example of this chapter. The code then displays the contents of the cache and waits for you to press a key.

```
' Add items to the cache using the key string names in the DemoCacheKeys array.
defaultCache.Add(DemoCacheKeys(0), "A cached item that never expires", _
            CacheItemPriority.NotRemovable, Nothing, never)
defaultCache.Add(DemoCacheKeys(1), "A cached item that depends on both " _
            & "a disk file and an hourly extended time expiration.", _
            CacheItemPriority.Normal, Nothing, expirations)
defaultCache.Add(DemoCacheKeys(2), "Another cached item")
defaultCache.Add(DemoCacheKeys(3), "And yet another cached item.")

ShowCacheContents(defaultCache)
Console.Write("Press any key to delete the text file...")
Console.ReadKey(True)
```

The following is the output you see at this point in the execution.

```
Created a 'never expired' dependency.
Created a text file named ATextFile.txt to use as a dependency.
Created an expiration for 30 minutes past every hour.

The cache contains the following 4 item(s):
Item key 'ItemOne' (System.String) = A cached item that never expires
Item key 'ItemTwo' (System.String) = A cached item that depends on both a disk
file and an hourly extended time expiration.
Item key 'ItemThree' (System.String) = Another cached item
Item key 'ItemFour' (System.String) = And yet another cached item.
```

When you press a key, the code continues by deleting the text file, and then re-displaying the contents of the cache. Then, as in earlier examples, it waits for the items to be scavenged from the cache. The output you see is shown here.

```
Cache contains the following 4 item(s):
Item key 'ItemOne' (System.String) = A cached item that never expires
Item with key 'ItemTwo' has been invalidated.
Item key 'ItemThree' (System.String) = Another cached item
Item key 'ItemFour' (System.String) = And yet another cached item.

Waiting for the dependent item to be scavenged from the cache...
Waiting... Waiting... Waiting... Waiting...
```

```
Cache contains the following 3 item(s):
Item key 'ItemOne' (System.String) = A cached item that never expires
Item key 'ItemThree' (System.String) = Another cached item
Item key 'ItemFour' (System.String) = And yet another cached item.
```

You can see that deleting the text file caused the item with key **ItemTwo** that depended on it to be invalidated and removed during the next scavenging cycle.

At this point, the code is again waiting for you to press a key. When you do, it continues by calling the **Remove** method of the cache manager to remove the item having the key **ItemOne**, and displays the cache contents again. Then, after you press a key for the third time, it calls the **Flush** method of the cache manager to remove all the items from the cache, and again calls the method that displays the contents of the cache. This is the code for this part of the example.

```
Console.Write("Press any key to remove {0} from the cache...", DemoCacheKeys(0))
Console.ReadKey(True)
defaultCache.Remove(DemoCacheKeys(0))
ShowCacheContents(defaultCache)

Console.Write("Press any key to flush the cache...")
Console.ReadKey(True)
defaultCache.Flush()
ShowCacheContents(defaultCache)
```

The result you see as this code executes is shown here.

```
Press any key to remove ItemOne from the cache...
Cache contains the following 2 item(s):
Item key 'ItemThree' (System.String) = Another cached item
Item key 'ItemFour' (System.String) = And yet another cached item.

Press any key to flush the cache...
The cache is empty.
```

REFRESHING THE CACHE

So far, when we used the **Add** method to add items to the cache, we passed a null value for the **refreshAction** parameter. You can use this parameter to detect when an item is removed from the cache, and discover the value of that item and the reason it was removed.

You must create a class that implements the **ICacheItemRefreshAction** interface, and contains a method named Refresh that accepts as parameters the key of the item being removed, the value as an **Object** type, and a value from the **CacheItemRemoved Reason** enumeration. The values from this enumeration are **Expired**, **Removed** (typically by your code or a dependency), **Scavenged** (typically in response to shortage of available memory), and **Unknown** (a reserved value you should avoid using).

Therefore, inside your **Refresh** method, you can query the parameter values passed to it to obtain the key and the final cached value of the item, and see why it was removed from the cache. At this point, you can make a decision on what to do about it. In some cases, it may make sense to insert the item into the cache again (such as when a file on which the item depends has changed, or if the data is vital to your application). Of course, you should generally only do this if it expired or was removed. If items are being scavenged because your machine is short of memory, you should think carefully about what you want to put back into the cache!

The example, *Detect and refresh expired or removed cache items,* illustrates how you can capture items being removed from the cache, and re-cache them when appropriate. The example uses the following implementation of the **ICacheItemRefreshAction** interface to handle the case when the cache contains instances of the **Product** type. For a general situation where you cache different types, you would probably want to check the type before attempting to cast it to the required target type. Also notice that the class carries the **Serializable** attribute. All classes that implement the **ICacheItemRefreshAction** interface must be marked as serializable.

```vb
<Serializable()> _
Public Class MyCacheRefreshAction
  Implements ICacheItemRefreshAction

  Public Sub Refresh(ByVal key As String, ByVal expiredValue As Object, _
                ByVal removalReason As CacheItemRemovedReason) _
                Implements ICacheItemRefreshAction.Refresh

    ' Item has been removed from cache. Perform desired actions here, based on
    ' the removal reason (for example, refresh the cache with the item).
    Dim expiredItem As Product = DirectCast(expiredValue, Product)
    Console.WriteLine("Cached item {0} was expired in the cache with " _
                & "the reason '{1}'", key, removalReason)
    Console.WriteLine("Item values were: ID = {0}, Name = '{1}', " _
                & "Description = {2}", expiredItem.ID, _
                expiredItem.Name, expiredItem.Description)

    ' Refresh the cache if it expired, but not if it was explicitly removed
    If removalReason = CacheItemRemovedReason.Expired Then
      Dim defaultCache As CacheManager _
        = EnterpriseLibraryContainer.Current.GetInstance(Of _
                                    CacheManager)("InMemoryCacheManager")
      defaultCache.Add(key, New Product(10, "Exciting Thing", _
                "Useful for everything"), CacheItemPriority.Low, _
                New MyCacheRefreshAction(), _
                New SlidingTime(New TimeSpan(0, 0, 10)))
      Console.WriteLine("Refreshed the item by adding it to the cache again.")
    End If
```

```
        End Sub
End Class
```

To use the implementation of the **ICacheItemRefreshAction** interface, you simply specify it as the **refreshAction** parameter of the **Add** method when you add an item to the cache. The example uses the following code to cache an instance of the **Product** class that will expire after three seconds.

```
defaultCache.Add(DemoCacheKeys(0), New Product(10, "Exciting Thing", _
            "Useful for everything"), _
            CacheItemPriority.Low, New MyCacheRefreshAction(), _
            New SlidingTime(New TimeSpan(0, 0, 3)))
```

The code then does the same as the earlier examples: it displays the contents of the cache, waits five seconds for the item to expire, displays the contents again, waits five more seconds until the item is scavenged, and then displays the contents for the third time. However, this time the Caching block executes the **Refresh** method of our **ICacheItem RefreshAction** callback as soon as the item is removed from the cache. This callback displays a message indicating that the cached item was removed because it had expired, and that it has been added back into the cache. You can see it in the final listing of the cache contents shown here.

```
The cache contains the following 1 item(s):
Item key 'ItemOne' (CachingExample.Product) = CachingExample.Product

Waiting... Waiting... Waiting... Waiting...

The cache contains the following 1 item(s):
Item with key 'ItemOne' has expired.

Cached item ItemOne was expired in the cache with the reason 'Expired'
Item values were: ID = 10, Name = 'Exciting Thing', Description = Useful for
everything
Refreshed the item by adding it to the cache again.

Waiting... Waiting...

The cache contains the following 1 item(s):
Item key 'ItemOne' (CachingExample.Product) = CachingExample.Product
```

LOADING THE CACHE

If you have configured a persistent backing store for a cache manager, the Caching block will automatically load the in-memory cache from the backing store when you instantiate that cache manager. Usually, this will occur when the application starts up. This is an example of **proactive cache loading**. Proactive cache loading is useful if you know that the data will be required, and it is unlikely to change much. Another approach is to create a class with a method that reads data you require from some data source, such as a database or an XML file, and loads this into the cache by calling the **Add** method for each item. If you execute this on a background or worker thread, you can load the cache without affecting the interactivity of the application or blocking the user interface.

Alternatively, you may prefer to use **reactive cache loading**. This approach is useful for data that may or may not be used, or data that is relatively volatile. In this case (if you are using a persistent backing store), you may choose to instantiate the cache manager only when you need to load the data. Alternatively, you can flush the cache (probably when your application ends) and then load specific items into it as required and when required. For example, you might find that you need to retrieve the details of a specific product from your corporate data store for display in your application. At this point, you could choose to cache it if it may be used again within a reasonable period and is unlikely to change during that period.

Proactive Cache Loading

The example, *Load the cache proactively on application startup,* provides a simple demonstration of proactive cache loading. In the startup code of your application you add code to load the cache with the items your application will require. The example creates a list of **Product** items, and then iterates through the list calling the **Add** method of the cache manager for each one. You would, of course, fetch the items to cache from the location (such as a database) appropriate for your own application. It may be that the items are available as a list, or—for example—by iterating through the rows in a **DataSet** or a **DataReader**.

```
' Create a list of products - may come from a database or other repository
Dim products As New List(Of Product)()
products.Add(New Product(42, "Exciting Thing", _
            "Something that will change your view of life."))
products.Add(New Product(79, "Useful Thing", _
            "Something that is useful for everything."))
products.Add(New Product(412, "Fun Thing", _
            "Something that will keep the grandchildren quiet."))


' Iterate the list loading each one into the cache
Dim i As Integer = 0
While i < products.Count
  theCache.Add(DemoCacheKeys(i), products(i))
  System.Math.Max(System.Threading.Interlocked.Increment(i), i - 1)
End While
```

Reactive Cache Loading

Reactive cache loading simply means that you check if an item is in the cache when you actually need it, and—if not—fetch it and then cache it for future use. You may decide at this point to fetch several items if the one you want is not in the cache. For example, you may decide to load the complete product list the first time that a price lookup determines that the products are not in the cache.

The example, *Load the cache reactively on demand,* demonstrates the general pattern for reactive cache loading. After displaying the contents of the cache (to show that it is, in fact, empty) the code attempts to retrieve a cached instance of the **Product** class. Notice that this is a two-step process in that you must check that the returned value is not **Nothing**. As we explained in the section "What's In My Cache?" earlier in this chapter, the **Contains** method may return true if the item has recently expired or been removed.

If the item is in the cache, the code displays the values of its properties. If it is not in the cache, the code executes a routine to load the cache with all of the products. This routine is the same as you saw in the previous example of loading the cache proactively.

```
Console.WriteLine("Getting an item from the cache...")
Dim theItem As Product = DirectCast(defaultCache.GetData(DemoCacheKeys(1)), _
                                    Product)


' You could test for the item in the cache using CacheManager.Contains(key)
' method, but you still must check if the retrieved item is null even
' if the Contains method indicates that the item is in the cache:
If Not theItem Is Nothing Then

    Console.WriteLine("Cached item values are: ID = {0}, Name = '{1}', " _
                      & "Description = {2}", theItem.ID, theItem.Name, _
                      theItem.Description)
Else

    Console.WriteLine("The item could not be obtained from the cache.")

    ' Item not found, so reactively load the cache
    LoadCacheWithProductList(defaultCache)
    Console.WriteLine("Loaded the cache with the list of products.")
    ShowCacheContents(defaultCache)
End If
```

After displaying the contents of the cache after loading the list of products, the example code then continues by attempting once again to retrieve the value and display its properties. You can see the entire output from this example here.

```
The cache is empty.

Getting an item from the cache...
The item could not be obtained from the cache.
```

```
Loaded the cache with the list of products.

The cache contains the following 3 item(s):
Item key 'ItemOne' (CachingExample.Product) = CachingExample.Product
Item key 'ItemTwo' (CachingExample.Product) = CachingExample.Product
Item key 'ItemThree' (CachingExample.Product) = CachingExample.Product

Getting an item from the cache...
Cached item values are: ID = 79, Name = 'Useful Thing', Description = Something
that is useful for everything.
```

In general, the pattern for a function that performs reactive cache loading is:

1. Check if the item is in the cache and the value returned is not **Nothing**.

2. If it is found in the cache, return it to the calling code.

3. If it is not found in the cache, create or obtain the object or value and cache it.

4. Return this new value or object to the calling code.

Extending Your Cache Advance

The Caching block, like all the other blocks in Enterprise Library, contains extension points that allow you to create custom providers and integrate them with the block. You can also replace the default cache manager if you want to use a different caching mechanism, or modify the source code to otherwise change the behavior of the block.

The cache manager is responsible for loading items from a persistent backing store into memory when you instantiate the application block. It also exposes the methods that manipulate the cache. If you want to change the way that the Caching block loads or manages cached items, for example to implement a distributed or specialist caching mechanism, or perform asynchronous or delayed cache loading, you can use the **ICacheManager** interface and implement the methods and properties it defines.

Alternatively, if you just want to use a different backing store or add a new expiration policy, you can create custom backing store providers and expiration policies and use these instead of the built-in providers and policies. To create a custom backing store provider, you can implement the **IBackingStore** interface or inherit from the **Base BackingStore** abstract class. To create a custom expiration policy, you can implement the **ICacheItemExpiration** interface and, optionally, the **ICacheItemRefreshAction** interface for a class that refreshes an expired cache item.

For more information about extending the Caching block, see the online documentation and the help files installed with Enterprise Library.

Summary

This chapter looked at the ways that you can implement caching across your application and your enterprise in a consistent and configurable way by using the Caching Application Block. The block provides a non-distributed cache that can cache items in memory, and optionally in a persistent backing store such as isolated storage or a database. You can also easily add new backing stores if required, and even replace the cache manager if you want to create a mechanism that does support other features, such as distributed caching.

The Caching block is flexible in order to meet most requirements for most types of applications. You can define multiple caches and partition each one, which is useful if you want to use a single database for multiple caches. And you can easily add encryption to the caching mechanism for items stored in a persistent backing store.

The block also provides a wide range of expiration mechanisms, including several time-based expirations as well as file-based expiration. Unlike some caching mechanisms, you can specify multiple expirations for each cached item, and even create your own custom expiration policies.

On top of all of this flexibility, the block makes it easy for administrators and operators to change the behavior through configuration using the configuration tools provided with Enterprise Library. They can change the settings for the cache, such as the polling frequency, change the backing stores that the block uses, and change the algorithms that it uses to encrypt cached data.

This chapter discussed all of these features, and contained detailed examples of how you can use the block in your own applications. For more information about the Caching block, see the online documentation and the help files installed with Enterprise Library.

6 Banishing Validation Complication

Introduction

If you happen to live in the U.S. and I told you that the original release date of version 2.0 of Enterprise Library was 13/01/2006, you'd wonder if I'd invented some new kind of calendar. Perhaps they added a new month to the calendar without you noticing (which I'd like to call Plutember in honor of the now-downgraded ninth planet). Of course, in many other countries around the world, 13/01/2006 is a perfectly valid date in January. This validation issue is well known and the solution probably seems obvious, but I once worked with an application that used dates formatted in the U.S. mm/dd/yyyy pattern for the filenames of reports it generated, and defaulted to opening the report for the previous day when you started the program. Needless to say, on my machines set up to use U.K. date formats, it never did manage to find the previous day's report.

Even better, when I tried to submit a technical support question on their Web site, it asked me for the date I purchased the software. The JavaScript validation code in the Web page running on my machine checked the format of my answer (27/04/2008) and accepted it. But the server refused to believe that there are twenty seven months in a year, and blocked my submission. I had to lie and say I purchased it on May 1 instead.

The problem is that validation can be an onerous task, especially when you need to do it in so many places in your applications, and for a lot of different kinds of values. It's extremely easy to end up with repeated code scattered throughout your classes, and yet still leave holes where unexpected input can creep into your application and possibly cause havoc.

Robust validation can help to protect your application against malicious users and dangerous input (including SQL injection attacks), ensure that it processes only valid data and enforces business rules, and improve responsiveness by detecting invalid data before performing expensive processing tasks.

So, how do you implement comprehensive and centralized validation in your applications? One easy solution is to take advantage of the Enterprise Library Validation block. The Validation block is a highly flexible solution that allows you to specify validation rules in configuration, with attributes, or in code, and have that validation applied to objects, method parameters, fields, and properties. It even includes features that integrate with Windows® Forms, Windows Presentation Foundation (WPF), ASP.NET, and Windows Communication Foundation (WCF) applications to present validation errors within the user interface or have them handled automatically by the service.

Techniques for Validation

Before we explore the Validation block, it's worth briefly reviewing some validation good practices. In general, there are three factors you should consider: where you are going to perform validation, what data should you validate, and how you will perform this validation.

WHERE SHOULD I VALIDATE?

Validation should, of course, protect your entire application. However, it is often the case that you need to apply validation in more than one location. If your application consists of layers, distributed services, or discrete components, you probably need to validate at each boundary. This is especially the case where individual parts of the application could be called from more than one place (for example, a business layer that is used by several user interfaces and other services).

It is also a really good idea to validate at trust boundaries, even if the components on each side of the boundary are not physically separated. For example, your business layer may run under a different trust level or account context than your data layer (even if they reside on the same machine). Validation at this boundary can prevent code that is running in low trust and which may have been compromised, from submitting invalid data to code that runs in higher trust mode.

Finally, a common scenario: validation in the user interface. Validating data on the client can improve application responsiveness, especially if the UI is remote from the server. Users do not have to wait for the server to respond when they enter or submit invalid data, and the server does not need to attempt to process data that it will later reject. However, remember that even if you do validate data on the client or in the UI you must always revalidate on the server or in the receiving service. This protects against malicious users who may circumvent client-side validation and submit invalid data.

WHAT SHOULD I VALIDATE?

To put it simply, everything. Or, at least any input values you will use in your application that may cause an error, involve a security risk, or could result in incorrect processing. Remember that Web page and service requests may contain data that the user did not enter directly, but could be used in your application. This can include cookies, header information, credentials, and context information that the server may use in various ways. Treat all input data as suspicious until you have validated it.

HOW SHOULD I VALIDATE?

For maximum security, your validation process should be designed to accept only data that you can directly determine to be valid. This approach is known as positive validation and generally uses an allow list that specifies data that satisfies defined criteria, and rejects all other data. Examples are rules that check if a number is between two predefined limits, or if the submitted value is within a list of valid values. Use this approach whenever possible.

The alternative and less-secure approach is to use a block list containing values that are not valid. This is called negative validation, and generally involves accepting only data that does not meet specific criteria. For example, as long as a string does not contain any of the specified invalid characters, it would be accepted. You should use this approach cautiously and as a secondary line of defense, because it is very difficult to create a complete list of criteria for all known invalid input—which may allow malicious data to enter your system.

Finally, consider sanitizing data. While this is not strictly a validation task, you can as an extra precaution attempt to eliminate or translate characters in an effort to make the input safe. However, do not rely on this technique alone because, as with negative validation, it can be difficult to create a complete list of criteria for all known invalid input unless there is a limited range of invalid values.

What Does the Validation Block Do?

The Validation block consists of a broad range of validators, plus a mechanism that executes these validators and collects and correlates the results to provide an overall validation result (true/valid or false/invalid). The Validation block can use individual attributes applied to classes and class members that the application uses (both the validation attributes provided with the Validation block and data annotation attributes from the **System.ComponentModel.DataAnnotations** namespace), in addition to rule sets defined in the configuration of the block, which specify the validation rules to apply.

The typical scenario when using the Validation block is to define rule sets through configuration or attributes applied to your classes. Each rule set specifies the set of individual validators and combinations of these validators that implement the validation rules you wish to apply to that class. Then you use a **ValidatorFactory** (or one of the equivalent implementations of this factory) to create a type validator for the class, optionally specifying the rule set it should use. If you don't specify a rule set, it uses the default rules. Then you can call the **Validate** method of the type validator. This method returns an instance of the **ValidationResults** class that contains details of all the validation errors detected. Figure 1 illustrates this process.

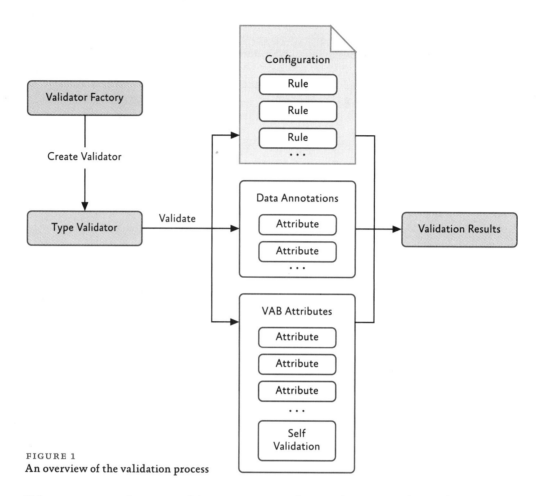

FIGURE 1
An overview of the validation process

When you use a rule set to validate an instance of a specific type or object, the block can apply the rules to:

- The type itself
- The values of public readable properties
- The values of public fields
- The return values of public methods that take no parameters

Notice that you can validate the values of method parameters and the return type of methods that take parameters when that method is invoked, only by using the validation call handler (which is part of the Validation block) in conjunction with the Unity dependency injection and interception mechanism. The validation call handler will validate the parameter values based on the rules for each parameter type and any validation attributes applied to the parameters. We don't cover the use of the validation call handler in this guide, as it requires you to be familiar with Unity interception techniques. For more information about interception and the validation call handler, see the Unity interception documentation installed with Enterprise Library or available online at http://go.microsoft.com/fwlink/?LinkId=188875.

Alternatively, you can create individual validators programmatically to validate specific values, such as strings or numeric values. However, this is not the main focus of the block—though we do include samples in this chapter that show how you can use individual validators.

In addition, the Validation block contains features that integrate with Windows® Forms, Windows Presentation Foundation (WPF), ASP.NET, and Windows Communication Foundation (WCF) applications. These features use a range of different techniques to connect to the UI, such as a proxy validator class based on the standard ASP.NET **Validator** control that you can add to a Web page, a **ValidationProvider** class that you can specify in the properties of Windows Forms controls, a **ValidatorRule** class that you can specify in the definition of WPF controls, and a behavior extension that you can specify in the **<system.ServiceModel>** section of your WCF configuration. You'll see more details of these features later in this chapter.

THE RANGE OF VALIDATORS

Validators implement functionality for validating Microsoft® .NET Framework data types. The validators included with the Validation block fall into three broad categories: value validators, composite validators, and type (object) validators. The value validators allow you to perform specific validation tests such as verifying:

- The length of a string, or the occurrence of a specified set of characters within it.
- Whether a value lies within a specified range, including tests for dates and times relative to a specified date/time.
- Whether a value is one of a specified set of values, or can be converted to a specific data type or enumeration value.
- Whether a value is null, or is the same as the value of a specific property of an object.
- Whether the value matches a specified regular expression.

The composite validators are used to combine other validators when you need to apply more complex validation rules. The Validation block includes an **AND** validator and an **OR** validator, each of which acts as a container for other validators. By nesting these composite validators in any combination and populating them with other validators, you can create very comprehensive and very specific validation rules.

Table 1 describes the complete set of validators provided with the Validation block.

TABLE 1 **The validators provided with the Validation block**

Validator type	Validator name	Description
Value Validators	Contains Characters Validator	Checks that an arbitrary string, such as a string entered by a user in a Web form, contains any or all of the specified characters.
	Date Time Range Validator	Checks that a DateTime object falls within a specified range.
	Domain Validator	Checks that a value is one of the specified values in a specified set.
	Enum Conversion Validator	Checks that a string can be converted to a value in a specified enumeration type.
	Not Null Validator	Checks that the value is not null.
	Property Comparison Validator	Compares the value to be checked with the value of a specified property.
	Range Validator	Checks that a value falls within a specified range.
	Regular Expression Validator	Checks that the value matches the pattern specified by a regular expression.
	Relative Date Time Validator	Checks that the DateTime value falls within a specified range using relative times and dates.
	String Length Validator	Checks that the length of the string is within the specified range.
	Type Conversion Validator	Checks that a string can be converted to a specific type.
Type Validators	Object Validator	Causes validation to occur on an object reference. All validators defined for the object's type will be invoked.
	Object Collection Validator	Checks that the object is a collection of the specified type and then invokes validation on each element of the collection.
Composite Validators	And Composite Validator	Requires all validators that make up the composite validator to be true.
	Or Composite Validator	Requires at least one of the validators that make up the composite validator be true.
Single Member Validators	Field Value Validator	Validates a field of a type.
	Method Return Value Validator	Validates the return value of a method of a type.
	Property Value Validator	Validates the value of a property of a type.

For more details on each validator, see the documentation installed with Enterprise Library or available online at http://go.microsoft.com/fwlink/?LinkId=188874. You will see examples that use many of these validators throughout this chapter.

VALIDATING WITH ATTRIBUTES

If you have full access to the source code of your application, you can use attributes within your classes to define your validation rules. You can apply validation attributes in the following ways:

- To a **field**. The Validation block will check that the field value satisfies all validation rules defined in validators applied to the field.
- To a **property**. The Validation block will check that the value of the get property satisfies all validation rules defined in validators applied to the property.
- To a **method that takes no parameters**. The Validation block will check that the return value of the method satisfies all validation rules defined in validators applied to the method.
- To an entire **Class**, using only the **NotNullValidator, ObjectCollection Validator, AndCompositeValidator**, and **OrCompositeValidator**). The Validation block can check if the object is null, that it is a member of the specified collection, and that any validation rules defined within it are satisfied.
- To a **parameter in a WCF Service Contract**. The Validation block will check that the parameter value satisfies all validation rules defined in validators applied to the parameter.
- To **parameters of methods that are intercepted**, by using the validation call handler in conjunction with the Policy Injection application block. For more information on using interception, see Appendix C, "Policy Injection in Enterprise Library."

Each of the validators described in the previous section has a related attribute that you apply in your code, specifying the values for validation (such as the range or comparison value) as parameters to the attribute. For example, you can validate a property that must have a value between 0 and 10 inclusive by applying the following attribute to the property definition, as seen in the following code.

```
<RangeValidator(0, RangeBoundaryType.Inclusive, 10, RangeBoundaryType.Inclusive)>
```

DataAnnotations Attributes

In addition to using the built-in validation attributes, the Validation block will perform validation defined in the vast majority of the validation attributes in the **System. ComponentModel.DataAnnotations** namespace. These attributes are typically used by frameworks and object/relational mapping (O/RM) solutions that auto-generate classes that represent data items. They are also generated by the ASP.NET validation controls that perform both client-side and server-side validation. While the set of validation attributes provided by the Validation block does not map exactly to those in the **DataAnnotations** namespace, the most common types of validation are supported. A typical use of data annotations is shown here.

```
<System.ComponentModel.DataAnnotations.Required( _
        ErrorMessage: = "You must specify a value for the product ID.")> _
<System.ComponentModel.DataAnnotations.StringLength(6, _
        ErrorMessage: = "Product ID must be 6 characters.")> _
<System.ComponentModel.DataAnnotations.RegularExpression("[A-Z]{2}[0-9]{4}", _
        ErrorMessage: = "Product ID must be 2 capital letters and 4 numbers.")> _
Public Property ID() As String
...
End Property
```

In reality, the Validation block validation attributes *are* data annotation attributes, and can be used (with some limitations) whenever you can use data annotations attributes— for example, with ASP.NET Dynamic Data applications. The main difference is that the Validation block attribute validation occurs only on the server, and not on the client.

Also keep in mind that, while DataAnnotations supports most of the Validation block attributes, not all of the validation attributes provided with the Validation block are supported by the built-in .NET validation mechanism. For more information, see the documentation installed with Enterprise Library, and the topic "System.Component Model.DataAnnotations Namespace" at http://msdn.microsoft.com/en-us/library/system.componentmodel.dataannotations.aspx.

SELF-VALIDATION

Self-validation might sound as though you should be congratulating yourself on your attractiveness and wisdom, and your status as fine and upstanding citizen. However, in Enterprise Library terms, self-validation is concerned with the use of classes that contain their own validation logic.

For example, a class that stores spare parts for aircraft might contain a function that checks if the part ID matches a specific format containing letters and numbers. You add the **HasSelfValidation** attribute to the class, add the **SelfValidation** attribute to any validation functions it contains, and optionally add attributes for the built-in Validation block validators to any relevant properties. Then you can validate an instance of the class using the Validation block. The block will execute the self-validation method.

> *Self-validation cannot be used with the UI validation integration features for Windows Forms, WPF, or ASP.NET.*

Self-validation is typically used where the validation rule you want to apply involves values from different parts of your class or values that are not publicly exposed by the class, or when the validation scenario requires complex rules that even a combination of composed validators cannot achieve. For example, you may want to check if the sum of the number of products on order and the number already in stock is less than a certain value before allowing a user to order more. The following extract from one of the examples you'll see later in this chapter shows how self-validation can be used in this case.

```
<HasSelfValidation()> _
Public Class AnnotatedProduct

  ...
  ... code to implement constructor and properties goes here
  ...

  <SelfValidation()> _
  Public Sub Validate(ByVal results As ValidationResults)
    Dim msg As String = String.Empty
    If InStock + OnOrder > 100 Then
      msg = "Total inventory (in stock and on order) cannot exceed 100 items."
      results.AddResult(New ValidationResult(msg, Me, "ProductSelfValidation", _
                        "", Nothing))
    End If
  End Sub
End Class
```

The Validation block calls the self-validation method when you validate this class instance, passing to it a reference to the collection of **ValidationResults** that it is populating with any validation errors found. The code above simply adds one or more new **Validation Result** instances to the collection if the self-validation method detects an invalid condition. The parameters of the **ValidationResult** constructor are:

* The validation error message to display to the user or write to a log. The **ValidationResult** class exposes this as the **Message** property.
* A reference to the class instance where the validation error was discovered (usually the current instance). The **ValidationResult** class exposes this as the **Target** property.
* A string value that describes the location of the error (usually the name of the class member, or some other value that helps locate the error). The **ValidationResult** class exposes this as the **Key** property.
* An optional string tag value that can be used to categorize or filter the results. The **ValidationResult** class exposes this as the **Tag** property.
* A reference to the validator that performed the validation. This is not used in self-validation, though it will be populated by other validators that validate individual members of the type. The **ValidationResult** class exposes this as the **Validator** property.

VALIDATION RULE SETS

A validation rule set is a combination of all the rules with the same name, which may be located in a configuration file or other configuration source, in attributes defined within the target type, and implemented through self-validation. In other words, a rule set includes any type of validation rule that has a specified name.

Rule set names are case-sensitive. *The two rule sets named* **MyRuleset** *and* **MyRuleSet** *are different!*

How do you apply a name to a validation rule? And what happens if you don't specify a name? In fact, the way it works is relatively simple, even though it may appear complicated when you look at configuration and attributes, and take into account how these are actually processed.

To start with, every validation rule is a member of some rule set. If you do not specify a name, that rule is a member of the default rule set; effectively, this is the rule set whose name is an empty string. When you do specify a name for a rule, it becomes part of the rule set with that name.

Assigning Validation Rules to Rule Sets

You specify rule set names in a variety of ways, depending on the location and type of the rule:

- **In configuration**. You define a type that you want to apply rules to, and then define one or more rule sets for that type. To each rule set you add the required combination of validators, each one representing a validation rule within that rule set. You can specify one rule set for each type as the default rule set for that type. The rules within this rule set are then treated as members of the default (unnamed) rule set, as well as that named rule set.
- **In Validation block validator attributes applied to classes and their members**. Every validation attribute will accept a rule set name as a parameter. For example, you specify that a **NotNullValidator** is a member of a rule set named **MyRuleset**, like this.

```
<NotNullValidator(MessageTemplate:="Cannot be null", _
            Ruleset:="MyRulesetName")>
```

- **In SelfValidation attributes within a class**. You add the **Ruleset** parameter to the attribute to indicate which rule set this self-validation rule belongs to. You can define multiple self-validation methods in a class, and add them to different rule sets if required.

```
<SelfValidation(Ruleset:="MyRulesetName")>
```

Configuring Validation Block Rule Sets

The Enterprise Library configuration console makes it easy to define rule sets for specific types that you will validate. Each rule set specifies a type to which you will apply the rule set, and allows you to specify a set of validation rules. You can then apply these rules as a complete set to an instance of an object of the defined type.

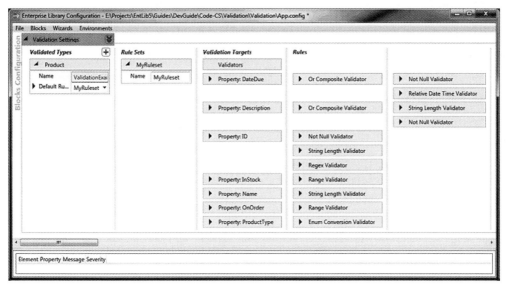

FIGURE 2
The configuration for the examples

Figure 2 shows the configuration console with the configuration used in the example application for this chapter. It defines a rule set named **MyRuleset** for the validated type (the **Product** class). **MyRuleset** is configured as the default rule set, and contains a series of validators for all of the properties of the **Product** type. These validators include two Or Composite Validators (which contain other validators) for the **DateDue** and **Description** properties, three validators that will be combined with the **And** operation for the **ID** property, and individual validators for the remaining properties.

> *When you highlight a rule, member, or validator in the configuration console, it shows connection lines between the configured items to help you see the relationships between them.*

Specifying Rule Sets When Validating

You can specify a rule set name when you create a type validator that will validate an instance of a type. If you use the **ValidatorFactory** facade to create a type validator for a type, you can specify a rule set name as a parameter of the **CreateValidator** method. If you create an Object Validator or an Object Collection Validator programmatically by calling the constructor, you can specify a rule set name as a parameter of the constructor. Finally, if you resolve a validator for a type through the Enterprise Library Container, you can specify a rule set name as the string key value. We look in more detail at the options for creating validators later in this chapter.

- **If you specify a rule set name** when you create a validator for an object, the Validation block will apply only those validation rules that are part of the specified rule set. It will, by default, apply all rules with the specified name that it can find in configuration, attributes, and self-validation.

- **If you do not specify a rule set name** when you create a validator for an object, the Validation block will, by default, apply all rules that have no name (effectively, rules with an empty string as the name) that it can find in configuration, attributes, and self-validation. If you have specified one rule set in configuration as the default rule set for the type you are validating (by setting the **DefaultRule** property for that type to the rule set name), rules within this rule set are also treated as being members of the default (unnamed) rule set.

The one time that this default mechanism changes is if you create a validator for a type using a facade other than **ValidatorFactory**. As you'll see later in this chapter you can use the **ConfigurationValidatorFactory**, **AttributeValidatorFactory**, or **Validation AttributeValidatorFactory** to generate type validators. In this case, the validator will only apply rules that have the specified name and exist in the specified location.

For example, when you use a **ConfigurationValidatorFactory** and specify the name **MyRuleset** as the rule set name when you call the **CreateValidator** method, the validator you obtain will only process rules it finds in configuration that are defined within a rule set named **MyRuleset** for the target object type. If you use an **AttributeValidator Factory**, the validator will only apply Validation block rules located in attributes and self-validation methods of the target class that have the name **MyRuleset**.

> *Configuring multiple rule sets for the same type is useful when the type you need to validate is a primitive type such as a String. A single application may have dozens of different rule sets that all target String.*

How Do I Use The Validation Block?

In the remainder of this chapter, we'll show you in more detail how you can use the features of the Validation block you have seen in previous sections. In this section, we cover three topics that you should be familiar with when you start to use the block in your applications: preparing your application to use the block, choosing a suitable approach for validation, the options available for creating validators, accessing and displaying validation errors, and understanding how you can use template tokens in validation messages.

PREPARING YOUR APPLICATION

To use the Validation block, you must reference the required assemblies. In addition to the assemblies required in every application that uses Enterprise Library (listed in Chapter 1, "Introduction"), you require the main Validation block assembly, **Microsoft.Practices. EnterpriseLibrary.Validation.dll**. If you intend to use the integration features for ASP. NET, Windows Forms, WPF, or WCF, you must also reference the relevant assembly that contains these features.

Then you can edit your code to specify the namespaces used by the Validation block and, optionally, the integration features if you need to integrate with WCF or a UI technology.

> *If you are using WCF integration, you should add a reference to the System.Service Model namespace.*

CHOOSING A VALIDATION APPROACH

Before you start to use the Validation block, you should consider how you want to perform validation. As you've seen, there are several approaches you can follow. Table 2 summarizes these, and will help you to choose one, or a combination, most suited to your requirements.

TABLE 2 **Validation approaches**

Validation approach	Advantages	Considerations
Rule sets in configuration	Supports the full capabilities of the Validation block validators. Validation rules can be changed without requiring recompilation and redeployment. Validation rules are more visible and easier to manage.	Rules are visible in configuration files unless the content is encrypted. May be open to unauthorized alteration if not properly protected. Type definitions and validation rule definitions are stored in different files and accessed using different tools, which can be confusing.
Validation block attributes	Supports the full capabilities of the Validation block validators. Validation attributes may be defined in separate metadata classes. Rules can be extracted from the metadata for a type by using reflection.	Requires modification of the source code of the types to validate. Some complex rule combinations may not be possible—only a single **And** or **Or** combination is available for multiple rules. Hides validation rules from administrators and operators.
Data annotation attributes	Allows you to apply validation rules defined by .NET data annotation attributes, which may be defined in separate metadata classes. Typically used with technologies such as LINQ, for which supporting tools might be used to generate code. Technologies such as ASP.NET Dynamic Data that use these attributes can perform partial client-side validation. Rules can be extracted from the metadata for a type by using reflection.	Requires modification of the source code. Does not support all of the powerful validation capabilities of the Validation block.
Self-validation	Allows you to create custom validation rules that may combine values of different members of the class.	Requires modification of the source code. Hides validation rules from administrators and operators. Rules cannot be extracted from the metadata for a type by using reflection.
Validators created programmatically	A simple way to validate individual values as well as entire objects. Useful if you only need to perform small and specific validation tasks, especially on value types held in variables.	Requires additional code and is generally more difficult to manage for complex validation scenarios. Hides validation rules from administrators and operators. More difficult to administer and manage.

If you decide to use attributes to define your validation rules within classes but are finding it difficult to choose between using the Validation block attributes and the Microsoft .NET data annotation attributes, you should consider using the Validation block attributes approach as this provides more powerful capabilities and supports a far wider range of validation operations. However, you should consider the data annotations approach in the following scenarios:

- When you are working with existing applications that already use data annotations.
- When you require validation to take place on the client.
- When you are building a Web application where you will use the ASP.NET Data Annotation Model Binder, or you are using ASP.NET Dynamic Data to create data-driven user interfaces.
- When you are using a framework such as the Microsoft Entity Framework, or another object/relational mapping (O/RM) technology that auto-generates classes that include data annotations.

OPTIONS FOR CREATING VALIDATORS PROGRAMMATICALLY

There are several ways that you can create the validators you require, whether you are creating a type validator that will validate an instance of your class using a rule set or attributes, or you are creating individual value validators:

- **Use the ValidatorFactory facade to create validators**. This approach makes it easy to create type validators that you can use, in conjunction with rule sets, to validate multiple members of an object instance. This is generally the recommended approach. You also use this approach to create validators that use only validation attributes or data annotations within the classes you want to validate, or only rule sets defined in configuration. You can resolve an instance of the **ValidatorFactory** using a single line of code, as you will see later in this chapter.
- **Create individual validators programmatically** by calling their constructor. The constructor parameters allow you to specify most of the properties you require for the validator. You can then set additional properties, such as the **Tag** or the resource name and type if you want to use a resource file to provide the message template. You can also build combinations of validators using this approach to implement complex validation rules.
- **Resolve individual validators through the Enterprise Library Container**. This approach allows you to obtain a validator instance using dependency injection; for example, by simply specifying the type of validator you require in the constructor of a class that you resolve through the container. If you specify a name when you resolve the instance, this is interpreted as the name of the rule set for that validator to use when validating objects. See Appendix A, "Dependency Injection with Unity" and Appendix B, "Using Dependency Injection in Enterprise Library" for more information about using a container to resolve and populate the dependencies of objects.

*Previous versions of Enterprise Library used static facades named **Validation** and **ValidationFactory** (as opposed to **ValidatorFactory** described above) to create validators and perform validation. While these facades are still available for backwards compatibility, you should use the approaches described above for creating validators as you write new code.*

PERFORMING VALIDATION AND DISPLAYING VALIDATION ERRORS

To initiate validation, you call the **Validate** method of your validator. There are two overloads of this method: one that creates and returns a populated **ValidationResults** instance, and one that accepts an existing **ValidationResults** instance as a parameter. The second overload allows you to perform several validation operations, and collect all of the errors in one **ValidationResults** instance.

You can check if validation succeeded, or if any validation errors were detected, by examining the **IsValid** property of a **ValidationResults** instance, and displaying details of any validation errors that occurred. The following code shows a simple example of how you can display the most relevant details of each validation error. See the section on self-validation earlier in this chapter for a description of the properties of each individual **ValidationResult** within the **ValidationResults**.

```
' Check if the ValidationResults detected any validation errors.
If results.IsValid Then
  Console.WriteLine("There were no validation errors.")
Else
  Console.WriteLine("The following {0} validation errors were detected:", _
                    results.Count)
  ' Iterate through the collection of validation results.
  For Each item As ValidationResult In results
    ' Show the target member name and current value.
    Console.WriteLine("Target:'{0}' Key:'{1}' Tag:'{2}' Message:'{3}'", _
                      item.Target, item.Key, item.Tag, item.Message)
  Next
End If
```

Alternatively, you can extract more information about the validation result for each individual validator where an error occurred. The example application we provide demonstrates how you can do this, and you'll see more details later in this chapter.

UNDERSTANDING MESSAGE TEMPLATE TOKENS

One specific and very useful feature of the individual validators you define in your configuration or attributes is the capability to include tokens in the message to automatically insert values of the validator's properties. This applies no matter how you create your validator—in rule sets defined in configuration, as validation attributes, or when you create validators programmatically.

The **Message** property of a validator is actually a template, not just a simple text string that is displayable. When the block adds an individual **ValidationResult** to the **ValidationResults** instance for each validation error it detects, it parses the value of the **Message** property looking for tokens that it will replace with the value of specific properties of the validator that detected the error.

The value injected into the placeholder tokens, and the number of tokens used, depends on the type of validator—although there are three tokens that are common to all validators. The token **{0}** will be replaced by the value of the object being validated (ensure that you escape this value before you display or use it in order to guard against injection attacks). The token **{1}** will contain the name of the member that was being validated, if available, and is equivalent to the **Key** property of the validator. The token **{2)** will contain the value of the **Tag** property of the validator.

The remaining tokens depend the on the individual validator type. For example, in the case of the Contains Characters validator, the tokens **{3}** and **{4}** will contain the characters to check for and the **ContainsCharacters** value (**All** or **Any**). In the case of a range validator, such as the String Length validator, the tokens **{3}** to **{6}** will contain the values and bound types (**Inclusive**, **Exclusive**, or **Ignore**) for the lower and upper bounds you specify for the validator. For example, you may define a String Length validator like this:

```
<StringLengthValidator(5, RangeBoundaryType.Inclusive, 20, _
    RangeBoundaryType.Inclusive, _
    MessageTemplate:= "{1} must be between {3} and {5} characters.")>
```

If this validator is attached to a property named **Description**, and the value of this property is invalid, the **ValidationResults** instance will contain the error message **Description must be between 5 and 20 characters.**

Other validators use tokens that are appropriate for the type of validation they perform. The documentation installed with Enterprise Library lists the tokens for each of the Validation block validators. You will also see the range of tokens used in the examples that follow.

Diving in With Some Simple Examples

The remainder of this chapter shows how you can use the Validation block in a variety of situations within your applications. We provide a simple console-based example application implemented as the Microsoft Visual Studio® solution named **Validation**. You can open it in Visual Studio to view the code, or run the application directly from the bin\Debug folder.

The application uses three versions of a class that stores product information. All of these implement an interface named **IProduct**, as illustrated in Figure 3. Each has a string property that is designed to be set to a value from an enumeration called **ProductType** that defines the valid set of product type names.

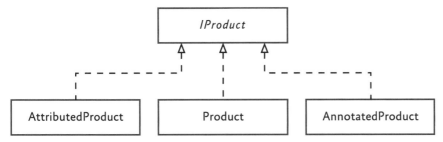

FIGURE 3
The product classes used in the examples

The **Product** class is used primarily with the example that demonstrates using a configured rule set, and contains no validation attributes. The **AttributedProduct** class contains Validation block attributes, while the **AnnotatedProduct** class contains .NET Data Annotation attributes. The latter two classes also contain self-validation routines—the extent depending on the capabilities of the type of validation attributes they contain. You'll see more on this topic when we look at the use of validation attributes later in this chapter.

The following sections of this chapter will help you understand in detail the different ways that you can use the Validation block:

- **Validating Objects and Collections of Objects**. This is the core topic for using the Validation block, and is likely to be the most common scenario in your applications. It shows how you can create type validators to validate instances of your custom classes, how you can dive deeper into the **ValidationResults** instance that is returned, how you can use the Object Validator, and how you can validate collections of objects.
- **Using Validation Attributes**. This section describes how you can use attributes applied to your classes to enable validation of members of these classes. These attributes use the Validation block validators and the .NET Data Annotation attributes.

- **Creating and Using Individual Validators**. This section shows how you can create and use the validators provided with the block to validate individual values and members of objects.
- **WCF Service Validation Integration**. This section describes how you can use the block to validate parameters within a WCF service.

Finally, we'll round off the chapter by looking briefly at how you can integrate the Validation block with user interface technologies such as Windows Forms, WPF, and ASP. NET.

VALIDATING OBJECTS AND COLLECTIONS OF OBJECTS

The most common scenario when using the Validation block is to validate an instance of a class in your application. The Validation block uses the combination of rules defined in a rule set and validators added as attributes to test the values of members of the class, and the result of executing any self-validation methods within the class.

The Validation block makes it easy to validate entire objects (all or a subset of its members) using a specific type validator or by using the Object validator. You can also validate all of the objects in a collection using the Object Collection validator. We will look at the Object validator and the Object Collection validator later. For the moment, we'll concentrate on creating and using a specific type validator.

Creating a Type Validator using the ValidatorFactory

You can resolve a **ValidatorFactory** instance through the Enterprise Library container and use it to create a validator for a specific target type. This validator will validate objects using a rule set, and/or any attributes and self-validation methods the target object contains. To obtain an instance of the **ValidatorFactory** class, you can use the following code.

```
Dim valFactory As ValidatorFactory _
    = EnterpriseLibraryContainer.Current.GetInstance(Of ValidatorFactory)()
```

You can then create a validator for any type you want to validate. For example, this code creates a validator for the **Product** class and then validates an instance of that class named **myProduct**.

```
Dim pValidator As Validator(Of Product) _
    = valFactory.CreateValidator(Of Product)()
Dim valResults As ValidationResults = pValidator.Validate(myProduct)
```

By default, the validator will use the default rule set defined for the target type (you can define multiple rule sets for a type, and specify one of these as the default for this type). If you want the validator to use a specific rule set, you specify this as the single parameter to the **CreateValidator** method, as shown here.

```
Dim productValidator As Validator(Of Product) _
    = valFactory.CreateValidator(Of Product)("RuleSetName")
Dim valResults As ValidationResults = productValidator.Validate(myProduct)
```

The example named *Using a Validation Rule Set to Validate an Object* creates an instance of the **Product** class that contains invalid values for all of the properties, and then uses the code shown above to create a type validator for this type and validate it. It then displays details of the validation errors contained in the returned **ValidationResults** instance. However, rather than using the simple technique of iterating over the **ValidationResults** instance displaying the top-level errors, it uses code to dive deeper into the results to show more information about each validation error, as you will see in the next section.

Delving Deeper into ValidationResults

You can check if validation succeeded, or if any validation error were detected, by examining the **IsValid** property of a **ValidationResults** instance and displaying details of any validation errors that occurred. However, when you simply iterate over a **Validation Results** instance (as we demonstrated in the section "Performing Validation and Displaying Validation Errors" earlier in this chapter), we displayed just the top-level errors. In many cases, this is all you will require. If the validation error occurs due to a validation failure in a composite (**And** or **Or**) validator, the error this approach will display is the message and details of the composite validator.

However, sometimes you may wish to delve deeper into the contents of a **Validation Results** instance to learn more about the errors that occurred. This is especially the case when you use nested validators inside a composite validator. The code we use in the example provides richer information about the errors. When you run the example, it displays the following results (we've removed some repeated content for clarity).

```
The following 6 validation errors were detected:
+ Target object: Product, Member: DateDue
  - Detected by: OrCompositeValidator
  - Tag value: Date Due
  - Validated value was: '23/11/2010 13:45:41'
  - Message: 'Date Due must be between today and six months time.'
  + Nested validators:
    - Detected by: NotNullValidator
    - Validated value was: '23/11/2010 13:45:41'
    - Message: 'Value can be NULL or a date.'
    - Detected by: RelativeDateTimeValidator
    - Validated value was: '23/11/2010 13:45:41'
    - Message: 'Value can be NULL or a date.'
+ Target object: Product, Member: Description
  - Detected by: OrCompositeValidator
  - Validated value was: '-'
  - Message: 'Description can be NULL or a string value.'
  + Nested validators:
    - Detected by: StringLengthValidator
    - Validated value was: '-'
    - Message: 'Description must be between 5 and 100 characters.'
    - Detected by: NotNullValidator
```

```
      - Validated value was: '-'
      - Message: 'Value can be NULL.'
...
+ Target object: Product, Member: ProductType
  - Detected by: EnumConversionValidator
  - Tag value: Product Type
  - Validated value was: 'FurryThings'
  - Message: 'Product Type must be a value from the 'ProductType' enumeration.'
```

You can see that this shows the target object type and the name of the member of the target object that was being validated. It also shows the type of the validator that performed the operation, the **Tag** property values, and the validation error message. Notice also that the output includes the validation results from the validators nested within the two **OrCompositeValidator** validators. To achieve this, you must iterate recursively through the **ValidationResults** instance because it contains nested entries for the composite validators.

The code we used also contains a somewhat contrived feature: to be able to show the value being validated, some examples that use this routine include the validated value at the start of the message using the **{0}** token in the form: **[{0}]** *validation error message*. The example code parses the **Message** property to extract the value and the message when it detects that this message string contains such a value. It also encodes this value for display in case it contains malicious content.

While this may not represent a requirement in real-world application scenarios, it is useful here as it allows the example to display the invalid values that caused the validation errors and help you understand how each of the validators works. We haven't listed the code here, but you can examine it in the example application to see how it works, and adapt it to meet your own requirements. You'll find it in the **ShowValidationResults**, **ShowValidatorDetails**, and **GetTypeNameOnly** routines located in the region named Auxiliary routines at the end of the main program file.

Using the Object Validator

An alternative approach to validating objects is to programmatically create an Object Validator by calling its constructor. You specify the type that it will validate and, optionally, a rule set to use when performing validation. If you do not specify a rule set name, the validator will use the default rule set. When you call the **Validate** method of the Object validator, it creates a type-specific validator for the target type you specify, and you can use this to validate the object, as shown here.

```
Dim pValidator As Validator = New ObjectValidator(GetType(Product), "RuleSetName")
Dim valResults As ValidationResults = pValidator.Validate(myProduct)
```

Differences Between the Object Validator and the Factory-Created Type Validators

While the two approaches you've just seen to creating or obtaining a validator for an object achieve the same result, there are some differences in their behavior:

- If you do not specify a target type when you create an Object Validator programmatically, you can use it to validate any type. When you call the **Validate** method, you specify the target instance, and the Object validator creates a type-specific validator for the type of the target instance. In contrast, the validator you obtain from a factory can only be used to validate instances of the type you specify when you obtain the validator. However, it can also be used to validate subclasses of the specified type, but it will use the rules defined for the specified target type.
- The Object Validator will always use rules in configuration for the type of the target object, and attributes and self-validation methods within the target instance. In contrast, you can use a specific factory class type to obtain validators that only validate the target instance using one type of rule source (in other words, just configuration rule sets, or just one type of attributes).
- The Object Validator will acquire a type-specific validator of the appropriate type each time you call the **Validate** method, even if you use the same instance of the Object validator every time. In contrast, a validator obtained from one of the factory classes does not need to do this, and will offer improved performance.

As you can see from the flexibility and performance advantages listed above, you should generally consider using the **ValidatorFactory** approach for creating validators to validate objects rather than creating individual Object Validator instances.

Validating Collections of Objects

Before we leave the topic of validation of objects, it is worth looking at how you can validate collections of objects. The Object Collection validator can be used to check that every object in a collection is of the specified type, and to perform validation on every member of the collection. You can apply the Object Collection validator to a property of a class that is a collection of objects using a Validation block attribute if you wish, as shown in this example that ensures that the **ProductList** property is a collection of **Product** instances, and that every instance in the collection contains valid values.

```
<ObjectCollectionValidator(GetType(Product))> _
ReadOnly Property ProductList(ByVal products() As ProductList)
   Get
     Return theProductList
   End Get
End Property
```

You can also create an Object Collection validator programmatically, and use it to validate a collection held in a variable. The example named *Validating a Collection of Objects* demonstrates this approach. It creates a **List** named **productList** that contains two instances of the **Product** class, one of which contains all valid values, and one that contains invalid values for some of its properties. Next, the code creates an Object Collection validator for the **Product** type and then calls the **Validate** method.

```
' Create an Object Collection Validator for the collection type.
Dim collValidator As Validator _
        = New ObjectCollectionValidator(GetType(AttributedProduct))

' Validate all of the objects in the collection.
Dim results As ValidationResults = collValidator.Validate(productList)
```

Finally, the code displays the validation errors using the same routine as in earlier examples. As the invalid Product instance contains the same values as the previous example, the result is the same. You can run the example and view the code to verify that this is the case.

USING VALIDATION ATTRIBUTES

Having seen how you can use rule sets defined in configuration, and how you can display the results of a validation process, we can move on to explore the other ways you can define validation rules in your applications. The example application contains two classes that contain validation attributes and a self-validation method. The **AttributedProduct** class contains Validation block attributes, while the **AnnotatedProduct** class contains data annotation attributes.

Using the Validation Block Attributes

The example, *Using Validation Attributes and Self-Validation*, demonstrates use of the Validation block attributes. The **AttributedProduct** class has a range of different Validation block attributes applied to the properties of the class, applying the same rules as the **MyRuleset** rule set defined in configuration and used in the previous examples.

For example, the **ID** property carries attributes that add a Not Null validator, a String Length validator, and a Regular Expression validator. These validation rules are, by default, combined with an **And** operation, so all of the conditions must be satisfied if validation will succeed for the value of this property.

```
<NotNullValidator(MessageTemplate:="You must specify a product ID.")> _
<StringLengthValidator(6, RangeBoundaryType.Inclusive, _
                    6, RangeBoundaryType.Inclusive, _
                    MessageTemplate:="Product ID must be {3} characters.")> _
<RegexValidator("[A-Z]{2}[0-9]{4}", _
            MessageTemplate:="Product ID must be 2 letters and 4 numbers.")> _
Public Property ID() As String Implements IProduct.ID
    ...
End Property
```

Other validation attributes used within the **AttributedProduct** class include an Enum Conversion validator that ensures that the value of the **ProductType** property is a member of the **ProductType** enumeration, shown here. Note that the token **{3}** for the String Length validator used in the previous section of code is the lower bound value, while the token **{3}** for the Enum Conversion validator is the name of the enumeration it is comparing the validated value against.

```
<EnumConversionValidator(GetType(ProductType), _
  MessageTemplate:="Product type must be a value from the '{3}' enumeration.")> _
Public Property ProductType() As String Implements IProduct.ProductType
  ...
End Property
```

Combining Validation Attribute Operations

One other use of validation attributes worth a mention here is the application of a composite validator. By default, multiple validators defined for a member are combined using the **And** operation. If you want to combine multiple validation attributes using an **Or** operation, you must apply the **ValidatorComposition** attribute first and specify **CompositionType.Or**. The results of all validation operations defined in subsequent validation attributes are combined using the operation you specify for composition type.

The example class uses a **ValidatorComposition** attribute on the nullable **DateDue** property to combine a Not Null validator and a Relative DateTime validator. The top-level error message that the user will see for this property (when you do not recursively iterate through the contents of the **ValidationResults**) is the message from the **ValidatorComposition** attribute.

```
<ValidatorComposition(CompositionType.[Or], _
        MessageTemplate:="Date due must be between today and six months time.")> _
<NotNullValidator(Negated:=True, _
        MessageTemplate:="[{0}]Value can be NULL or a date.")> _
<RelativeDateTimeValidator(0, DateTimeUnit.Day, 6, DateTimeUnit.Month, _
        MessageTemplate:="[{0}]Value can be NULL or a date.")> _
Public Property DateDue() As System.Nullable(Of DateTime)
  ...
End Property
```

If you want to allow null values for a member of a class, you can apply the **IgnoreNulls** attribute.

Applying Self-Validation

Some validation rules are too complex to apply using the validators provided with the Validation block or the .NET Data Annotation validation attributes. It may be that the values you need to perform validation come from different places, such as properties, fields, and internal variables, or involve complex calculations.

In this case, you can define self-validation rules as methods within your class (the method names are irrelevant), as described earlier in this chapter in the section "Self-Validation." We've implemented a self-validation routine in the **AttributedProduct** class in the example application. The method simply checks that the combination of the values of the **InStock**, **OnOrder**, and **DateDue** properties meets predefined rules. You can examine the code within the **AttributedProduct** class to see the implementation.

Results of the Validation Operation

The example creates an invalid instance of the **AttributedProduct** class shown above, validates it, and then displays the results of the validation process. It creates the following output, though we have removed some of the repeated output here for clarity. You can run the example yourself to see the full results.

```
Created and populated a valid instance of the AttributedProduct class.

Created and populated an invalid instance of the AttributedProduct class.
The following 7 validation errors were detected:
+ Target object: AttributedProduct, Member: ID
  - Detected by: RegexValidator
  - Validated value was: '12075'
  - Message: 'Product ID must be 2 capital letters and 4 numbers.'
...
...
+ Target object: AttributedProduct, Member: ProductType
  - Detected by: EnumConversionValidator
  - Validated value was: 'FurryThings'
  - Message: 'Product type must be a value from the 'ProductType' enumeration.'
...
...
+ Target object: AttributedProduct, Member: DateDue
  - Detected by: OrCompositeValidator
  - Validated value was: '19/08/2010 15:55:16'
  - Message: 'Date due must be between today and six months time.'
  + Nested validators:
    - Detected by: RelativeDateTimeValidator
    - Validated value was: '18/11/2010 13:36:02'
    - Message: 'Value can be NULL or a date.'
    - Detected by: NotNullValidator
    - Validated value was: '18/11/2010 13:36:02'
    - Message: 'Value can be NULL or a date.'
+ Target object: AttributedProduct, Member: ProductSelfValidation
  - Detected by: [none]
  - Tag value:
  - Message: 'Total inventory (in stock and on order) cannot exceed 100 items.'
```

Notice that the output includes the name of the type and the name of the member (property) that was validated, as well as displaying type of validator that detected the error, the current value of the member, and the message. For the **DateDue** property, the output shows the two validators nested within the Or Composite validator. Finally, it shows the result from the self-validation method. The values you see for the self-validation are those the code in the self-validation method specifically added to the **Validation Results** instance.

Validating Subclass Types

While discussing validation through attributes, we should briefly touch on the factors involved when you validate a class that inherits from the type you specified when creating the validator you use to validate it. For example, if you have a class named **SaleProduct** that derives from **Product**, you can use a validator defined for the **Product** class to validate instances of the **SaleProduct** class. The **Validate** method will also apply any relevant rules defined in attributes in both the **SaleProduct** class and the **Product** base class.

If the derived class inherits a member from the base class and does not override it, the validators for that member defined in the base class apply to the derived class. If the derived class inherits a member but overrides it, the validators defined in the base class for that member do not apply to the derived class.

Validating Properties that are Objects

In many cases, you may have a property of your class defined as the type of another class. For example, your **OrderLine** class is likely to have a property that is a reference to an instance of the **Product** class. It's common for this property to be defined as a base type or interface type, allowing you to set it to an instance of any class that inherits or implements the type specified for the property.

You can validate such a property using an **ObjectValidator** attribute within the class. However, by default, the validator will validate the property using rules defined for the type of the property—in this example the type **IProduct**. If you want the validation to take place based on the actual type of the object that is currently set as the value of the property, you can add the **ValidateActualType** parameter to the **ObjectValidator** attribute, as shown here.

```
Public Class OrderLine

  <ObjectValidator(ValidateActualType:=True)> _
  Public Property OrderProduct(ByVal oProduct As IProduct)

    ...

  End Property
  ...
End Class
```

Using Data Annotation Attributes

The System.ComponentModel.DataAnnotations namespace in the .NET Framework contains a series of attributes that you can add to your classes and class members to signify metadata for these classes and members. They include a range of validation attributes that you can use to apply validation rules to your classes in much the same way as you can with the Validation block attributes. For example, the following shows how you can use the Range attribute to specify that the value of the property named **OnOrder** must be between 0 and 50.

```
<Range(0, 50, ErrorMessage:="Quantity on order must be between 0 and 50.")> _
Public Property OnOrder() As Integer
```

```
...
End Property
```

Compared to the validation attributes provided with the Validation block, there are some limitations when using the validation attributes from the DataAnnotations namespace:

- The range of supported validation operations is less comprehensive, though there are some new validation types available in.NET Framework 4.0 that extend the range. However, some validation operations such as property value comparison, enumeration membership checking, and relative date and time comparison are not available when using data annotation validation attributes.
- There is no capability to use **Or** composition, as there is with the Or Composite validator in the Validation block. The only composition available with data annotation validation attributes is the **And** operation.
- You cannot specify rule sets names, and so all rules implemented with data annotation validation attributes belong to the default rule set.
- There is no simple built-in support for self-validation, as there is in the Validation block.

You can, of course, include both data annotation and Validation block attributes in the same class if you wish, and implement self-validation using the Validation block mechanism in a class that contains data annotation validation attributes. The validation methods in the Validation block will process both types of attributes.

For more information about data annotations, see http://msdn.microsoft.com/en-us/library/system.componentmodel.dataannotations.aspx (.NET Framework 3.5) and http://msdn.microsoft.com/en-us/library/system.componentmodel.dataannotations(VS.100).aspx (.NET Framework 4.0).

An Example of Using Data Annotations

The examples we provide for this chapter include one named *Using Data Annotation Attributes and Self-Validation*. This uses only the range of data annotation attributes in version 3.5 of the .NET Framework, so you can run it on machines that do not have Visual Studio 2010 or version 4.0 of the .NET Framework installed.

The class named **AnnotatedProduct** contains data annotation attributes to implement the same rules as those applied by Validation block attributes in the **Attributed Product** class (which you saw in the previous example). However, due to the limitations with data annotations, the self-validation method within the class has to do more work to achieve the same validation rules.

For example, it has to check the minimum value of some properties as the data annotation attributes in version 3.5 of the .NET Framework only support validation of the maximum value (in version 4.0, they do support minimum value validation). It also has to check the value of the **DateDue** property to ensure it is not more than six months in the future, and that the value of the **ProductType** property is a member of the **ProductType** enumeration.

To perform the enumeration check, the self-validation method creates an instance of the Validation block Enum Conversion validator programmatically, and then calls its **DoValidate** method (which allows you to pass in all of the values required to perform the validation). The code passes to this method the value of the **ProductType** property, a reference to the current object, the name of the enumeration, and a reference to the **ValidationResults** instance being use to hold all of the validation errors.

```
Dim enumConverterValidator = New EnumConversionValidator(GetType(ProductType), _
                "Product type must be a value from the '{3}' enumeration.")
enumConverterValidator.DoValidate(ProductType, Me, "ProductType", results)
```

The code that creates the object to validate, validates it, and then displays the results is the same as you saw in the previous example, with the exception that it creates an invalid instance of the **AnnotatedProduct** class, rather than the **AttributedProduct** class. The result when you run this example is also similar to that of the previous example, but with a few exceptions. We've listed some of the output here.

```
Created and populated an invalid instance of the AnnotatedProduct class.
The following 7 validation errors were detected:
+ Target object: AnnotatedProduct, Member: ID
  - Detected by: [none]
  - Tag value:
  - Message: 'Product ID must be 6 characters.'
...
+ Target object: AnnotatedProduct, Member: ProductSelfValidation
  - Detected by: [none]
  - Tag value:
  - Message: 'Total inventory (in stock and on order) cannot exceed 100 items.'
+ Target object: AnnotatedProduct, Member: ID
  - Detected by: ValidationAttributeValidator
  - Message: 'Product ID must be 2 capital letters and 4 numbers.'
+ Target object: AnnotatedProduct, Member: InStock
  - Detected by: ValidationAttributeValidator
  - Message: 'Quantity in stock cannot be less than 0.'
```

You can see that validation failures detected for data annotations contain less information than those detected for the Validation block attributes, and validation errors are shown as being detected by the **ValidationAttributeValidator** class—the base class for data annotation validation attributes. However, where we performed additional validation using the self-validation method, there is extra information available.

Defining Attributes in Metadata Classes

In some cases, you may want to locate your validation attributes (both Validation block attributes and .NET Data Annotation validation attributes) in a file separate from the one that defines the class that you will validate. This is a common scenario when you are using tools that generate the class files, and would therefore overwrite your validation attributes. To avoid this you can locate your validation attributes in a separate file that forms a partial class along with the main class file. This approach makes use of the **MetadataType** attribute from the System.ComponentModel.DataAnnotations namespace.

You apply the **MetadataType** attribute to your main class file, specifying the type of the class that stores the validation attributes you want to apply to your main class members. You must define this as a partial class, as shown here. The only change to the content of this class compared to the attributed versions you saw in the previous sections of this chapter is that it contains no validation attributes.

```
<MetadataType(GetType(ProductMetadata))> _
Partial Public Class Product
   ... Existing members defined here, but without attributes or annotations ...
End Class
```

You then define the metadata type as a normal class, except that you declare simple properties for each of the members to which you want to apply validation attributes. The actual type of these properties is not important, and is ignored by the compiler. The accepted approach is to declare them all as type **Object**. As an example, if your **Product** class contains the **ID** and **Description** properties, you can define the metadata class for it, as shown here.

```
Public Class ProductMetadata

  <Required(ErrorMessage:="ID is required.")> _
  <RegularExpression("[A-Z]{2}[0-9]{4}", _
        ErrorMessage:="Product ID must be 2 capital letters and 4 numbers.")> _
  Public ID As Object

  <StringLength(100, ErrorMessage:="Description must be less than 100 chars.")> _
  Public Description As Object

End Class
```

Specifying the Location of Validation Rules

When you use a validator obtained from the **ValidatorFactory**, as we've done so far in the example, validation will take into account any applicable rule sets defined in configuration and in attributes and self-validation methods found within the target object. However, you can resolve different factory types if you want to perform validation using only rule sets defined in configuration, or using only attributes and self-validation. The specialized types of factory you can use are:

- **ConfigurationValidatorFactory**. This factory creates validators that only apply rules defined in a configuration file, or in a configuration source you provide. By default it looks for configuration in the default configuration file (App.config or Web.config). However, you can create an instance of a class that implements the **IConfigurationSource** interface, populate it with configuration data from another file or configuration storage media, and use this when you create this validator factory.
- **AttributeValidatorFactory**. This factory creates validators that only apply rules defined in Validation block attributes located in the target class, and rules defined through self-validation methods.
- **ValidationAttributeValidatorFactory**. This factory creates validators that only apply rules defined in .NET Data Annotations validation attributes.

For example, to obtain a validator for the **Product** class that validates using only attributes and self-validation methods within the target instance, and validate an instance of this class, you resolve an instance of the **AttributeValidatorFactory** from the container, as shown here.

```
Dim attrFactory As AttributeValidatorFactory = _
  EnterpriseLibraryContainer.Current.GetInstance(Of AttributeValidatorFactory)()
Dim pValidator As Validator(Of Product) _
    = attrFactory.CreateValidator(Of Product)()
Dim valResults As ValidationResults = pValidator.Validate(myProduct)
```

CREATING AND USING INDIVIDUAL VALIDATORS

You can create an instance of any of the validators included in the Validation block directly in your code, and then call its **Validate** method to validate an object or value. For example, you can create a new Date Time Range validator and set the properties, such as the upper and lower bounds, the message, and the **Tag** property. Then you call the **Validate** method of the validator, specifying the object or value you want to validate. The example, *Creating and Using Validators Directly,* demonstrates the creation and use of some of the individual and composite validators provided with the Validation block.

Validating Strings for Contained Characters

The example code first creates a **ContainsCharactersValidator** that specifies that the validated value must contain the characters c, a, and t, and that it must contain all of these characters (you can, if you wish, specify that it must only contain **Any** of the characters). The code also sets the **Tag** property to a user-defined string that helps to identify the validator in the list of errors. The overload of the **Validate** method used here returns a new **ValidationResults** instance containing a **ValidationResult** instance for each validation error that occurred.

```
' Create a Contains Characters Validator and use it to validate a string.
Dim charsValidator As New ContainsCharactersValidator("cat", _
                   ContainsCharacters.All, _
                   " Value must contain {4} of the characters '{3}'.")
charsValidator.Tag = "Validating the String value 'disconnected'"
Dim valResults As ValidationResults = charsValidator.Validate("disconnected")
```

Validating Integers within a Domain

Next, the example code creates a new **DomainValidator** for integer values, specifying an error message and an array of acceptable values. Then it can be used to validate an integer, with a reference to the existing **ValidationResults** instance passed to the **Validate** method this time.

```
' Create a Domain Validator and use it to validate an Integer value.
Dim integerValidator As Validator = New DomainValidator(Of Integer)( _
                        "Value must be in the list 1, 3, 7, 11, 13.", _
                        New Integer() {1, 3, 7, 11, 13})
```

```
integerValidator.Tag = "Validating the Integer value '42'"
integerValidator.Validate(42, valResults)
```

Validating with a Composite Validator

To show how you can create composite validators, the next section of the example creates an array containing two validators: a **NotNullValidator** and a **StringLengthValidator**. The first parameter of the **NotNullValidator** sets the **Negated** property. In this example, we set it to true so that the validator will allow null values. The **StringLengthValidator** specifies that the string it validates must be exactly five characters long. Notice that range validators such as the **StringLengthValidator** have properties that specify not only the upper and lower bound values, but also whether these values are included in the valid result set (**RangeBoundaryType.Inclusive**) or excluded (**RangeBoundaryType.Exclusive**). If you do not want to specify a value for the upper or lower bound of a range validator, you must set the corresponding property to **RangeBoundaryType.Ignore**.

```
Dim valArray As Validator() = New Validator() _
{ _
  New NotNullValidator(True, "Value can be NULL."), _
  New StringLengthValidator(5, RangeBoundaryType.Inclusive, _
                     5, RangeBoundaryType.Inclusive, _
                     "Must be between {3} ({4}) and {5} ({6}) chars.") _
}
```

Having created an array of validators, we can now use this to create a composite validator. There are two composite validators, the **AndCompositeValidator** and the **Or CompositeValidator**. You can combine these as well to create any nested hierarchy of validators you require, with each combination returning a valid result if all (with the **AndCompositeValidator**) or any (with the **OrCompositeValidator**) of the validators it contains are valid. The example creates an **OrCompositeValidator**, which will return true (valid) if the validated string is either null or contains exactly five characters. Then it validates a null value and an invalid string, passing into the **Validate** method the existing **ValidationResults** instance.

```
Dim orValidator As Validator = New OrCompositeValidator( _
                     "Value can be NULL or a string of 5 characters.", _
                     valArray)

' Validate two values with the Or Composite Validator.
orValidator.Validate(null, valResults)
orValidator.Validate("MoreThan5Chars", valResults)
```

Validating Single Members of an Object

The Validation block contains three validators you can use to validate individual members of a class directly, instead of validating the entire type using attributes or rule sets. Although you may not use this approach very often, you might find it to be useful in some scenarios. The Field Value validator can be used to validate the value of a field of a type.

The Method Return Value validator can be used to validate the return value of a method of a type. Finally, the Property Value validator can be used to validate the value of a property of a type.

The example shows how you can use a Property Value validator. The code creates an instance of the **Product** class that has an invalid value for the ID property, and then creates an instance of the **PropertyValueValidator** class, specifying the type to validate and the name of the target property. This second parameter of the constructor is the validator to use to validate the property value—in this example a Regular Expression validator. Then the code can initiate validation by calling the **Validate** method, passing in the existing **ValidationResults** instance, as shown here.

```
Dim productWithID As IProduct = New Product()
PopulateInvalidProduct(productWithID)
Dim propValidator As Validator = New PropertyValueValidator(Of Product)("ID", _
    New RegexValidator("[A-Z]{2}[0-9]{4}", _
                    "Product ID must be 2 capital letters and 4 numbers."))
propValidator.Validate(productWithID, valResults)
```

If required, you can create a composite validator containing a combination of validators, and specify this composite validator in the second parameter. A similar technique can be used with the Field Value validator and Method Return Value validator.

After performing all of the validation operations, the example displays the results by iterating through the **ValidationResults** instance that contains the results for all of the preceding validation operations. It uses the same **ShowValidationResults** routine we described earlier in this chapter. This is the result:

```
The following 4 validation errors were detected:
+ Target object: disconnected, Member:
  - Detected by: ContainsCharactersValidator
  - Tag value: Validating the String value 'disconnected'
  - Message: 'Value must contain All of the characters 'cat'.'
+ Target object: 42, Member:
  - Detected by: DomainValidator`1[System.Int32]
  - Tag value: Validating the Integer value '42'
  - Message: 'Value must be in the list 1, 3, 7, 11, 13.'
+ Target object: MoreThan5Chars, Member:
  - Detected by: OrCompositeValidator
  - Message: 'Value can be NULL or a string of 5 characters.'
  + Nested validators:
    - Detected by: NotNullValidator
    - Message: 'Value can be NULL.'
    - Detected by: StringLengthValidator
    - Message: 'Value must be between 5 (Inclusive) and 5 (Inclusive) chars.'
+ Target object: Product, Member: ID
  - Detected by: RegexValidator
  - Message: 'Product ID must be 2 capital letters and 4 numbers.'
```

You can see how the message template tokens create the content of the messages that are displayed, and the results of the nested validators we defined for the Or Composite validator. If you want to experiment with individual validators, you can modify and extend this example routine to use other validators and combinations of validators.

WCF SERVICE VALIDATION INTEGRATION

This section of the chapter demonstrates how you can integrate your validation requirements for WCF services with the Validation block. The Validation block allows you to add validation attributes to the parameters of methods defined in your WCF service contract, and have the values of these automatically validated each time the method is invoked by a client.

To use WCF integration, you edit your service contract, edit the WCF configuration to add the Validation block and behaviors, and then handle errors that arise due to validation failures. In addition to the other assemblies required by Enterprise Library and the Validation block, you must add the assembly named Microsoft.Practices.Enterprise Library.Validation.Integration.WCF to your application and reference them all in your service project.

The example, *Validating Parameters in a WCF Service*, demonstrates validation in a simple WCF service. It uses a service named **ProductService** (defined in the **Example Service** project of the solution). This service contains a method named **AddNewProduct** that accepts a set of values for a product, and adds this product to its internal list of products.

Defining Validation in the Service Contract

The service contract, shown below, carries the **ValidationBehavior** attribute, and each service method defines a fault contract of type **ValidationFault**.

```
<ServiceContract()> _
<ValidationBehavior()> _
Public Interface IProductService

  <OperationContract()> _
  <FaultContract(GetType(ValidationFault))> _
  Function AddNewProduct( _
    <NotNullValidator(MessageTemplate:="Must specify a product ID.")> _
    <StringLengthValidator(6, RangeBoundaryType.Inclusive, _
        6, RangeBoundaryType.Inclusive, _
        MessageTemplate:=" Product ID must be {3} characters.")> _
    <RegexValidator("[A-Z]{2}[0-9]{4}", _
        MessageTemplate:="Product Product ID must be 2 letters and 4 numbers.")> _
    ByVal id As String, _
    ...
    <IgnoreNulls(MessageTemplate:="Description can be NULL or a string value.")> _
    <StringLengthValidator(5, RangeBoundaryType.Inclusive, _
        100, RangeBoundaryType.Inclusive, _
```

```
      MessageTemplate:="Description must be between {3} and {5} characters.")> _
   ByVal description As String, _
   <EnumConversionValidator(GetType(ProductType), _
      MessageTemplate:="Must be a value from the '{3}' enumeration.")> _
   ByVal prodType As String, _
   ...
   <ValidatorComposition(CompositionType.Or, _
      MessageTemplate:="Date must be between today and six months time.")> _
   <NotNullValidator(Negated:=True, _
      MessageTemplate:="Value can be NULL or a date.")> _
   <RelativeDateTimeValidator(0, DateTimeUnit.Day, 6, DateTimeUnit.Month, _
      MessageTemplate:="Value can be NULL or a date.")> _
   ByVal dateDue As System.Nullable(Of DateTime)) _
   As Boolean

End Interface
```

You can see that the service contract defines a method named **AddNewProduct** that takes as parameters the value for each property of the **Product** class we've used throughout the examples. Although the previous listing omits some attributes to limit duplication and make it easier to see the structure of the contract, the rules applied in the example service we provide are the same as you saw in earlier examples of validating a **Product** instance. The method implementation within the WCF service is simple—it just uses the values provided to create a new **Product** and adds it to a generic **List**.

Editing the Service Configuration

After you define the service and its validation rules, you must edit the service configuration to force validation to occur. The first step is to specify the Validation block as a behavior extension. You will need to provide the appropriate version information for the assembly, which you can obtain from the configuration file generated by the configuration tool for the client application, or from the source code of the example, depending on whether you are using the assemblies provided with Enterprise Library or assemblies you have compiled yourself.

```
<extensions>
  <behaviorExtensions>
    <add name="validation"
         type="Microsoft.Practices...WCF.ValidationElement,
               Microsoft.Practices...WCF" />
  </behaviorExtensions>

  ... other existing behavior extensions here ...

</extensions>
```

Next, you edit the **<behaviors>** section of the configuration to define the validation behavior you want to apply. As well as turning on validation here, you can specify a rule set name (as shown) if you want to perform validation using only a subset of the rules defined in the service. Validation will then only include rules defined in validation attributes that contain the appropriate **Ruleset** parameter (the configuration for the example application does not specify a rule set name here).

```
<behaviors>
  <endpointBehaviors>
    <behavior name="ValidationBehavior">
      <validation enabled="true" ruleset="MyRuleset" />
    </behavior>
  </endpointBehaviors>

  ... other existing behaviors here ...

</behaviors>
```

> *Note that you cannot use a configuration rule set with a WCF service—all validation rules must be in attributes.*

Finally, you edit the **<services>** section of the configuration to link the **ValidationBehavior** defined above to the service your WCF application exposes. You do this by adding the **behaviorConfiguration** attribute to the service element for your service, as shown here.

```
<services>
  <service behaviorConfiguration="ExampleService.ProductServiceBehavior"
         name="ExampleService.ProductService">
    <endpoint address="" behaviorConfiguration="ValidationBehavior"
            binding="wsHttpBinding" contract="ExampleService.IProductService">
      <identity>
        <dns value="localhost" />
      </identity>
    </endpoint>
    <endpoint address="mex" binding="mexHttpBinding" contract="IMetadataExchange" />
  </service>
  ...
</services>
```

Using the Product Service and Detecting Validation Errors

At last you can use the WCF service you have created. The example uses a service reference added to the main project, and initializes the service using the service reference in the usual way. It then creates a new instance of a **Product** class, populates it with valid values, and calls the **AddNewProduct** method of the WCF service. Then it repeats the process, but this time by populating the product instance with invalid values. You can examine the code in the example to see this if you wish.

However, one important issue is the way that service exceptions are handled. The example code specifically catches exceptions of type **FaultException<ValidationFault>**. This is the exception generated by the service, and **ValidationFault** is the type of the fault contract we specified in the service contract.

Validation errors detected in the WCF service are returned in the **Details** property of the exception as a collection. You can simply iterate this collection to see the validation errors. However, if you want to combine them into a **ValidationResults** instance for display, especially if this is part of a multi-step process that may cause other validation errors, you must convert the collection of validation errors returned in the exception.

The example application does this using a method named **ConvertToValidation Results**, as shown here. Notice that the validation errors returned in the **ValidationFault** do not contain information about the validator that generated the error, and so we must use **Nothing** for this when creating each **ValidationResult** instance.

```
' Convert the validation details in the exception to individual
' ValidationResult instances and add them to the collection.
Dim adaptedResults As New ValidationResults()
For Each result As ValidationDetail In results
  adaptedResults.AddResult(New ValidationResult(result.Message, target, _
                                        result.Key, result.Tag, Nothing))
Next
Return adaptedResults
```

When you execute this example, you will see a message indicating the service being started—this may take a while the first time, and may even time out so that you need to try again. Then the output shows the result of validating the valid **Product** instance (which succeeds) and the result of validating the invalid instance (which produces the now familiar list of validation errors shown here).

```
The following 6 validation errors were detected:
...
+ Target object: Product, Member:
  - Detected by: [none]
  - Tag value: id
  - Message: 'Product ID must be two capital letters and four numbers.'
...
+ Target object: Product, Member:
  - Detected by: [none]
  - Tag value: description
  - Message: 'Description must be between 5 and 100 characters.'
+ Target object: Product, Member:
  - Detected by: [none]
  - Tag value: prodType
  - Message: 'Product type must be a value from the 'ProductType' enumeration.'
...
+ Target object: Product, Member:
```

```
- Detected by: [none]
- Tag value: dateDue
- Message: 'Date due must be between today and six months time.'
```

Again, we've omitted some of the duplication so that you can more easily see the result. Notice that there is no value available for the name of the member being validated or the validator that was used. This is a form of exception shielding that prevents external clients from gaining information about the internal workings of the service. However, the **Tag** value returns the name of the parameter that failed validation (the parameter names are exposed by the service), allowing you to see which of the values you sent to the service actually failed validation.

USER INTERFACE VALIDATION INTEGRATION

The Validation block contains integration components that make it easy to use the Validation block mechanism and rules to validate user input within the user interface of ASP.NET, Windows Forms, and WPF applications. While these technologies do include facilities to perform validation, this validation is generally based on individual controls and values.

When you integrate the Validation block with your applications, you can validate entire objects, and collections of objects, using sets of rules you define. You can also apply complex validation using the wide range of validators included with the Validation block. This allows you to centrally define a single set of validation rules, and apply them in more than one layer and when using different UI technologies.

> *The UI integration technologies provided with the Validation block do not instantiate the classes that contain the validation rules. This means that you cannot use self-validation with these technologies.*

ASP.NET User Interface Validation

The Validation block includes the **PropertyProxyValidator** class that derives from the ASP.NET **BaseValidator** control, and can therefore take part in the standard ASP.NET validation cycle. It acts as a wrapper that links an ASP.NET control on your Web page to a rule set defined in your application through configuration, attributes, and self-validation.

To use the **PropertyProxyValidator**, you add the assembly named Microsoft. Practices.EnterpriseLibrary.Validation.Integration.AspNet to your application, and reference it in your project. You must also include a **Register** directive in your Web pages to specify this assembly and the prefix for the element that will insert the **PropertyProxy Validator** into your page.

```
<% @Register TagPrefix="EntLibValidators"
Assembly="Microsoft.Practices.EnterpriseLibrary.Validation.Integration.AspNet"
Namespace="Microsoft.Practices.EnterpriseLibrary.Validation.Integration.AspNet"
%>
```

Then you can define the validation controls in your page. The following shows an example that validates a text box that accepts a value for the **FirstName** property of a **Customer** class, and validates it using the rule set named **RuleSetA**.

```
<EntLibValidators:PropertyProxyValidator id="firstNameValidator"
   runat="server" ControlToValidate="firstNameTextBox"
   PropertyName="FirstName" RulesetName="RuleSetA"
   SourceTypeName="ValidationQuickStart.BusinessEntities.Customer" />
```

One point to be aware of is that, unlike the ASP.NET validation controls, the Validation block **PropertyProxyValidator** control does not perform client-side validation. However, it does integrate with the server-based code and will display validation error messages in the page in the same way as the ASP.NET validation controls.

For more information about ASP.NET integration, see the documentation installed with Enterprise Library and available online at http://go.microsoft.com/fwlink/ ?LinkId=188874.

Windows Forms User Interface Validation

The Validation block includes the **ValidationProvider** component that extends Windows Forms controls to provide validation using a rule set defined in your application through configuration, attributes, and self-validation. You can handle the **Validating** event to perform validation, or invoke validation by calling the **PerformValidation** method of the control. You can also specify an **ErrorProvider** that will receive formatted validation error messages.

To use the **ValidationProvider**, you add the assembly named Microsoft.Practices. EnterpriseLibrary.Validation.Integration.WinForms to your application, and reference it in your project.

For more information about Windows Forms integration, see the documentation installed with Enterprise Library and available online at http://go.microsoft.com/ fwlink/?LinkId=188874.

WPF User Interface Validation

The Validation block includes the **ValidatorRule** component that you can use in the binding of a WPF control to provide validation using a rule set defined in your application through configuration, attributes, and self-validation. To use the **ValidatorRule**, you add the assembly named Microsoft.Practices.EnterpriseLibrary.Validation.Integration.WPF to your application, and reference it in your project.

As an example, you can add a validation rule directly to a control, as shown here.

```
<TextBox x:Name="TextBox1">
  <TextBox.Text>
    <Binding Path="ValidatedStringProperty" UpdateSourceTrigger="PropertyChanged">
      <Binding.ValidationRules>
        <vab:ValidatorRule SourceType="{x:Type test:ValidatedObject}"
                           SourcePropertyName="ValidatedStringProperty"/>
      </Binding.ValidationRules>
    </Binding>
  </TextBox.Text>
</TextBox>
```

You can also specify a rule set using the **RulesetName** property, and use the **Validation SpecificationSource** property to refine the way that the block creates the validator for the property.

For more information about WPF integration, see the documentation installed with Enterprise Library and available online at http://go.microsoft.com/fwlink/?LinkId= 188874.

Creating Custom Validators

While the wide range of validators included with the Validation block should satisfy most requirements, you can easily create your own custom validators and integrate them with the block. This may be useful if you have some specific and repetitive validation task that you need to carry out, and which is more easily accomplished using custom code.

The easiest way to create a custom validator is to create a class that inherits from one of the abstract base classes provided with the Validation block. Depending on the type of validation you need to perform, you may choose to inherit from base types such as the **ValueValidator** or **MemberAccessValidator** classes, the **Validator(Of T)** base class (for a strongly typed validator) or from the **Validator** class (for a loosely typed validator).

You can also create your own custom validation attributes that will apply custom validators you create. The base class, **ValidatorAttribute,** provides a good starting point for this.

For more information on extending Enterprise Library and creating custom providers, see the documentation installed with Enterprise Library and available online at http:// go.microsoft.com/fwlink/?LinkId=188874.

Summary

In this chapter we have explored the Enterprise Library Validation block and shown you how easy it is to decouple your validation code from your main application code. The Validation block allows you to define validation rules and rule sets; and apply them to objects, method parameters, properties, and fields of objects you use in your application. You can define these rules using configuration, attributes, or even using custom code and self-validation within your classes.

Validation is a vital crosscutting concern, and should occur at the perimeter of your application, at trust boundaries, and (in most cases) between layers and distributed components. Robust validation can help to protect your applications and services from malicious users and dangerous input (including SQL injection attacks); ensure that it processes only valid data and enforces business rules; and improve responsiveness.

The ability to centralize your validation mechanism and the ability to define rules through configuration also make it easy to deploy and manage applications. Administrators can update the rules when required without requiring recompilation, additional testing, and redeployment of the application. Alternatively, you can define rules, validation mechanisms, and parameters within your code if this is a more appropriate solution for your own requirements.

7 Relieving Cryptography Complexity

Introduction

How secret are your secrets? We all know how important it is to encrypt information that is sensitive, whether it is stored in a database or a disk file, passed over the network (especially the Internet), or even sitting around in memory. Handing over a list of your customers' credit card numbers to some geek sitting in his bedroom hacking your online store is not a great way to build customer confidence. Neither is allowing some disenfranchised administrator to leave your company with a plain-text copy of all your trading partners' network passwords.

The trouble is that writing all that extra code from scratch to perform reliable and secure encryption is complicated and soaks up valuable development time. Even the names of the encryption algorithms are impenetrable, such as AES, 3DES, and RC5. And when it comes to hashing algorithms, there's even more of an assortment. How do you implement routines to use the HMAC, MD5, RIPEMD, and SHA algorithms?

The Microsoft® .NET Framework provides a range of managed code hashing and encryption mechanisms, but you still need to write a good deal of code to use them. Thankfully, the Cryptography Application Block makes it all very much easier. Like all of the other application blocks in Enterprise Library, the Cryptography block is completely configurable and manageable, and offers a wide range of hashing and encryption options using many of the common (and some not so common) algorithms.

What Does the Cryptography Block Do?

The Cryptography block provides mechanisms to perform two basic activities: symmetric encryption/decryption of data, and creating hash values from data. It contains a range of providers that make use of the platform functions for a range of encryption and hashing algorithms. These providers have a simple API that makes it easy to perform common actions, without requiring you to be familiar with the individual algorithms or the process of interacting with the platform functionality.

A SECRET SHARED

One important point you must be aware of is that there are two basic types of encryption: symmetric (or shared key) encryption, and asymmetric (or public key) encryption. The Cryptography block supports only symmetric encryption. The patterns & practices guide "Data Confidentiality" at http://msdn.microsoft.com/en-us/library/aa480570.aspx provides an overview of both types of encryption and lists the factors you should consider when using encryption.

Is a secret still secret when you tell it to somebody else? When using symmetric encryption, you don't have a choice. Unlike asymmetric encryption, which uses different public and private keys, symmetric encryption uses a single key to both encrypt and decrypt the data. Therefore, you must share the encryption key with the other party so that they (or it, in the case of code) can decrypt the data.

In general, this means that the key should be long and complex (the name of your dog is not a great example of an encryption key). Depending on the algorithm you choose, this key will usually be a minimum of 128 bits—the configuration tools in Enterprise Library can generate random keys for you, as you'll see in the section "Configuring Cryptographic Providers" later in this chapter. Alternatively, you can configure the encryption providers to use your existing keys.

MAKING A HASH OF IT

Hashing is useful when you need to store a value or data in a way that hides the original content with no option of reconstructing the original content. An obvious example is when storing passwords in a database. Of course, the whole point of creating a hash is to prevent the initial value from being readable; thus, the process is usually described as a one-way hashing function. Therefore, as you can't get the original value back again, you can only use hashing where it is possible to compare hashed values. This is why many systems allow users only to reset (but not retrieve) their passwords; because the system itself has no way to retrieve the original password text.

In the case of stored passwords, the process is easy. You just hash the password the user provides when they log in and compare it with the hash stored in your database or repository. Just be aware that you cannot provide a forgotten password function that allows users to retrieve a password. Sending them the hashed value would not be of any help at all.

Other examples for using hashing are to compare two long string values or large objects. Hashing effectively generates a unique key for such a value or object that is considerably smaller, or shorter, than the value itself.

HOW DOES THE CRYPTOGRAPHY BLOCK MANAGE ENCRYPTION KEYS?

The keys required for both encryption and decryption are stored in separate files, one for each key, on your machine. The full physical path and name of each key file is stored in the configuration of your application. If you move your application or key files, you must update this path.

One vitally important issue you must be aware of when using encryption (both symmetric providers and some hashing algorithms) is that, if a malicious user or attacker obtains access to your keys, they can use them to decrypt your data. Therefore, to protect the keys, the key files are encrypted automatically using the Windows® Data Protection application programming interface (DPAPI), which relies on either a machine key or a user key that is auto-generated by the operating system. If you lose a key file, or if a malicious user or attacker damages it, you will be unable to decrypt the data you encrypted with that key.

Therefore, ensure that you protect your key files from malicious access, and keep backup copies. In particular, protect your keys with access control lists (ACL) that grant only the necessary permissions to the identities that require access to the key file, and avoid allowing remote debugging if the computer runs in a high-risk environment (such as a Web server that allows anonymous access).

For more information on DPAPI, and a description of how it works, see "Windows Data Protection" at http://msdn.microsoft.com/en-us/library/ms995355.aspx.

HOW DOES THE CRYPTOGRAPHY BLOCK INTEGRATE WITH OTHER BLOCKS?

The Cryptography block integrates with the Caching block, where it can be used to encrypt cached data. When you add a symmetric storage encryption provider to the Caching block, it automatically adds the Cryptography block to your application configuration.

The Security block uses the Caching block to store credentials. When you add a caching store provider to a security cache for the Security block, you can configure that caching store provider to use one of your configured cache managers. If that cache manager uses a persistent backing store, you should ensure that you use a symmetric storage encryption provider for that cache manager.

How Do I Use the Cryptography Block?

Like all of the Enterprise Library application blocks, you start by configuring your application to use the block, as demonstrated in Chapter 1, "Introduction." Then you add one or more hash algorithm providers and one or more symmetric encryption providers, depending on the requirements of your application. For each of the providers that you add, you select a specific cryptographic provider (algorithm type) and set the relevant properties for each provider. If none of the built-in hash and symmetric encryption providers meets your requirements, you can create custom providers and add these to your application configuration.

After you add the hash algorithm providers and symmetric encryption providers you want to use to your configuration, you can specify which of each of these is the default—the one that the block will use if you don't specify a provider by name in your application code. You just use the drop-down lists for the **DefaultHashProvider** and **Default SymmetricCryptoProvider** properties of the Cryptography Application Block node to select the default providers.

Of course, as part of the configuration task, you still need to decide which algorithms to use. For a **Hash Algorithm Provider**, you can specify if the provider will use a SALT value (a random string pre-pended to the plain-text before hashing to improve the security of the algorithm). In addition, for some of the hash algorithms, you can specify or generate a key for the algorithm. Other providers, such as SHA and MD5, do not require a key. As a general recommendation, you should aim to use at minimum the SHA256 algorithm for hashing, and preferably a more robust version such as SHA384 or SHA512.

You can use two different types of **Symmetric Encryption Provider** in the Cryptography block (in addition to custom providers that you create). You can choose the DPAPI provider, or one of the well-known symmetric algorithms such as AES or 3DES. As a general recommendation, you should aim to use the AES (Rijndael) algorithm for encryption.

> *Comprehensive information about the many different encryption and hashing algorithms is contained in the Handbook of Applied Cryptography (Menezes, Alfred J., Paul C. van Oorschot and Scott A. Vanstone, CRC Press, October 1996, ISBN: 0-8493-8523-7). See http://www.cacr.math.uwaterloo.ca/hac/ for more information. You will also find a list of publications that focus on cryptography at "Additional Documentation on Cryptography" (http://msdn.microsoft.com/en-us/library/aa375543(VS.85).aspx).*

CONFIGURING CRYPTOGRAPHIC PROVIDERS

In addition to the obvious properties for each cryptographic provider you add to your configuration, such as the name, some providers require you to specify an encryption key. If you already have a DPAPI-encrypted key file for the selected algorithm type, you can use this. Alternatively, you can copy an existing plain text value of the appropriate size and use that as the key value. The third approach is to allow the Enterprise Library configuration to generate a new key for you.

When you add a provider that requires a key to your configuration, the configuration tool starts the Cryptographic Key Wizard. This makes it easy to select or create the key you need and save it to a file and to set the appropriate values in the configuration. The only page you may find confusing is the final one where you must specify either Machine mode or User mode access to the key.

You should select **Machine** mode if your application runs on its own dedicated server that is not shared with other applications, or when you have multiple applications that run on the same server and you want those applications to be able to share sensitive information.

Select **User** mode if you run your application in a shared hosting environment and you want to make sure that your application's sensitive data is not accessible to other applications on the server. In this situation, each application should run under a separate identity, and the resources for the application—such as files and databases—should be restricted to that identity.

If you add a DPAPI symmetric cryptography provider to your list of symmetric providers, you can specify the Protection Scope as either **CurrentUser** or **LocalMachine**. Current user means that DPAPI uses a loaded user profile to generate the key, and only that user account can decrypt the encrypted data. Local machine means that any code running on the machine has access to the protected key, and can decrypt any secret encrypted in the same mode.

ADDING THE REQUIRED REFERENCES

To use the Cryptography block features in your application, you must reference the required assemblies and then instantiate the objects you want to use in your code. In addition to the Enterprise Library assemblies you require in every Enterprise Library project (listed in Chapter 1, "Introduction"), you should reference or add to your bin folder the following assemblies:

- Microsoft.Practices.EnterpriseLibrary.Security.Cryptography.dll
- Microsoft.Practices.EnterpriseLibrary.Security.Caching.dll

To make it easier to use the objects in the Cryptography block, you can add references to the relevant namespaces to your project. Then you are ready to write some code. The following sections demonstrate the tasks you can accomplish, and provide more details about how the block helps you to implement a common and reusable strategy for cryptography.

However, before you start to use the objects in the block, you must resolve an instance of the **CryptographyManager** class. This class exposes the API that you interact with to use the cryptography providers (symmetric and hash providers) in your code. The simplest approach is to use the **GetInstance** method of the Enterprise Library container, as shown here.

```
' Resolve the default CryptographyManager object from the container.
Dim defaultCrypto As CryptographyManager _
    = EnterpriseLibraryContainer.Current.GetInstance(Of CryptographyManager)()
```

Diving in with an Example

You can download an example application (a simple console-based application) that demonstrates all of the scenarios you will see in the remainder of this chapter. You can run this directly from the bin\debug folder, or open the solution named **Cryptography** in Microsoft® Visual Studio® to see all of the code as you run the examples.

> *Before you attempt to run the example, you must create new encryption keys for the block to use to encrypt the data when using a symmetric encryption provider. This is because the key is tied to either the user or the machine, and so the key included in the sample files will not work on your machine. In the configuration console, select the **AesManaged** symmetric provider, and click the "..." button in the **Key** property to start the Key wizard. Use this wizard to generate a new key, save the key file, and automatically update the content of App.config. Then repeat this procedure for the **RijndaelManager** symmetric provider. Rijndael is an implementation of the AES algorithm. However, we will demonstrate both as we show you how to encrypt and decrypt both value types and objects.*

ENCRYPTING AND DECRYPTING DATA USING A SYMMETRIC PROVIDER

To encrypt and decrypt information, you use a symmetric encryption provider. As you saw earlier, the Cryptography block includes several symmetric encryption providers. The examples we provide use two of these: the AES managed symmetric algorithm provider and the Rijndael managed symmetric algorithm provider. The examples demonstrate how to use these providers to encrypt both a text string and an object (in our example this is a simple class named **Product**), and how to decrypt the encrypted item.

The Cryptography Manager exposes two methods for working with symmetric encryption providers:

- The **EncryptSymmetric** method takes as parameters the name of a symmetric provider configured in the Cryptography block for the application, and the item to encrypt. There are two overloads of this method. One accepts a string and returns a base-64 encoded string containing the encrypted text. The second overload accepts the data to encrypt as a byte array, and returns a byte array containing the encrypted data.
- The **DecryptSymmetric** method takes as parameters the name of a symmetric provider configured in the Cryptography block for the application, and the item to decrypt. There are two overloads of this method. One accepts a base-64 encoded string containing the encrypted text and returns the decrypted text. The second overload accepts a byte array containing the encrypted data and returns a byte array containing the decrypted item.

Encrypting and Decrypting a Text String

The first example, *Encrypt and Decrypt a Text String using a Symmetric Algorithm*, uses the AES managed symmetric algorithm provider to encrypt and decrypt a text string.

The code shown below creates a text string and then calls the **EncryptSymmetric** method of the Cryptography Manager, passing to it the name of the AES managed symmetric algorithm provider defined in the configuration of the application, and the text string to encrypt. To decrypt the resulting string, the code then calls the **Decrypt Symmetric** method of the Cryptography Manager, passing to it (as before) the name of the AES managed symmetric algorithm provider defined in the configuration of the application, and the encrypted base-64 encoded string. We've removed some of the lines of code that simply write values to the console screen to make it easier to see the code that actually does the work.

```
' Define the text string instance to encrypt.
Dim sampleText As String = "This is some text to encrypt."


' Use the AES Symmetric Algorithm Provider.
' The overload of the EncryptSymmetric method that takes a
' string returns the result as a Base-64 encoded string.
Dim encrypted As String = defaultCrypto.EncryptSymmetric("AesManaged", sampleText)


' Now decrypt the result string.
```

```
Dim decrypted As String = defaultCrypto.DecryptSymmetric("AesManaged", encrypted)

' Destroy any in-memory variables that hold sensitive information.
encrypted = Nothing
decrypted = Nothing
```

Notice that the last lines of the code destroy the in-memory values that hold the sensitive information used in the code. This is good practice as it prevents any leakage of this information should an error occur elsewhere in the application, and prevents any attacker from being able to dump the memory contents and view the information. If you store data in a string, set it to **Nothing**, allowing the garbage collector to remove it from memory during its next run cycle. If you use an array, call the static **Array.Clear** method (passing in the array you used) to remove the contents after use.

> *You may also consider storing values in memory using the* **SecureString** *class, which is part of the Microsoft .NET Framework. However, in the current release of Enterprise Library, the methods of the Security block do not accept or return* **SecureString** *instances, and so you must translate them into strings when interacting with the block methods. For more information about using the* **SecureString** *class, see "SecureString Class" at http://msdn.microsoft.com/en-us/library/system.security.securestring.aspx.*

When you run this example, you'll see the output shown below. You can see the value of the original string, the base-64 encoded encrypted data, and the result after decrypting this value.

```
Text to encrypt is 'This is some text to encrypt.'

Encrypted and Base-64 Encoded result is '+o3zulnEOeggpIqUeiHRD2ID4E85TSPxCjS/D6k
II4CUCjedFvlNOXjrqjna7ZWWbJp5yfyh/VrHw7oQPzUtUaxlXNdyiqSvDGcU814NNq4='

Decrypted string is 'This is some text to encrypt.'
```

Encrypting and Decrypting an Object Instance

The second example, *Encrypt and Decrypt Data using a Symmetric Algorithm*, uses the Rijndael managed symmetric algorithm provider to encrypt and decrypt an instance of the **Product** class defined within the example project.

The code shown below first creates a new instance of the **Product** class. We need to pass this to the **EncryptSymmetric** method of the Cryptography Manager, along with the name of the Rijndael managed symmetric algorithm provider defined in the configuration of the application, as an array of bytes. The easiest way to perform the conversion to a byte array is to take advantage of the **SerializationUtility** class in the Caching block. This class exposes two methods: **ToBytes** and **ToObject**. We use the **ToBytes** method to convert the **Product** instance into a byte array before passing it the **EncryptSymmetric** method.

Then the code decrypts the resulting byte array using the **DecryptSymmetric** method of the Cryptography Manager, passing to it (as before) the name of the Rijndael managed symmetric algorithm provider defined in the configuration of the application, and the encrypted byte array. The **ToObject** method of the **SerializationUtility** class then converts this back into an instance of the Product class. Again, we've removed some of the lines of code that simply write values to the console screen to make it easier to see the code that actually does the work.

```vb
' Create the object instance to encrypt.
Dim sampleObject As New Product(42, "Fun Thing", _
                        "Something to keep the grandchildren quiet.")


' Use the Rijndael Symmetric Algorithm Provider.
' Must serialize the object to a byte array first. One easy way is to use
' the methods of the SerializationUtility class from the Caching block.
Dim serializedObject As Byte() = SerializationUtility.ToBytes(sampleObject)


' The overload of the EncryptSymmetric method that takes a
' byte array returns the result as a byte array.
Dim encrypted As Byte() = defaultCrypto.EncryptSymmetric("RijndaelManaged", _
                                                serializedObject)


' Now decrypt the result byte array and deserialize the
' result to get the original object.
Dim decrypted As Byte() = defaultCrypto.DecryptSymmetric("RijndaelManaged", _
                                                encrypted)
Dim decryptedObject As Product _
    = DirectCast(SerializationUtility.ToObject(decrypted), Product)


' Destroy any in-memory variables that hold sensitive information.
Array.Clear(encrypted, 0, encrypted.Length)
Array.Clear(decrypted, 0, decrypted.Length)
Array.Clear(serializedObject, 0, serializedObject.Length)
decryptedObject = Nothing
```

If you run this example, you'll see the output shown below. You can see the value of the properties of the Product class we created, the encrypted data (we base-64 encoded it for display), and the result after decrypting this data.

```
Object to encrypt is 'CryptographyExample.Product'
 - Product.ID = 42
 - Product.Name = Fun Thing
 - Product.Description = Something to keep the grandchildren quiet.
```

```
Encrypted result is 'System.Byte[]'
Contents (when Base-64 encoded for display) are:
OEnp9yOP6LInmsfFDaGfVR7RJbwU4/TQskYtIPsqXKcx4UhxMctzBPWXuUX8Q+RgKqYdGAZVVbSCR2Vx
yTmSDdYQNdiSohA5Fo6bWOqhOR5V0uxdcfNUgKhUhuIAhl5RZ8W5WD8M2CdMiqG1gPgQjJC2afwf1mJn
F/4ZB/oD9QcCyQf5d5F1Ww==

Decrypted object is 'CryptographyExample.Product'
 - Product.ID = 42
 - Product.Name = Fun Thing
 - Product.Description = Something to keep the grandchildren quiet.
```

OBTAINING AND COMPARING HASH VALUES

To create and compare hash values, you use a hash provider. As you saw earlier, the Cryptography block includes several hash providers. The examples we provide use two of these: the SHA512 hash algorithm provider and the MD5Cng hash algorithm provider. The examples demonstrate how to use these providers to create a hash for both a text string and an object (in our example this is a simple class named Product), and how to compare the generated hashes with the original and other text strings and object instances.

The Cryptography Manager exposes two methods for working with hash providers:

- The **CreateHash** method takes as parameters the name of a hash provider configured in the Cryptography block for the application, and the item for which it will create the hash value. There are two overloads of this method. One accepts a string and returns the hash as a string. The second overload accepts the data to encrypt as a byte array, and returns a byte array containing the hash value.

- The **CompareHash** method takes as parameters the name of a hash provider configured in the Cryptography block for the application, the un-hashed item to compare the hash with, and the hash value to compare to the un-hashed item. There are two overloads of this method. One accepts the un-hashed item and the hash as strings. The second overload accepts the un-hashed item and the hash as byte arrays.

Creating and Comparing Hash Values for Text Strings

The example *Create and Compare Hash Values for Text Strings* uses the SHA512 hash algorithm provider to create a hash of three text strings. It then compares these hashes with the original and other values to demonstrate how even a minor difference between the original strings creates different hash values.

The code shown below creates three text strings that will be hashed. Notice that the second and third vary only in the letter case of two words. Then the code uses the **CreateHash** method of the Cryptography Manager to create the hashes of these three strings. In each case, the code passes to the CreateHash method the name of the SHA512 hash algorithm provider defined in the configuration of the application, and the text string.

Next, the code performs three comparisons of the hash values using the **CompareHash** method of the Cryptography Manager. It compares the hash of the first string with first string itself, to prove that they are equivalent. Then it compares the hash of the first string with the second string, to provide that they are not equivalent. Finally, it compares the hash of the second string with the third string, which varies only in letter case, to prove that these are also not equivalent.

As in earlier examples, we've removed some of the lines of code that simply write values to the console screen to make it easier to see the code that actually does the work.

```vbnet
' Define the text strings instance to encrypt.
Dim sample1Text As String = "This is some text to hash."
Dim sample2Text As String = "This is some more text to hash."
Dim sample3Text As String = "This is Some More text to hash."


' Create the hash values using the SHA512 Hash Algorithm Provider.
' The overload of the CreateHash method that takes a
' string returns the result as a string.
Dim hashed1Text As String _
    = defaultCrypto.CreateHash("SHA512CryptoServiceProvider", sample1Text)
Dim hashed2Text As String _
    = defaultCrypto.CreateHash("SHA512CryptoServiceProvider", sample2Text)
Dim hashed3Text As String _
    = defaultCrypto.CreateHash("SHA512CryptoServiceProvider", sample3Text)


' Compare the strings with some of the hashed values.
Console.WriteLine("Comparing the string '{0}' with the hash of this string:", _
                sample1Text)
Console.WriteLine("- result is {0}", _
                defaultCrypto.CompareHash("SHA512CryptoServiceProvider", _
                                        sample1Text, hashed1Text))

Console.WriteLine("Comparing the string '{0}' with hash of the string  '{1}'", _
                sample1Text, sample2Text)
Console.WriteLine("- result is {0}", _
                defaultCrypto.CompareHash("SHA512CryptoServiceProvider", _
                                        sample2Text, hashed1Text))

Console.WriteLine("Comparing the string '{0}' with hash of the string  '{1}'", _
                sample2Text, sample3Text)
Console.WriteLine("- result is {0}", _
                defaultCrypto.CompareHash("SHA512CryptoServiceProvider", _
                                        sample3Text, hashed2Text))
```

If you run this example, you'll see the output shown below. You can see the hash values of the three text strings, and the result of the three hash comparisons.

```
Text strings to hash and the resulting hash values are:

This is some text to hash.
v38snPJbuCtwfMUSNRjsgDqu4PB7ok7LQ2id4RJMZUGlhn+LTgX3FNEVuUbauokCpiCzzfZI2d9sNjlo
56NmuZ/8FY2sknxrD262TLSSYSQ=

This is some more text to hash.
braokQ/wraq9WVnKSqBROBUNG2lBwiICwX0lTGPSaooaJXL7/WcJvUCtBry8+0iRg+Rij5Xiz56jD4Zm
xcKrp7kGVDeWuA7jHeYiFZmGbOU=

This is Some More text to hash.
aw3anokiiBXPJfxZ5kf2SrlTEN3lokVlT+46t0V1B7der1wsNTD4dPxKQly8SDAjoCgCWwzSCh4k+OUf
O6/y6JIpFtWpQDqHO3JH+Rj25K0=

Comparing the string 'This is some text to hash.' with the hash of this string:
- result is True

Comparing the string 'This is some text to hash.' with hash of the string  'This
 is some more text to hash.'
- result is False

Comparing the string 'This is some more text to hash.' with hash of the string
'This is Some More text to hash.'
- result is False
```

Creating and Comparing Hash Values for Object Instances

The example *Create and Compare Hash Values for Data Items* uses the MD5Cng hash algorithm provider to create a hash of two instances of the Product class defined within the example project, demonstrating how different property values produce a different hash value. It then compares the second object instance with the hash of the first to show that they are different.

The code shown below starts by creating an instance of the **Product** class, and then serializes it using the **ToBytes** method of the **SerializationUtility** class. Then it calls the **CreateHash** method of the Cryptography Manager, passing to it the name of the MD5Cng hash algorithm provider defined in the configuration of the application, and the byte array generated from the **Product** class instance.

Next, the code repeats the process with another new instance of the **Product** class, with different values for its properties, and displays the hash of this to show that it is different from the other instance of the **Product** class created previously. Finally, the code compares the hash of the first instance of the **Product** class with the second instance of the same class to prove that they are not equivalent.

As in earlier examples, we've removed some of the lines of code that simply write values to the console screen to make it easier to see the code that actually does the work.

```vb
' Create the object instance to encrypt.
Dim sample1Object As New Product(42, "Exciting Thing", _
                        "Something to keep you on your toes.")

' Create the hash values using the SHA512 Hash Algorithm Provider.
' Must serialize the object to a byte array first. One easy way is to use
' the methods of the SerializationUtility class from the Caching block.
Dim serializedObject As Byte() = SerializationUtility.ToBytes(sample1Object)

' The overload of the CreateHash method that takes a
' byte array returns the result as a byte array.
Dim hashed1Object As Byte() = defaultCrypto.CreateHash("MD5Cng", serializedObject)

' Do the same to generate a hash for another similar object with
' different property values.
Dim sample2Object As New Product(79, "Fun Thing", _
                        "Something to keep the grandchildren quiet.")

serializedObject = SerializationUtility.ToBytes(sample2Object)
Dim hashed2Object As Byte() = defaultCrypto.CreateHash("MD5Cng", serializedObject)

' Compare the hashed values.
Console.WriteLine("Comparing second object with hash of the first object:")
Console.WriteLine("- result is {0}", _
                    defaultCrypto.CompareHash("MD5Cng", _
                                        serializedObject, hashed1Object))
```

If you run this example, you'll see the output shown below. You can see the hash values of the two instances of the Product class, and the result of the hash comparison.

```
First object to hash is 'CryptographyExample.Product'
 - Product.ID = 42
 - Product.Name = Exciting Thing
 - Product.Description = Something to keep you on your toes.
Generated hash (when Base-64 encoded for display) is:
Gd2V77Zau/pgOcg1A2A5zk6RTd5zFFnHKXfhVx8LEi4=
```

```
Second object to hash is 'CryptographyExample.Product'
 - Product.ID = 79
 - Product.Name = Fun Thing
 - Product.Description = Something to keep the grandchildren quiet.
Generated hash (when Base-64 encoded for display) is:
1Eyal+AHf3e2QyEB+sqsGDOdux1Iom4z0zGLYlHlC78=


Comparing second object with hash of the first object:
 - result is False
```

Creating Custom Cryptography Providers

While the Cryptography block contains providers for a range of hashing and encryption algorithms, you may find that you have specific requirements that none of these algorithms can satisfy. For example, you may wish to perform some company-specific encryption technique, or implement a non-standard hashing algorithm. You may even want to apply multiple levels of encryption based on business requirements or data handling standards relevant to your industry.

> *Be aware that you may introduce vulnerabilities into your application by using non-standard or custom encryption algorithms. The strength of any algorithm you use must be verified as being suitable for your requirements, and rechecked regularly to ensure that new decryption techniques or known vulnerabilities do not compromise your application.*

You can implement a custom hashing provider or a custom encryption provider, and integrate them with Enterprise Library. The Cryptography block contains two interfaces, **IHashProvider** and **ISymmetricCryptoProvider**, that define hashing and encryption provider requirements. For a custom hashing provider, you must implement the **Create Hash** and **CompareHash** methods based on the hashing algorithm you choose. For a custom encryption provider, you must implement the **Encrypt** and **Decrypt** methods based on the encryption algorithm you choose.

One other way that you may want to modify the block is to change the way that it creates and stores keys. By default, it stores keys that you provide or generate for the providers in DPAPI-encrypted disk files. You can modify the **KeyManager** class in the block to change this behavior, and modify the Wizard that helps you to specify the key in the configuration tools.

For more information about extending and modifying the Cryptography block, see the online documentation and the help files installed with Enterprise Library.

Summary

This chapter looked at the Cryptography Application Block. It began by discussing cryptographic techniques and strategies for which the block is suitable, and helped you decide how you might use the block in your applications. The two most common scenarios are symmetric encryption/decryption of data, and creating hash values from data. Symmetric encryption is useful whenever you need to protect data that you are storing or sending across a network. Hashing is useful for tasks such as storing passwords so that you can confirm user identity without allowing the passwords to be visible to anyone who may access the database or intercept the passwords as they pass over a network.

Many types of cryptographic algorithms that you may use with the Cryptography block require access to a key for both encryption and decryption. **It is vitally important that you protect this key** both to prevent unauthorized access to the data and to allow you to encrypt it when required. The Cryptography block protects key files using DPAPI encryption.

The bulk of the chapter then explored the main techniques for using the block. This includes encrypting and decrypting data, creating a hash value, and comparing hash values (for example, when verifying a submitted user password). As you have seen, the block makes these commonly repeated tasks much simpler, while allowing the configuration to be easily managed post-deployment and at run time by administrators and operations staff.

8   An Authentic Approach to Token Identity

Introduction

I guess most people have seen a sitcom on TV where some unfortunate member of the cast is faced with a large red button carrying a sign that says "Do not press this button." You know that, after the requisite amount of facial contortions and farcical fretting, they are going to press the button and some comedic event will occur. So it's reasonably certain that any user authorization strategy you adopt that contains an element that simply asks the user not to press that button unless he is a manager or administrator is not likely to provide a secure environment for your enterprise application.

User authorization—controlling what your users can and cannot do with your application—is a vital ingredient of a robust security strategy. In general, an application UI should prevent users from attempting actions for which they are not eligible; usually by disabling or even hiding controls that, depending on their permissions within the application, they are not permitted to use. And, of course, the application should check that users are authorized to carry out all operations that they initiate, whether it is through a UI or as a call from another layer or segment of the application.

The Security Application Block provides features that can help you to implement authorization for your applications, and can simplify the task by allowing you to maintain consistent security practices across the entire application and your enterprise as a whole. It makes it easier for you to implement authorization using standard practices, and you can extend the block to add specific functionality that you require for your own scenarios.

What Does the Security Block Do?

The Security Application Block implements two related features. It provides the capability to configure and manage sets of authorization rules using a variety of rule providers, and can help you to cache credentials for your application to use where it must make repeated authorization checks. These two features combine to provide an environment for implementing authorization in a flexible way, while allowing the details of the authorization policies (the sets of rules) to be administered without requiring changes to the application—eliminating the requirement to recompile, test, and redeploy the application as the policies change. It also means that administrators can manage the policies using Group Policy if required.

In your application code, you can quickly and easily create tokens for users, cache these tokens, expire them, and check if users are authorized to perform specific tasks or operations. These features make use of one or more authorization rule providers and security caches that you define for your application, and even use across multiple applications. The following sections of this chapter explain what an authorization rule provider and a security cache are, and how they help you to implement a security strategy for your applications.

WHAT ARE AUTHORIZATION RULE PROVIDERS?

An authorization rule provider is a component or service that allows you to define rules. Using a rule you specify a task or operation that users may perform, and you then allocate users and groups to this task or operation. The Security block uses these rules to determine whether a specific user or role is authorized to execute a specified task or operation.

The Security block includes a rule provider that stores the information as a series of expressions, one for each task or operation, in the application configuration file. You can encrypt this section of the configuration file to prevent anyone who can access it from being able to see the expressions. Alternatively, you can use the Windows® Authorization Manager (AzMan) provider, part of the current Microsoft® Windows operating systems, which allows you to store the authorization rules in a variety of locations, and include Windows users and groups in the rules. Enterprise Library includes an assembly named Microsoft.Practices.EnterpriseLibrary.Security.AzMan.dll that allows it to interact with AzMan.

About Authorization Manager (AzMan)

While it's useful to be able to define your security roles and authorization rules in the application configuration file, what would be really cool is to be able to make use of the groups, roles, and user accounts already defined on your system or network, and store the rules in some portable format such as an XML file or (perhaps less portable) a database. The details of Windows users and groups are stored in Active Directory®, and—while you can write code to access the information—using Active Directory is not a trivial exercise. Windows Authorization Manager (AzMan) gives you a way to access this information, and administer security rules in other locations, without requiring complex code. It even provides a GUI that you can use to create authorization rules and administer these rules.

The Windows AzMan provider is part of the operating system in Windows XP Professional and Windows Server® 2003 and later. The GUI is part of the operating system in Windows Vista® and Windows Server 2003 and later. In Windows Vista, Windows Server® 2008, and Windows 7, AzMan provides additional capabilities. For more information about AzMan, see the following resources:

- "Authorization Manager" (Overview) at http://technet.microsoft.com/en-us/library/cc732290.aspx.
- "Authorization Manager" (Details) at http://technet.microsoft.com/en-us/library/cc732077(WS.10).aspx.
- "How to install and administer the Authorization Manager in Windows Server 2003" at http://support.microsoft.com/kb/324470.

AzMan allows you to define an application, the roles for that application, and the operations (such as submit order or approve expenses) that the application exposes. For each operation, you can define users and groups that can execute that operation. You can include local and domain user accounts and account groups stored in Active Directory. You can store your authorization rules in Active Directory, in an XML file, or in a database.

WHY DO I NEED A SECURITY CACHE?

Unless all of the features of your application are meant to be completely available to anonymous users, you will need to authenticate users and definitively identify each one. You can then determine what that user is and is not permitted to do inside your application. Common approaches to authentication include logon dialogs where users enter their user name and password (and, perhaps, additional information that helps to confirm their identity), and other mechanisms such as smart card readers, fingerprint readers, and more.

You may force users to authenticate when they first access the application, or at some later stage when they try to execute some activity that has limited permissions. This really depends on whether you want to hide or disable elements of the UI, or you are happy to accept requests and then authenticate at that point in your application. For example, a Web service application will usually authenticate users when a request is received, while a Windows Forms application will usually authenticate users when they start the application.

What you don't want to do is continually annoy users by forcing them to reauthenticate every time they try to execute some operation or carry out some task. For example, if you are browsing a shopping Web site and adding to your cart all of those science fiction DVDs you want to be able to watch over and over again, you wouldn't expect to have to enter your account logon details for every item. Once your application knows who a user is, it should reuse the results of the initial authentication if possible.

To be able to do this, you must cache the user's credentials for a predetermined period when you first authenticate them, and generate a token that represents the user. You may decide to cache the credentials for the duration a Windows Forms application is running, or for the duration of the user's session in ASP.NET. You may even decide to persist them in a cache that survives application and machine restarts (such as the user-specific isolated storage mechanism) if you want to allow the logged-on user of the machine to be able to access the application without reauthenticating. An example is the Windows operating system, which forces you to log on when you first start it up, but can then reuse persistently cached credentials to connect to other resources such as mapped drives.

The Security Application Block allows you to configure one or more Security Caches that use an in-memory cache, and optionally a persistent backing store, to cache user credentials for specific periods and obtain a token that you can use to check the user's identity at some future stage in your application.

An alternative approach to caching identities you may consider is to use the Microsoft .NET Framework version 4.0 System.Runtime.Caching capabilities. However, you would then need to implement suitable methods that accept and return identities, and ensure that you correctly secure the stored content.

How Do I Configure the Security Block?

Like all of the Enterprise Library application blocks, you start by configuring your application to use the block, as demonstrated in Chapter 1, "Introduction." The Security Settings section of the configuration for the Security block contains three areas, shown in Figure 1. The first is where you specify the authorization providers you want to use. Below that is the area where you configure one or more security caches for your security tokens. Your code can store tokens in this cache, and retrieve them when required. You can even persist the credentials across application restarts by defining backing stores for credentials. The third area is where you configure the authorization rules that define the users, groups, and operations related to your application.

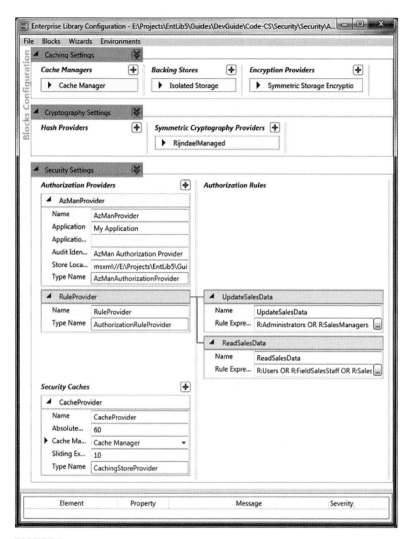

FIGURE 1
The security settings section

Figure 1 shows the configuration for the example application we provide for this chapter. You can see the areas where we defined the authorization providers and the security cache. Because we specified the Caching Application Block as the security cache, the configuration tool added the Caching block to the configuration automatically. We added an isolated storage backing store to the Caching block to persist credentials, and specified a symmetric storage provider for this store to protect the persisted credentials. This automatically added the Cryptography block to the configuration, and we specified a DPAPI symmetric crypto provider to perform the encryption.

For more information about configuring the Caching block, see Chapter 5, "A Cache Advance for your Applications." For more information about configuring the Cryptography block, see Chapter 7 "Relieving Cryptography Complexity."

CONFIGURING AUTHORIZATION RULES

The way that you configure your authorization rules depends on the type of authorization provider you are using. If you use the AzMan provider, you must configure the authorization rules using the AzMan GUI, or through the command line or scripting. If you choose to use the standard authorization rule provider instead, you must configure the authorization rules for this provider.

Each rule equates to a task or operation that your users may perform, and for which you want to be able to authorize these users to check if they should be allowed to execute "... that task. Click the "..." button in the Rule Expression property of an Authentication Rule to open the Rule Expression Editor dialog, which makes it easier to generate the expressions for each of the rules you define. It helps you to insert the appropriate tokens that indicate individual identities, roles, and anonymous users; plus the operators that allow you to specify compound rules. For example, the following expression identifies users who are members of the Managers role or have the names Alice or Bob, but excludes any managers who are also members of the ITAdmin role:

(R:Managers OR I:Alice OR I:Bob) AND NOT R:ITAdmin

If you specify this expression for a rule named Update Database, you can use the **Authorize** method of the Security block to ensure that only users for whom the expression evaluates to true can execute this task. You'll see how in the following sections of this chapter.

How Do I Use the Security Block?

After you configure the block, as described in the previous sections of this chapter, you can write code in your application that uses the features of the block. However, first, you must add references to the appropriate Enterprise Library assemblies to your project. In addition to the Enterprise Library assemblies you require in every Enterprise Library project (listed in Chapter 1, "Introduction"), you should reference or add to your bin folder the following assemblies:

- Microsoft.Practices.EnterpriseLibrary.Security.dll
- Microsoft.Practices.EnterpriseLibrary.Security.Cryptography.dll
- Microsoft.Practices.EnterpriseLibrary.Security.Cache.CachingStore.dll
- Microsoft.Practices.EnterpriseLibrary.Security.Caching.dll
- Microsoft.Practices.EnterpriseLibrary.Security.Caching.Cryptography.dll
- Microsoft.Practices.EnterpriseLibrary.Security.AzMan.dll

You need the caching assemblies only if you are using a cache to store credentials. You need the AzMan assembly only if you are using the AzMan rule store.

Now, after adding references to the relevant namespaces to your project, you are ready to write some code. The following sections demonstrate the tasks you can accomplish, and provide more details of the way the block helps you to implement a common and reusable strategy for security.

Diving in With an Example

You can download an example application (a simple console-based application) that demonstrates all of the scenarios you will see in the remainder of this chapter. You can run this directly from the bin\debug folder, or open the solution named **Security** in Microsoft Visual Studio® to see all of the code as you run the examples.

> *Before you attempt to run the example, you must create a new encryption key for the block to use to encrypt the data when using a symmetric encryption provider. This is because the key is tied to either the user or the machine, and so the key included in the sample files will not work on your machine. In the configuration console, select the* **RijndaelManager** *symmetric provider and click the "..." button in the* **Key** *property to start the Key Wizard. Use this wizard to generate a new key, save the key file, and automatically update the contents of App.config.*
>
> *You must also edit the path in the* **Store Location** *property of the AzMan authentication provider so that it reflects the location of the file named Example.xml. This file is included in the examples, and is located in the same folder as the main program files, which is [path-to-samples]\Security\Security.*

Before you start to use the objects in the block, you must resolve an instance of the security cache and authorization providers you want to use in your application. The example we provide uses the simplest approach—the **GetInstance** method of the Enterprise Library container, as shown here.

```
' Resolve the cache and auth provider objects from the container.
Dim secCache As ISecurityCacheProvider _
   = EnterpriseLibraryContainer.Current.GetInstance(Of ISecurityCacheProvider) _
                                        ("CacheProvider")

Dim ruleAuth As IAuthorizationProvider _
   = EnterpriseLibraryContainer.Current.GetInstance(Of IAuthorizationProvider) _
                                        ("RuleProvider")

Dim azmanAuth As IAuthorizationProvider _
   = EnterpriseLibraryContainer.Current.GetInstance(Of IAuthorizationProvider) _
                                        ("AzManProvider")
```

CACHING A USER IDENTITY AND OBTAINING
A TEMPORARY TOKEN

The first example, *Authenticate a user and cache the identity*, shows how you can use the Security block to cache both an authenticated identity and a user principal, and return temporary tokens that serve as an alternative to user credentials for the duration of the user session. The following code, taken from the example, first checks that the user is authenticated within the operating system and, if so, displays details of the user's identity using a separate routine named **ShowUserIdentityDetails**. We'll look at that routine in a short while.

The code then caches this Windows identity in the security cache to obtain the token, and displays details of this token. Then it generates a new generic principal for this identity, defining it as a member of a role named **FieldSalesStaff**, and displays the details of this new principal using another routine named **ShowGenericPrincipalDetails**. Again, we'll look at this routine in a short while. Next, the code caches the generic principal, collects the token from the security cache, and displays details of this token.

```
' Get current Windows Identity and check if authenticated.
Dim identity As WindowsIdentity = WindowsIdentity.GetCurrent()
If identity.IsAuthenticated Then
  Console.WriteLine("Current user identity obtained from Windows:")
  ShowUserIdentityDetails(identity)

  ' Cache the Windows Identity and save the token in a variable.
  identityToken = secCache.SaveIdentity(identity)
  Console.WriteLine("Current user identity has been cached.")
  Console.WriteLine("The IIdentity security token is '{0}'.", _
                    identityToken.Value)
  Console.WriteLine()

  ' Generate a Generic Principal for this identity and save in cache.
  Dim principal As IPrincipal = New GenericPrincipal(identity, _
                                New String() {"FieldSalesStaff"})
  Console.WriteLine("Created a new Generic Principal for this user:")
  ShowGenericPrincipalDetails(principal)
  principalToken = secCache.SavePrincipal(principal)
  Console.WriteLine("Current user principal has been cached.")
  Console.WriteLine("The IPrincipal security token is '{0}'.", _
                    principalToken.Value)
Else
  Console.WriteLine("Current user is not authenticated.")
End If
```

The tokens are stored in program-wide variables and are therefore available to code in the other examples for this chapter.

You can also use the **SaveProfile** method of the security cache to store a user's profile (such as the user's ASP.NET profile), and obtain a token that you can use to access it again when required.

Displaying User Identity Details

The previous code uses a separate routine named **ShowUserIdentityDetails** that does just that. It displays the values of the two properties common to all types that implement the **IIdentity** interface, and then checks if the identity is actually an instance of the **WindowsIdentity** class. If it is, the code displays the values of the additional properties that are specific to this type.

```
Sub ShowUserIdentityDetails(ByVal identity As Object)
  Dim iid As IIdentity = TryCast(identity, IIdentity)
  Console.WriteLine("- Current user {0} is authenticated.", iid.Name)
  Console.WriteLine("- Authentication type: {0}.", iid.AuthenticationType)

  If TypeOf identity Is WindowsIdentity Then
    Dim winIdentity As WindowsIdentity = TryCast(identity, WindowsIdentity)
    Console.WriteLine("- Impersonation level: {0}.", _
                      winIdentity.ImpersonationLevel)
    Console.WriteLine("- Is the Guest account: {0}.", winIdentity.IsGuest)
    Console.WriteLine("- Is the System account: {0}.", winIdentity.IsSystem)
    Console.WriteLine("- SID value: '{0}'.", winIdentity.User.Value)
    Console.WriteLine("- Member of {0} account groups.", _
                      winIdentity.Groups.Count)
  End If
End Sub
```

Displaying Generic Principal Details

The code you saw earlier uses a separate routine named **ShowGenericPrincipalDetails** that displays details of a generic principal. It shows the identity name, and then calls the **IsInRole** method to check if this principal is defined for two roles named **SalesManagers** and **FieldSalesStaff**.

```
Sub ShowGenericPrincipalDetails(ByVal principal As IPrincipal)
  Console.WriteLine("- Current user is {0}.", principal.Identity.Name)
  Console.WriteLine("- IsInRole 'SalesManagers': {0}.", _
                    principal.IsInRole("SalesManagers"))
  Console.WriteLine("- IsInRole 'FieldSalesStaff': {0}.", _
                    principal.IsInRole("FieldSalesStaff"))
End Sub
```

When you run the example, you will see output like that below. Of course, the identity details will differ for your logged-on account. Notice, however, that the output shows that the principal is a member of only one of the two roles we tested for. You can also see the value of the tokens generated by the security cache when we cached the identity and principal.

```
Current user identity obtained from Windows:
- Current user SOME-DOMAIN\username is authenticated.
- Authentication type: Kerberos.
- Impersonation level: None.
- Is the Guest account: False.
- Is the System account: False.
- SID value: 'S-1-5-21-xxxxxxx-117609710-xxxxxxxxx-1108'.
- Member of 12 account groups.
Current user identity has been cached.
The IIdentity security token is '02acc9a5-6dac-4b40-a82d-a16f3d9ddc37'.


Created a new Generic Principal for this user:
- Current user is SOME-DOMAIN\username.
- IsInRole 'SalesManagers': False.
- IsInRole 'FieldSalesStaff': True.
Current user principal has been cached.
The IPrincipal security token is 'ffcbc717-63ad-4a8b-82e2-26af54741ac1'.
```

AUTHENTICATING A USER USING A TOKEN

After you cache an identity and obtain a token, you can use this token to authenticate a
user throughout your application. At any point in your code, you can use the token to
obtain an identity or principal that you have stored in the cache.

The example *Retrieve a user's identity from the cache* shows how you can retrieve a
cached identity using a token. The code displays the value of the token, and then calls the
GetIdentity method to retrieve the matching identity from the cache. This method
returns **Nothing** if the identity is not found in the cache.

```
' Check if the user has run the option that caches the identity and principal.
If identityToken IsNot Nothing Then

    ' Check if the user has been authenticated and the identity has been cached.
    Console.WriteLine("The IIdentity security token is '{0}'.", identityToken.Value)
    Dim identity As [Object] = secCache.GetIdentity(identityToken)
    If identity IsNot Nothing Then

        ' Identity was found in cache.
        Console.WriteLine("User identity has been retrieved from the cache:")
        ShowUserIdentityDetails(identity)

    Else

        ' Identity removed from cache due to time expiration, or explicitly in code.
        Console.WriteLine("Identity was not found in cache for the specified token.")
    End If
```

```
Else
  Console.WriteLine("You must obtain a token by caching the current " _
              & "identity before you can retrieve it.")
End If
```

You can also use the **GetProfile** method of the security cache to retrieve a user's profile (such as the user's ASP.NET profile) by supplying a suitable token obtained from the security cache using the **SaveProfile** method.

The example produces output like the following, though the actual values will, of course, differ for your account identity.

```
The IIdentity security token is '02acc9a5-6dac-4b40-a82d-a16f3d9ddc37'.
User identity has been retrieved from the cache:
- Current user SOME-DOMAIN\username is authenticated.
- Authentication type: Kerberos.
- Impersonation level: None.
- Is the Guest account: False.
- Is the System account: False.
- SID value: 'S-1-5-21-xxxxxxx-117609710-xxxxxxxxx-1108'.
- Member of 12 account groups.
```

After you retrieve an identity, principal, or profile, you can compare the values with those of the current user or use it to authenticate a user for other processes or systems.

TERMINATING A USER SESSION AND EXPIRING THE TOKEN
When a user logs out of the application, or when you wish to invalidate the cached identity, you can use the methods of the security cache. As you would expect, the **ExpireIdentity** method expires a token corresponding to a cached identity, the **Expire Principal** method expires a token corresponding to a cached principal, and the **Expire Profile** method expires a token corresponding to a cached user profile. The example *Expire an authenticated user* demonstrates how you can expire a cached identity and a cached principal using these methods, as shown below.

```
' Check if the user has run the option that caches the identity and principal.
If identityToken IsNot Nothing Then
  Console.WriteLine("The IIdentity security token is '{0}'.", _
              identityToken.Value)

  ' Expire the identity token in the cache.
  secCache.ExpireIdentity(identityToken)
  Console.WriteLine("The identity for this token has been expired " _
              & "and removed from the cache.")
  Console.WriteLine("The IPrincipal security token is '{0}'.", _
              principalToken.Value)

  ' Expire the principal token in the cache.
```

```
    secCache.ExpirePrincipal(principalToken)
    Console.WriteLine("The principal for this token has been expired " _
                  & "and removed from the cache.")
Else
    Console.WriteLine("You do not have a token that you can use to " _
                  & "expire an identity.")
End If
```

When you run this example, you will see the values of the tokens before they are expired, and messages indicating that they were removed from the cache.

```
The IIdentity security token is 'e303fd67-331a-45b0-94d4-087e462cacda'.
The identity for this token has been expired and removed from the cache.


The IPrincipal security token is 'd6563752-78ed-489a-86fa-efd76c97a976'.
The principal for this token has been expired and removed from the cache.
```

CHECKING IF A USER IS AUTHORIZED TO PERFORM A TASK

One of the main reasons for using the Security block to manage identities is that it makes it easy to check if a user is authorized to perform a specified task or operation. The Security block contains two authorization providers, though you can create your own and integrate them with the Security block if you wish.

To check if a user is authorized, you call the **Authorize** method of an authorization provider, passing to it the user principal and the name of the task or operation. The **Authorize** method returns either **True** or **False**. The two providers included in the block are the authorization rule provider and the AzMan authorization provider (for details of these providers, see "What Are Authorization Rule Providers?" near the beginning of this chapter). The examples we present for this chapter include one that uses the authorization rule provider and one that uses the AzMan authorization provider.

Using Security Block Configured Rules

If you only need to store authorization rules within the configuration of your application and have them fully managed by the Security block, you can use the authorization rule provider. As you saw earlier in this chapter, you configure a series of authorization rules for your application. Each rule defines an expression that specifies which users can access a specific task or carry out a specific operation.

The example *Authorize a user for a process using a stored rule* demonstrates this approach to authorization. In the application configuration we defined two rules:
- The rule named **UpdateSalesData** uses the expression **"R:Administrators OR R:SalesManagers."** This allows a user who is a member of the **Administrators** role or the **SalesManagers** role to execute this task.
- The rule named **ReadSalesData** uses the expression **"R:Users OR R:FieldSalesStaff OR R:SalesManagers."** This allows a user who is a member of the **Users**, **FieldSalesStaff**, or **SalesManagers** role to execute this task.

The example code starts by displaying the value of the current principal token stored in the application-level variable (you must execute the first example to authenticate yourself and obtain a token before you can run this example). Then it retrieves the principal from the security cache using this token, and calls a separate routine named **AuthorizeUser WithRules** that performs the authorization.

The **AuthorizeUserWithRules** routine takes as parameters the generic principal as a type that implements the **IPrincipal** interface, and a reference to the authorization provider to use. In this example, this is the Security block authorization rule provider resolved from the Enterprise Library container and stored in the variable named **ruleAuth** when the example application starts. We showed how you can obtain instances of the two types of authorization provider in the section "Diving in With an Example," earlier in this chapter.

```
' Check if the user has run the option that caches the identity and principal.
If principalToken IsNot Nothing Then

  ' First try authorizing tasks using the cached Generic Principal.
  Console.WriteLine("The IPrincipal security token is '{0}'.", _
                  principalToken.Value)

  ' Retrieve the user principal from the security cache using the token.
  Dim principal As IPrincipal = secCache.GetPrincipal(principalToken)
  If principal IsNot Nothing Then
    ' Check if this user is authorized for tasks using the Rule Provider.
    AuthorizeUserWithRules(principal, ruleAuth)
  Else
    ' Identity removed from cache due to time expiration, or explicitly in code.
    Console.WriteLine("Principal not found in cache for the specified token.")
  End If

Else

  Console.WriteLine("You must obtain a token by caching the current identity " _
                  & "before you can use it to check authorization rules.")
End If
```

The following code shows the **AuthorizeUserWithRules** routine we used in the previous example. It simply calls the **Authorize** method of the authorization provider—once for the **UpdateSalesData** task and once for the **ReadSalesData** task—and displays the results.

```
Sub AuthorizeUserWithRules(ByVal principal As IPrincipal, _
                         ByVal authProvider As IAuthorizationProvider)

  ' Determine whether user is authorized for rule defined as "UpdateSalesData".
```

```
    Dim canUpdateSalesData As Boolean _
        = authProvider.Authorize(principal, "UpdateSalesData")
    Console.WriteLine("User can execute 'UpdateSalesData' task: {0}", _
                        canUpdateSalesData)

    ' Determine whether user is authorized for rule defined as "ReadSalesData".
    Dim canReadSalesData As Boolean _
        = authProvider.Authorize(principal, "ReadSalesData")
    Console.WriteLine("User can execute 'ReadSalesData' task: {0}", _
                        canReadSalesData)
End Sub
```

When you run this example, you will see output similar to that below. The code in the first example of this chapter, which authorizes the user and caches the identity and principal, defines the principal it generates as a member of only the **FieldSalesStaff** role, and so the user is authorized only for the **ReadSalesData** task.

```
The IPrincipal security token is '77a9c8af-9691-4ae4-abb5-0e964dc4610e'.
User can execute 'UpdateSalesData' task: False
User can execute 'ReadSalesData' task: True
```

Using AzMan Provider Rules

The second example of authorization, *Authorize a user for a process using AzMan rules*, uses the Windows Authorization Manager (AzMan) provider. In the example, we defined rules for the same two tasks you saw in the previous example: **UpdateSalesData** and **ReadSalesData**. However, AzMan depends on being able to access Windows account details using the security identifier (SID), and so rules in the file named Example.xml we provide with the examples may not be able to authenticate you on your machine. It will only work if you are using a local machine account or your current domain logon account can access the Active Directory® store to obtain information. You should open the Example.xml file in AzMan (a snap-in for the Microsoft Management Console (MMC)) and edit the rules it contains to specify your own local or domain accounts to experiment with AzMan authorization.

The example code is similar to what you saw when we used the Security block authorization rule provider in the previous example. It obtains the current user principal from the security cache using the token stored in the application-level variable, and calls the same **AuthorizeUserWithRules** method as the previous example to check if this principal is authorized for the **UpdateSalesData** and **ReadSalesData** tasks. This example then generates a **WindowsPrincipal** for the current user and checks if this is authorized for the **UpdateSalesData** and **ReadSalesData** tasks.

The main differences in the code for this example are that it passes a reference to the AzMan authorization provider created when the program starts to the **AuthorizeUser WithRules** routine, as shown here.

```
' First try authorizing tasks using the cached Generic Principal.
Dim genPrincipal As IPrincipal = secCache.GetPrincipal(principalToken)
If genPrincipal IsNot Nothing Then

  ' Check if this user is authorized for tasks using the AzMan provider.
  AuthorizeUserWithRules(genPrincipal, azmanAuth)
End If
...
```

```
' Now try checking for authorization for tasks using the cached WindowsIdentity
Dim identity As IIdentity = secCache.GetIdentity(identityToken)
If identity IsNot Nothing Then

  ' Generate a WindowsPrincipal from the IIdentity.
  Dim winPrincipal As IPrincipal = New WindowsPrincipal(TryCast(identity, _
                                                 WindowsIdentity))

  ' Check if this user is authorized for tasks using the AzMan provider.
  ' Note: this will only work if you are using a local machine account or your
  ' current domain account can access directory store to obtain information.
  AuthorizeUserWithRules(winPrincipal, azmanAuth)
End If
...
```

When you run this example, after configuring the AzMan rules to suit your own machine and account, you should be able to see a result similar to that shown here.

```
The IPrincipal security token is '77a9c8af-9691-4ae4-abb5-0e964dc4610e'.
User can execute 'UpdateSalesData' task: False
User can execute 'ReadSalesData' task: True

The IIdentity security token is '3b6eb4a7-b958-4cc2-b2b9-112cd58c566d'.
User can execute 'UpdateSalesData' task: False
User can execute 'ReadSalesData' task: True
```

Creating Custom Authorization Providers

Although the Security Application Block contains only two authorization providers and two caching providers, you can extend it easily to add new providers if none of those included are exactly right for your own scenarios. The block contains a base class named **AuthorizationProvider** that you can inherit from and extend to perform custom authorization. You simply need to implement the **Authorize** method, and then integrate your new provider with Enterprise Library.

You can also implement custom cache managers and cache backing stores and integrate these with the Caching Application Block to provide a custom caching mechanism for credentials, and implement a custom cryptography provider for the Cryptography Application Block that you can then use to encrypt cached credentials. For more information about creating custom providers, cache managers, and backing stores, see the online documentation and the help files installed with Enterprise Library and available online at http://go.microsoft.com/fwlink/?LinkId=188874.

Summary

This chapter described how you can use the Security Application Block to simplify common tasks such as caching authenticated user credentials and checking if users are authorized to perform specific tasks. While the code required to implement these tasks without using the Security block is not overly onerous, the block does save you the effort of writing and testing the same code in multiple locations. It also allows you to use a variety of different cache and authorization providers, depending on your requirements, and change the provider through configuration. Administrators and operators will find this feature useful when they come to deploy your applications in different environments.

The chapter described the scenarios for using the Security block, and explained the concepts of authorizing users and caching credentials. It then presented detailed examples of how you can use the features of the block in a sample application. You will find more details on specific tasks, such as configuration and deployment, in online documentation and the help files installed with Enterprise Library.

Appendix A   Dependency Injection with Unity

Modern business applications consist of custom business objects and components that perform specific or generic tasks within the application, in addition to components that individually address crosscutting concerns such as logging, authentication, authorization, caching, and exception handling. The key to successfully building these types of applications is to achieve a decoupled or very loosely coupled design. Loosely coupled applications are more flexible and easier to maintain. They are also easier to test during development.

What is Dependency Injection?

Dependency injection (DI) is a prime technique for building loosely coupled applications. It provides opportunities to simplify code, abstract and handle dependencies between objects, and automatically generate dependent object instances. Dependency injection describes the process of designing applications so that, rather than specifying concrete dependencies within the application at design time and creating the required objects in the code, the application decides at run time what objects it needs, and generates and injects these into the application.

The use of dependency injection provides several benefits, including:

- **Reducing coupling between classes**. Dependencies are clearly defined in each class. The configuration information, and mappings between interfaces or base classes and the actual concrete types, are stored in the container used by the dependency injection mechanism, and can be updated as required—without requiring any changes to the run-time code.
- **Making your code more discoverable**. You can easily tell from the types of the constructors, properties, or methods of your classes what objects they use and what dependencies they have. If you create instances using code inside the classes, it is more difficult to trace dependencies. Resolving dependencies at the surface of a class by specifying the types or interfaces it requires and taking advantage of dependency injection is the recommended approach.
- **Making testing easier**. If you resolve or obtain objects using code within your classes, you must provide a suitably configured container for use when unit testing these classes. If you take advantage of dependency injection, you can create simple mock test objects for your classes to use.

The Unity Dependency Injection and Interception Mechanism

Unity is a lightweight, flexible, configurable, and extensible dependency injection container that supports constructor, property setter, and method call injection (as well as instance and type interception). It is provided as an integral part of Enterprise Library and is also available as a stand-alone DI mechanism. Unity provides a comprehensive set of capabilities, and makes it easier to implement common dependency inversion patterns and techniques that are useful in application architecture, design, and development.

Unity provides a container that you use to store type mappings and registrations. You can create multiple containers, and nest these containers in a hierarchical fashion, if required. It also supports extensions that allow you to implement extra functionality for objects resolved through the container. Unity can generate instances of any object that has a public constructor (in other words, objects that you can create using the **New** operator).

As Unity creates each object, it inspects it for dependencies and automatically populates these. So, for example, if you specify a parameter for the constructor or a dependent property of a custom class to be of type **MyBusinessComponent**, Unity will create an instance of **MyBusinessComponent** and populate the constructor or property. However, if **MyBusinessComponent** defines a dependency on another class named **MyDataComponent**, Unity will create an instance of that class and populate that dependency, and so on. If there is no mapping in the container for the type specified in the parameter or property, Unity simply creates a new instance of the specified type by calling the constructor of that type that has the greatest number of parameters, and returns it.

Imagine that **MyDataComponent** requires a **LogWriter** to create log messages. If it contains a dependent parameter or property of type **LogWriter**, Unity will populate that as part of the instantiation process as well. This process (sometimes referred to as auto-wiring) can apply right across the defined dependencies in your application, as shown in Figure 1.

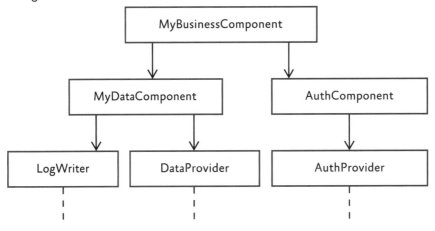

FIGURE 1
A possible object graph for a business component

SUMMARY OF UNITY FEATURES

Unity is more than just a simple dependency injection container. It provides advanced capabilities that allow you to satisfy a wide range of requirements that can help you build more decoupled applications. Unity allows you to:

- **Register mappings between interfaces or base classes and concrete object types**. When you resolve the interface or base type, Unity will return an instance of the concrete type. This may be a new or an existing instance, depending on the lifetime you specify for the registration.
- **Register instances of existing objects in the container**. When you resolve the type, Unity will return an instance of that type. This is useful when working with objects that must be instantiated as single instances (singletons), or must have a non-standard lifetime, such as services used by your application. Unity will return the existing instance.
- **Specify the lifetime of objects that will be resolved through the container**. Unity can resolve objects based on the singleton pattern; or with a weak reference when the object is managed by another process. It can also be configured to return instances on a per-thread basis, where a new instance is created for each thread while an existing instance is returned for calls on the same thread.
- **Define multiple named registrations for a type**. You can create more than one registration or mapping for a type as long as these registrations and mappings have a unique name. Registrations and mappings that do not have a name are known as default registrations and default mappings, where the name is effectively an empty string.
- **Construct an entire object graph for an application that will be resolved at run time**. Unity can automatically resolve the types specified in constructor and method parameters and properties at run time. The parameters of constructors or methods of objects that are resolved through the container, or the values for properties of objects resolved through the container, can be populated with an object resolved through another registration within the container, or an instance of the specified type if no matching registration exists.
- **Specify values for constructor and method parameters and properties**. These can be the parameters of constructors or methods of objects that are resolved through the container, or the values for properties of objects resolved through the container. The value can be specified directly, or it can be an object resolved through another registration within the container.
- **Define matching rules and behaviors as part of an interception policy**. These can be used to apply business rules or change the behavior of existing components. Calls to methods or properties of these objects will then pass through a policy pipeline containing one or more interception behaviors. This is a similar approach to that used in aspect-oriented programming (AOP).
- **Add custom extensions to the container**. These can extend or change the behavior of the container when resolving objects. Some Unity features, such as interception, are powered by a container extension that is included with the standard Unity installation.

Defining Dependencies with Unity

Unity provides three ways for you to define the dependencies for each of your custom types:

- You can define all of your dependency injection and interception requirements using a configuration file. At run time, you use a single line of code to read the configuration and load it into a Unity container.
- You can use the methods of the container that register types, type mappings, parameter and property values, and interception requirements in your code. You can also use these methods to modify any existing registrations in the container at run time.
- You can apply attributes to define dependencies for constructor and method parameters and properties of types that you will resolve through the container. This is a simple approach, but does not provide the same level of control as using a configuration file or the run-time container API.

You can also use a mixture of all of these techniques; for example, you can register a mapping in the container between an interface and a concrete implementation, then use an attribute to define a dependency for a property or parameter on an implementation of this interface.

Table 1 will help you to choose the best approach for your own requirements.

TABLE 1 **Defining dependencies**

Technique	Description	Considerations
Configuration-based	Define dependencies using registrations and mappings loaded into the container from a file or other configuration source.	Makes it easy to change the registrations and dependency mappings; often by just editing the configuration file. However, users of the classes do not see the dependencies in the source code. This approach is flexible and allows comprehensive configuration of injection of resolved type instances, fixed values, and arrays.
Dynamic registration	Define dependencies using registrations and mappings within the container by generating them dynamically at run time using code.	Changes to the registrations and dependency mappings require you edit the code, though this is usually only in one location in a startup file. However, users of the classes do not see the dependencies in the source code. This approach is flexible and allows comprehensive configuration of injection of resolved type instances, fixed values, and arrays.
Attribute-based	Use attributes applied to parameters and properties within the classes to define the dependencies.	Makes the dependencies obvious and easy to see in the source code of classes, but requires you to edit the source code when you need to change the dependencies. This approach is also less flexible and less comprehensive than the other approaches.

In addition, you can change the behavior of the dependency resolution mechanism in several ways:

- You can specify parameter overrides or dependency overrides that set the values of specific parameters.
- You can define optional dependencies, so that Unity will set the value of a parameter or property to **Nothing** if it cannot resolve the type of the dependency.
- You can use deferred resolution, so that the resolution does not take place until the target type is actually required or used in your code.
- You can specify a lifetime manager that will control the lifetime of the resolved type.

The following sections of this appendix describe some of the more common techniques for defining dependencies in your classes through constructor, property, and method call injection. We do not discuss interception in this appendix. For full details of all the capabilities and uses of Unity, see the Unity section of the documentation installed with Enterprise Library and available online at http://go.microsoft.com/fwlink/?LinkId= 188875.

CONSTRUCTOR INJECTION

By default, Unity will attempt to resolve and populate the types of every parameter of a class constructor when you resolve that type through the container. You do not need to configure or add attributes to a class for this to occur. Unity will choose the most complex constructor (usually the one with the largest number of parameters), resolve the type of each parameter through the container, and then create a new instance of the target type using the resolved values.

The following are some simple examples that demonstrate how you can define constructor injection for a type.

Automatic Constructor Injection

If you have a class that contains a non-default constructor, Unity will automatically populate any dependencies defined in the parameters of the constructor. For example, the following type has a dependency on a type named **Database**.

```
Public Class MyNewObject
  Public Sub New(defaultDB As Database)
    ' code to use the resolved Database instance here
  End Sub
End Class
```

If you need to change the behavior of the automatic constructor injection process, perhaps to specify the lifetime of the resolved type or to set the value or lifetime of the types resolved for the parameters, you can configure the container at design time using a configuration file or at run time using the container API.

Design-Time Configuration

Configuring constructor injection in a configuration file is useful when you need to exert control over the process. For example, consider the following class that contains a single constructor that takes two parameters.

```
Public Class MyNewObject
  Public Sub New(defaultDB As Database, departmentName As String)
    ...
  End Sub
End Class
```

The second parameter is a string, and Unity cannot generate an instance of a **String** type unless you have registered it in the container using a named instance registration. Therefore, you must override the default behavior of the automatic injection process. You can do this in a configuration file, and at the same time manage three aspects of the injection process: the resolved object lifetime, the value of parameters, and the choice of constructor when the type contains more than one constructor.

For example, you can use the following **register** directive in a configuration file to specify that the resolved instance of **MyNewObject** should be a singleton (with its lifetime managed by the container), that Unity should resolve the type **Database** of the parameter named **defaultDB** and inject the result, and that Unity should inject the string value "Customer Service" into the parameter named **departmentName**.

```
<register type="MyNewObject">
  <lifetime type="singleton" />
  <constructor>
    <param name="defaultDB" />
    <param name="departmentName" value="Customer Service" />
  </constructor>
</register>
```

When you specify constructor injection like this, you are also specifying which constructor Unity should use. Even if the **MyNewObject** class contains a more complex constructor, Unity will use the one that matches the list of parameters you specify in the **register** element.

To register your types using named registrations, you simply add the **name** attribute to the **register** element, as shown here.

```
<register type="MyNewObject" name="Special Customer Object">
  ...
</register>
```

To register mappings between an interface or base class and a type that implements the interface or inherits the base type, you add the **mapTo** attribute to the **register** element. You can, of course, define default (unnamed) and named mappings in the same way as you do type registrations. The following example shows registration of a named mapping.

```
<register type="IMyType" mapTo="MyImplementingType"
        name="Special Customer Object">
  ...
</register>
```

Run-Time Configuration

You can configure injection for the default or a specific constructor at run time by calling the **RegisterType** method of the Unity container. This approach also gives you a great deal of control over the process. The following code registers the **MyNewObject** type with a singleton (container-controlled) lifetime.

```
myContainer.RegisterType(Of MyNewObject)(New ContainerControlledLifetimeManager())
```

If you want to create a named registration, you add the name as the first parameter of the **RegisterType** method, as shown here.

```
myContainer.RegisterType(Of MyNewObject)("Special Customer Object", _
                New ContainerControlledLifetimeManager())
```

If you want to create a mapping, you specify the mapped type as the second generic type parameter, as shown here.

```
myContainer.RegisterType(Of IMyType, MyImplementingType)( _
                "Special Customer Object", _
                New ContainerControlledLifetimeManager())
```

If you need to specify the value of the constructor parameters, such as a **String** type (which Unity cannot create unless you register a **String** instance with the container), or specify which constructor Unity should choose, you include an instance of the **Injection Constructor** type in your call to the **RegisterType** method. For example, the following creates a registration named Special Customer Object for the **MyNewObject** type as a singleton, specifies that Unity should resolve the type **Database** of the parameter named **defaultDB** and inject the result, and that Unity should inject the string value "Customer Service" into the parameter named **departmentName**.

```
myContainer.RegisterType(Of MyNewObject)( _
        "Special Customer Object", _
        New ContainerControlledLifetimeManager(), _
        New InjectionConstructor(GetType(Database), "Customer Service") _
)
```

Configuration with Attributes

When you specify just the type in a constructor parameter, as shown earlier, the container will return the default concrete implementation of that type as defined in the registrations within the container. To specify a named registration when using constructor injection, you can add the **Dependency** attribute to the parameter definition, as shown below.

```
Public Class MyNewObject
  Public Sub New(<Dependency("CustomerDB")> customers As Database)
    ' code to use the resolved Database instance here
  End Sub
End Class
```

If your class has multiple constructors, and you want to specify the one Unity will use, you apply the **InjectionConstructor** attribute to that constructor, as shown in the code excerpt that follows. If you do not specify the constructor to use, Unity chooses the most complex (usually the one with the most parameters). This technique is useful if the most complex constructor has parameters that Unity cannot resolve.

```
Public Class MyNewObject

  Public Sub New(defaultDB As Database, departmentName As String)
    ...
  End Sub

  <InjectionConstructor> _
  Public Sub New(defaultDB As Database)
    ...
  End Sub

End Class
```

PROPERTY (SETTER) INJECTION

Property (setter) injection can populate one or more properties of your custom classes at run time. Unlike constructor injection, property injection does not occur by default. You must specify the dependency using a configuration file, programmatically at run time, or by applying an attribute to the property that holds the dependent type.

Design-Time Configuration

To define property injection using a configuration file, you simply specify the names of the properties that Unity should populate within the **register** element. If you want Unity to resolve the type specified by the property, you need do no more than that. If you want to specify a value, you can include this within the **property** element. If you want Unity to use a named registration within the container to resolve the type, you include the **dependencyName** attribute in the **property** element. Finally, if you want to resolve a type that is compatible with the property name, such as resolving an interface type for which you have named mappings already registered in the container, you specify the type to resolve using a **dependencyType** attribute.

The following excerpt from a configuration file specifies dependency injection for three public properties of a type named **MyOtherObject**. Unity will resolve whatever type the **BusinessComponent** property of the **MyOtherObject** type is defined as through the container and inject the result into that property. It will also inject the string value "CorpData42" into the property named **DataSource**, and resolve the type **ILogger** using a mapping named **StdLogger** and inject the result into the **Logger** property.

```
<register type="MyOtherObject">
  <property name="BusinessComponent" />
  <property name="DataSource" value="CorpData42" />
  <property name="Logger" dependencyName="StdLogger" dependencyType="ILogger" />
</register>
```

Run-Time Configuration

You can configure injection for any public property of the target class at run time by calling the **RegisterType** method of the Unity container. This gives you a great deal of control over the process. The following code performs the same dependency injection process as the configuration file example you have just seen. Notice the use of the **ResolvedParameter** type to specify the named mapping that Unity should use to resolve the **ILogger** interface.

```
myContainer.RegisterType(Of MyOtherObject)( _
          New InjectionProperty("BusinessComponent"), _
          New InjectionProperty("DataSource", "CorpData42"), _
          New InjectionProperty("Logger", _
              New ResolvedParameter(typeof(ILogger), "StdLogger") _
          ) _
)
```

You can use the **ResolvedParameter** type in constructor and method call injection as well as in property injection, and there are other types of injection parameter classes available for even more specialized tasks when configuring injection.

Configuration with Attributes

To specify injection for a property, you can alternatively apply the **Dependency** attribute to it to indicate that the type defined and exposed by the property is a dependency of the class. The following code demonstrates property injection for a class named **MyNewObject** that exposes as a property a reference to an instance of the type **Database**.

```
Public Class MyNewObject

  Private theDB As Database

  <Dependency> _
  Public Property CustomerDB() As Database
    Get
      Return theDB
    End Get
    Set(ByVal value As Database)
```

```
        theDB = value
    End Set
  End Property

End Class
```

When you apply the **Dependency** attribute without specifying a name, the container will return the type specified as the default (an unnamed registration) or a new instance of that type. To specify a named registration when using property injection with attributes, you include the name as a parameter of the **Dependency** attribute, as shown below.

```
Public Class MyNewObject

  Private theDB As Database

  <Dependency("LocalDB")> _
  Public Property NamedDB() As Database
    Get
      Return theDB
    End Get
    Set(ByVal value As Database)
      theDB = value
    End Set
  End Property

End Class
```

METHOD CALL INJECTION

Method call injection is a less common approach than constructor and property setter injection, but is useful in two specific situations. Firstly, constructor injection only works when you are instantiating new instances of objects (when the constructor is executed), whereas method call injection will work with existing instances of objects. For example, Unity will execute the method when it resolves an instance that is registered as a singleton, or when you call the **BuildUp** method of the container.

Secondly, while property setter injection also works with existing instances, it requires public properties to be exposed. Using method call injection means that you do not need to expose public properties to be able to inject values into existing instances of resolved types.

The usual approach is to expose a public initialization method that takes as parameters the objects you want to resolve and obtain references to. Unity will populate the parameters and then call the method. As the method executes, you store the resolved types in local variables of your class.

Method call injection does not occur by default, and must be configured using a configuration file, programmatically at run time, or by applying an attribute to the method.

Design-Time Configuration

The techniques for specifying dependency injection for method parameters is very similar to what you saw earlier for constructor parameters. The following excerpt from a configuration file defines the dependencies for the two parameters of a method named **Initialize** for a type named **MyNewObject**. Unity will resolve the type of the parameter named **customerDB** through the container and inject the result into that parameter of the target type. It will also inject the string value "Customer Services" into the parameter named **departmentName**.

```
<register type="MyNewObject">
  <method name="Initialize">
    <param name="customerDB" />
    <param name="departmentName" value="Customer Services" />
  </method>
</register>
```

You can also use the **dependencyName** and **dependencyType** attributes to specify how Unity should resolve the type for a parameter in exactly the same way as you saw for property injection. If you have more than one overload of a method in your class, Unity uses the set of parameters you define in your configuration to determine the actual method to populate and execute.

Run-Time Configuration

As with constructor and property injection, you can configure injection for any public method of the target class at run time by calling the **RegisterType** method of the Unity container. The following code achieves the same result as the configuration extract you have just seen.

```
myContainer.RegisterType(Of MyNewObject)( _
    New InjectionMethod("Initialize", GetType(Database), "CustomerServices") _
)
```

In addition, you can specify the lifetime of the type, and use named dependencies, in exactly the same way as you saw for constructor injection.

Configuration with Attributes

You can apply the **InjectionMethod** attribute to a method to indicate that any types defined in parameters of the method are dependencies of the class. The following code demonstrates the most common scenario, saving the dependent object instance in a class-level variable, for a class named **MyNewObject** that exposes a method named **Initialize** that takes as parameters instances of the type **Database** and an instance of a concrete type that implements the **ILogger** interface.

```
Public Class MyNewObject

  Private theDB As Database
  Private theLogger As ILogger
```

```
<InjectionMethod()> _
Public Sub Initialize(customerDB As Database, loggingComponent As ILogger)
  ' assign the dependent objects to class-level variables
  theDB = customerDB
  theLogger = loggingComponent
End Sub
```

End Class

You can also add the **Dependency** attribute to a parameter to specify the name of the registration Unity should use to resolve the parameter type, just as you saw earlier for constructor injection with attributes. And, as with constructor injection, all of the parameters of the method must be resolvable through the container. If any are value types that Unity cannot create, you must ensure that you have a suitable registration in the container for that type, or use a dependency override to set the value.

MORE DEPENDENCY INJECTION OPPORTUNITIES
In addition to the techniques we have shown here for defining dependencies, Unity allows you to specify both the type to resolve, and its dependencies, as generic types. You can also specify dependencies that are arrays of any type, including generic types. You can even have Unity resolve all the members of an array automatically, or specify individual members of the array yourself.

Resolving Populated Instances of Your Classes

After you have defined your object graph dependencies, you must resolve the type at the root of this hierarchy through the container to initiate the dependency injection process. In Unity, you use the **Resolve** method to kick off the process by specifying the type of the object whose dependencies you want Unity to populate. The following code resolves a populated instance of the **MyNewObject** type from the container.

```
Dim theInstance As MyNewObject = container.Resolve(Of MyNewObject)()
```

This returns the type registered as the default (no name was specified when it was registered). If you want to resolve a type that was registered with a name, you specify this name as a parameter of the **Resolve** method. You might also consider using implicit typing instead of specifying the type, to make your code less dependent on the results of the resolve process.

```
Dim theInstance = container.Resolve(Of MyNewObject)("Registration Name")
```

Alternatively, you may choose to define the returned type as the interface type when you are resolving a mapped type. For example, if you registered a type mapping between the interface **IMyType** and the concrete type **MyNewObject**, you should consider using the following code when you resolve it.

```
Dim theInstance As IMyType = container.Resolve(Of IMyType)()
```

Writing code that specifies an interface instead of a particular concrete type means that you can change the configuration to specify a different concrete type without needing to change your code. Unity will always return a concrete type (unless it cannot resolve an interface or abstract type that you specify; in which case an exception is thrown).

You can also resolve a collection of types that are registered using named mappings (not default unnamed mappings) by calling the **ResolveAll** method. This may be useful if you want to check what types are registered in your run-time code, or display a list of available types. However, Unity also exposes methods that allow you to iterate over the container and obtain information about all of the registrations.

We don't have room to provide a full guide to using Unity here. However, this discussion should have given you a taste of what you can achieve using dependency injection. For more detailed information about using Unity, see the documentation installed with Enterprise Library and available online at http://go.microsoft.com/fwlink/?LinkId=188874.

Appendix B   Dependency Injection in Enterprise Library

This appendix discusses some of the more advanced topics that will help you to obtain the maximum benefit from Enterprise Library in terms of creating objects and managing the dependency injection container. It includes the following:

- Loading configuration information into a Unity container
- Viewing the registrations in the container
- Populating entire object graphs at application startup
- Maintaining a reference to the container in request-based applications
- Using an alternative service locator or dependency injection container

These topics provide information about how you can use the more sophisticated dependency injection approach for creating instances of Enterprise Library objects, as described in Chapter 1, "Introduction." If you have decided not to use this approach, and you are using the Enterprise Library service locator and its **GetInstance** method to instantiate Enterprise Library types, they are not applicable to your scenario.

Loading Configuration Information into a Unity Container

Unlike many applications, and unlike the application blocks within Enterprise Library, Unity does not automatically load configuration information when it starts. This is intentional; it means that you can load configuration information into one or more new or existing containers, including containers that you create as a hierarchy of parent and child containers.

This also means that you can exert considerable control over how requests for types are handled. For example, you can use multiple containers to specify dependencies for different parts of your application, while allowing requests that cannot be satisfied in a child container to pass up through the hierarchy of parent containers until a suitable registration is found.

It also means that you can load configuration information from different sources. A typical example is loading configuration from a file other than App.config or Web.config, or by adding registrations programmatically by—for example—reading them from a database and applying them to the container.

The Unity container class exposes the **LoadConfiguration** method that you can use to populate a container. You can call this method with no parameters to read a **<unity>**

section from the current application configuration file (App.config or Web.config), as demonstrated in Chapter 1 of this guide. Alternatively, you can provide the method with a **UnityConfigurationSection** instance that contains the configuration information. The following code opens a configuration file using the methods of the Microsoft® .NET Framework configuration system, casts it to a **UnityConfigurationSection** type, and loads the registrations in the **<container>** section that has the name **MyContainerName** into a new Unity container.

```
' Read a specified config file using the .NET configuration system.
Dim map As New ExeConfigurationFileMap()
map.ExeConfigFilename = "c:\configfiles\myunityconfig.config"
Dim config As System.Configuration.Configuration _
                    = ConfigurationManager.OpenMappedExeConfiguration(map, _
                                              ConfigurationUserLevel.None)
' Get the unity configuration section.
Dim section As UnityConfigurationSection _
     = DirectCast(config.GetSection("unity"), UnityConfigurationSection)

' Create and populate a new UnityContainer with the configuration information.
Dim theContainer As IUnityContainer = New UnityContainer()
theContainer.LoadConfiguration(section, "MyContainerName")
```

You can define multiple containers within the **<unity>** section of a configuration file providing each has a unique name, and load each one into a separate container at run time. If you do not assign a name to a container in the configuration file, it becomes the default container, and you can load it by omitting the name parameter in the **LoadConfiguration** method.

To load a container programmatically in this way, you must add the System.Configuration.dll assembly and the Microsoft.Practices.Unity.Configuration.dll assembly to your project. You should also import the following namespaces:
- Microsoft.Practices.EnterpriseLibrary.Common.Configuration.Unity
- Microsoft.Practices.Unity

Viewing Registrations in the Container

Sometimes you may find that your application throws an error indicating that it cannot resolve a specific type. The error messages that Unity returns are detailed, and should help you to find the problem quickly. However, you may find it useful to be able to browse the contents of the container to see the registrations and mappings it contains.

The Unity container exposes the **Registrations** property, which returns a collection of **ContainerRegistration** instances; one for each registration or type mapping in the container. The following example code shows how you can extract details for each registration: the registered type, the type it maps to (if any), the name of the registration (if it is not a default registration), and the lifetime manager type.

```
For Each item As ContainerRegistration In theContainer.Registrations
  regType = item.RegisteredType.Name
  mapTo = item.MappedToType.Name
  regName = If(item.Name, "[default]")
  lifetime = item.LifetimeManagerType.Name
  If mapTo <> regType Then
    mapTo = " -> " & mapTo
  Else
    mapTo = String.Empty
  End If
  lifetime = lifetime.Substring(0, lifetime.Length - "LifetimeManager".Length)
  ' Display details of the registration as appropriate.
Next
```

Populating Entire Object Graphs at Application Startup

After you populate the container with your configuration information, both the Enterprise Library information and the registrations and mappings for your own custom types, you can resolve these custom types with all of their dependencies populated through dependency injection. You can define dependencies in three ways:

- **As one or more parameters of a constructor in the target class**. Unity will create instances of the appropriate types and populate the constructor parameters when the target object is instantiated. This is the approach you will typically use. For example, you can have Unity automatically create and pass into your constructor an instance of a **LogWriter** or an **ExceptionManager**, store the reference in a class variable or field, and use it within that class.
- **As one or more properties of the target class**. Unity will create an instance of the type defined by the property or in configuration and set that instance as the value of the property when the class is resolved through the container.
- **As one or more parameters of a method in the target class**. Unity will create instances of the appropriate types and populate the method parameters when the target object is instantiated, and then call that method. You can store the references passed in the parameters in a class variable or field for use within that class. This approach is typically used when you have an **Initialize** or similar method that should execute when the class is instantiated.

By taking advantage of this capability to populate an entire object graph, you may decide to have the container create and inject instances of the appropriate types for all of the dependencies defined in your entire application when it starts up (or, at least, a significant proportion of it).

While this may seem to be a strange concept, it means that you do not need to hold onto a reference to the container after you perform this initial population of dependencies. That doesn't mean you cannot hold onto the container reference as well, but resolving all of the required types at startup can improve run-time performance at the cost of slightly increased startup time. Of course, this also requires additional memory and resources to hold all of the resolved instances, and you must balance this against the expected improvement in run-time performance.

You can populate all of your dependencies by resolving the main form or startup class through the container. The container will automatically create the appropriate instances of the objects required by each class and inject them into the parameters and properties. However, it does rely on the container being able to create and return instances of types that are not registered in the container. The Unity container can do this. If you use an alternative container, you may need to preregister all of the types in your application, including the main form or startup class.

Typically, this approach to populating an entire application object graph is best suited to applications built using form-based or window-based technologies such as Windows® Presentation Foundation (WPF), Windows Forms, console applications, and Microsoft Silverlight® (using the version of Unity specifically designed for use in Silverlight applications).

For information about how you can resolve the main form, window, or startup class of your application, together with example code, see the documentation installed with Enterprise Library or available online at http://go.microsoft.com/fwlink/?LinkId=188874.

Maintaining a Container Reference in Request-Based Applications

When using the default Unity DI mechanism with Enterprise Library, all you need to do is initialize the container once on your application, and then use it to resolve (or obtain) instances of Enterprise Library objects or your own classes and objects. Initializing the container requires just the following single line of code.

```
' Create and populate the default container with application configuration.
Dim container = New UnityContainer() _
                .AddNewExtension(Of EnterpriseLibraryCoreExtension)()
```

However, to use the container to resolve types throughout your application, you must hold a reference to it. You can store the container in a global variable in a Windows Forms or WPF application, in the **Application** dictionary of an ASP.NET application, or in a custom extension to the **InstanceContext** of a Windows Communication Foundation (WCF) service.

Table 1 will help you to understand when and where you should hold a reference to the container in forms-based and rich client applications built using technologies such as Windows Forms, WPF, and Silverlight.

TABLE 1 Holding a reference to the container in forms-based and rich client applications

Task	When	Where
Create and configure container.	At application startup.	Main routine, startup events, application definition file, or as appropriate for the technology.
Obtain objects from the container.	At application startup, and later if required.	Where appropriate in the code.
Store a reference to the container.	At application startup.	Global application state.
Dispose the container.	When the application shuts down.	Where appropriate in the code or automatically when the application ends.

Table 2 will help you to understand when and where you should hold a reference to the container in request-based applications built using technologies such as ASP.NET Web applications and Web services.

TABLE 2 Holding a reference to the container in request-based applications

Task	When	Where
Create and configure container.	At application startup.	HTTP Module (ASP.NET and ASMX), InstanceContext extension (WCF).
Obtain objects from the container.	During each HTTP request.	In the request start event or load event. Objects are disposed when the request ends.
Store a reference to the container.	At application startup.	Global application state or service context.
Dispose the container.	When the application shuts down.	Where appropriate in the code.

For more detailed information about how you can maintain a reference to the container in different types of applications, in particular, request-based applications, and the code you can use to achieve this, see the documentation installed with Enterprise Library or available online at http://go.microsoft.com/fwlink/?LinkId=188874.

Using an Alternative Service Locator or Container

Enterprise Library, by default, uses the Unity dependency injection mechanism to create instances of Enterprise Library objects. If you are already using, or plan to use, a different dependency injection container in your application you may be able to use it to create Enterprise Library objects instead of using Unity.

For this to work, you can obtain or write your own configurator that can load the container with the Enterprise Library configuration information you specify, or create a type that implements the **IServiceLocator** interface and can expose the configuration information.

The default behavior of Enterprise Library is to create a new Unity container, create a new configurator for the container, and then read the configuration information from the application's default configuration file (App.config or Web.config). The following code extract shows the process that occurs.

```
Dim container = New UnityContainer()
Dim configurator = New UnityContainerConfigurator(container)


' Read the configuration files and set up the container.
EnterpriseLibraryContainer.ConfigureContainer(configurator, _
                          ConfigurationSourceFactory.Create())
' The container is now ready to resolve Enterprise Library objects
```

The task of the configurator is to translate the configuration file information into a series of registrations within the container. Enterprise Library contains only the **Unity ContainerConfigurator**, though you can write your own to suit your chosen container, or obtain one from a third party.

An alternative approach is to create a custom implementation of the **IServiceLocator** interface that may not use a configurator, but can read the application configuration and return the appropriate fully populated Enterprise Library objects on demand.

See http://commonservicelocator.codeplex.com for more information about the **IServiceLocator** interface.

To keep up with discussions regarding alternate configuration options for Enterprise Library, see the forums on CodePlex at http://www.codeplex.com/entlib/Thread/List.aspx.

Appendix C

Policy Injection in Enterprise Library

Policy injection describes a method for inserting code between the client and an object that the client uses, in order to change the behavior of the target object without requiring any changes to that object, or to the client. The general design pattern for this technique is called interception, and has become popular through the Aspect-Oriented Programming (AOP) paradigm.

Interception has been a feature of Enterprise Library since version 3.0. In previous releases of Enterprise Library, the manner in which you would enable interception was through the Policy Injection Application Block, which exposed static facades you could use to create wrapped instances of target objects and the appropriate proxy through which the client can access that target object.

The block also contained a series of call handlers that are inserted into the interception pipeline, between the client and the target object. The same set of call handlers as used in previous versions of Enterprise Library is included in version 5.0, though they are no longer located in the Policy Injection block (which is provided mainly for backwards compatibility with existing applications).

In version 5.0 of Enterprise Library, the recommended approach for implementing policy injection is through the Unity interception mechanism. This supports several different techniques for implementing interception, including the creation of derived classes rather than remoting proxies, and it has much less impact on application performance.

The call handlers you use with the Unity interception mechanism can instantiate application blocks, allowing you to apply the capabilities of the blocks for managing crosscutting concerns for the target object. The capabilities provided by interception and policy injection through Unity and Enterprise Library allow you to:

- Add validation capabilities by using the validation handler. This call handler uses the Validation block to validate the values passed in parameters to the target object. This is a useful approach to circumvent the limitations within the Validation block, which cannot validate parameters of method calls except in specific scenarios such as in Windows® Communication Foundation (WCF) applications.
- Add logging capabilities to objects by using the logging handler. This call handler uses the Logging block to generate log entries and write them to configured target sources.

- Add exception handling capabilities by using the exception handling handler. This call handler uses the Exception Handling block to implement a consistent strategy for handling, replacing, wrapping, and logging exceptions.
- Add authorization capabilities to objects by using the authorization handler. This call handler uses the Security block to check if the caller has the required permission to execute each call.
- Add performance measurement capabilities by using the performance counter handler. This call handler updates Windows® performance counters with each call, allowing you to measure performance and monitor target object activity.
- Add custom behavior to objects by creating your own interception call handlers.

For more information about using Unity to implement interception, see the documentation installed with Enterprise Library or available online at http://go.microsoft.com/fwlink/?LinkId=188874.

For information on how to use the Policy Injection block facade, see the documentation for version 4.1 of Enterprise Library on MSDN® at http://msdn.microsoft.com/en-us/library/dd139982.aspx.

Appendix D   Enterprise Library Configuration Scenarios

The comprehensive configuration capabilities of Enterprise Library—the result of the extensible configuration system and the configuration tools it includes—make Enterprise Library highly flexible and easy to use. The combination of these features allows you to:
- Read configuration information from a wide range of sources.
- Enforce common configuration settings across multiple applications.
- Share configuration settings between applications.
- Specify a core set of configuration settings that applications can inherit.
- Merge configuration settings that are stored in a shared location.
- Create different configurations for different deployment environments.

This appendix provides an overview of the scenarios for using these features and demonstrates how you can apply them in your own applications and environments. More information on the scenarios presented here is provided in the documentation installed with Enterprise Library and available online at http://go.microsoft.com/fwlink/?LinkId=188874.

About Enterprise Library Configuration

Enterprise Library configuration information is stored in instances of classes that implement the **IConfigurationSource** interface, and are typically known as *configuration sources*. Figure 1 shows a high-level view of the two types of information for a configuration source and the different ways that an application's configuration can be defined and applied.

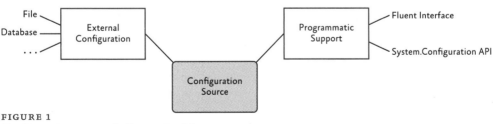

FIGURE 1
Configuration sources in Enterprise Library

EXTERNAL CONFIGURATION

External configuration encompasses the different ways that configuration information can reside in a persistent store and be applied to a configuration source at run time. Possible sources of persistent configuration information are files, a database, and other custom stores. Enterprise Library can load configuration information from any of these stores automatically. To store configuration in a database you can use the SQL configuration source that is available as a sample from the Enterprise Library community site at http://entlib.codeplex.com. You can also specify one or more configuration sources to satisfy more complex configuration scenarios, and create different configurations for different run-time environments. See the section "Scenarios for Advanced Configuration" later in this appendix for more information.

PROGRAMMATIC SUPPORT

Programmatic support encompasses the different ways that configuration information can be generated dynamically and applied to a configuration source at run time. Typically, in Enterprise Library this programmatic configuration takes place through the fluent interface specially designed to simplify dynamic configuration, or by using the methods exposed by the Microsoft® .NET Framework System.Configuration API.

Using the Fluent Interfaces

All of the application blocks except for the Validation Application Block and Policy Injection Application Block expose a fluent interface. This allows you to configure the block at run time using intuitive code assisted by Microsoft IntelliSense® in Visual Studio® to specify the providers and properties for the block. The following is an example of configuring an exception policy for the Exception Handling Application Block and loading this configuration into the Enterprise Library container.

```
Dim builder = New ConfigurationSourceBuilder()

builder.ConfigureExceptionHandling() _
        .GivenPolicyWithName("MyPolicy") _
        .ForExceptionType(Of NullReferenceException)() _
          .LogToCategory("General") _
            .WithSeverity(System.Diagnostics.TraceEventType.Warning) _
            .UsingEventId(9000) _
          .WrapWith(Of InvalidOperationException)() _
            .UsingMessage("MyMessage") _
          .ThenThrowNewException()

Dim configSource = New DictionaryConfigurationSource()
builder.UpdateConfigurationWithReplace(configSource)
EnterpriseLibraryContainer.Current _
  = EnterpriseLibraryContainer.CreateDefaultContainer
```

Scenarios for Advanced Configuration

The Enterprise Library stand-alone configuration console and the Visual Studio integrated configuration editor allow you to satisfy a range of advanced configuration scenarios based on external configuration sources such as disk files. When you use the configuration tools without specifying a configuration source, they default to using the System Configuration Source to create a single configuration file that contains the entire configuration for the application. Your application will expect this to be named App.config or Web.config (depending on the technology you are using), and will read it automatically.

You can select **Add Configuration Settings** on the **Blocks** menu to display the section that contains the default system configuration source. If you click the chevron arrow to the right of the **Configuration Sources** title to open the section properties pane you can see that this is also, by default, specified as the **Selected Source**—the configuration source to which the configuration generated by the tool will be written. When an application that uses Enterprise Library reads the configuration, it uses the settings specified for the selected source.

The following sections describe the common scenarios for more advanced configuration that you can accomplish using the configuration tools. Some of these scenarios require you to add additional configuration sources to the application configuration.

SCENARIO 1: USING THE DEFAULT APPLICATION CONFIGURATION FILE

This is the default and simplest scenario. You configure your application using the configuration tool without adding a **Configuration Sources** section or any configuration sources. You must specify either your application's App.config or Web.config file when you save the configuration, or use the configuration tool to edit an existing App.config or Web.config file.

SCENARIO 2: USING A NON-DEFAULT CONFIGURATION STORE

In this scenario, you want to store your configuration in a file or other type of store, instead of in the application's App.config or Web.config file. To achieve this you:

1. Use the configuration tools to add a suitable configuration source to the **Configuration Sources** section. If you want to use a standard format configuration file, add a file-based configuration source. To store the configuration information in a different type of store, you must install a suitable configuration source. You can use the sample SQL configuration source that is available from the Enterprise Library community site at http://entlib.codeplex.com to store your configuration in a database.

2. Set the relevant properties of the new configuration source. For example, if you are using the built-in file-based configuration source, set the **File Path** property to the path and name for the configuration file.

3. Set the **Selected Source** property in the properties pane for the **Configuration Sources** section to your new configuration source. This updates the application's default App.config or Web.config file to instruct Enterprise Library to use this as its configuration source.

SCENARIO 3: SHARING THE SAME CONFIGURATION BETWEEN MULTIPLE APPLICATIONS

In this scenario, you want to share configuration settings between multiple applications or application layers that run in different locations, such as on different computers. To achieve this, you simply implement the same configuration as described in the previous scenario, locating the configuration file or store in a central location. Then specify this file or configuration store in the settings for the configuration source (such as the built-in file-based configuration source) for each application.

SCENARIO 4: MANAGING AND ENFORCING CONFIGURATION FOR MULTIPLE APPLICATIONS

In this scenario, you not only want to share configuration settings between multiple applications or application layers that run on different computers (as in the previous scenario), but also be able to manage and enforce these configuration settings for this application or its layers on all machines within the same Active Directory® domain. To achieve this you:

1. Use the configuration tools to add a manageable configuration source to the **Configuration Sources** section.

2. Specify a unique name for the **Application Name** property that defines the application within the Active Directory repository and domain.

3. Set the **File Path** property to the path and name for the configuration file.

4. Set the **Selected Source** property in the properties pane for the **Configuration Sources** section to the new manageable configuration source. This updates the application's default App.config or Web.config file to instruct Enterprise Library to use this as its configuration file.

5. After you finish configuring the application blocks and settings for your application, right-click the title bar of the manageable configuration source and select **Generate ADM Template**. This creates a Group Policy template that you can install into Active Directory. The template contains the settings for the application blocks, and configuring them in Active Directory forces each application instance to use the centrally specified settings.

The manageable configuration source does not provide Group Policy support for the Validation Application Block, the Policy Injection Application Block, or Unity.

SCENARIO 5: SHARING CONFIGURATION SECTIONS
ACROSS MULTIPLE APPLICATIONS

In this scenario, you have multiple applications or application layers that must use the same shared configuration for some application blocks (or for some sections of the configuration such as instrumentation settings or connection strings). Effectively, you want to be able to redirect Enterprise Library to some shared configuration sections, rather than sharing the complete application configuration. For example, you may want to specify the settings for the Logging Application Block and share these settings between several applications, while allowing each application to use its own local settings for the Exception Handling Application Block. You achieve this by redirecting specific configuration sections to matching sections of a configuration store in a shared location. The steps to implement this scenario are as follows:

1. Use the configuration tools to add a suitable configuration source for your application to the **Configuration Sources** section. This configuration source should point to the shared configuration store. If you want to use a standard format configuration file as the shared configuration store, add a file-based configuration source. To store the shared configuration information in a different type of store, you must install a suitable configuration source. You can use the sample SQL configuration source that is available from the Enterprise Library community site at http://entlib.codeplex.com to store your configuration in a database.

2. Set the relevant properties of the shared configuration source. For example, if you are using the built-in file-based configuration source, set the **File Path** property to the path and name for the application's configuration file.

3. Set the **Selected Source** property in the properties pane for the **Configuration Sources** section to **System Configuration Source**.

4. Click the plus-sign icon in the **Redirected Sections** column and click **Add Redirected Section**. A redirected section defines one specific section of the local application's configuration that you want to redirect to the shared configuration source so that it loads the configuration information defined there. Any local configuration settings for this section are ignored.

5. In the new redirected section, select the configuration section you want to load from the shared configuration store using the drop-down list in the **Name** property. The name of the section changes to reflect your choice.

6. Set the **Configuration Source** property of the redirected section by selecting the shared configuration source you defined in your configuration. This configuration source will provide the settings for the configuration sections that are redirected.

7.   Repeat steps 4, 5, and 6 if you want to redirect other configuration sections to the shared configuration store. Configuration information for all sections for which you do not define a redirected section will come from the local configuration source.

8.   To edit the contents of the shared configuration store, you must open that configuration in the configuration tools or in a text editor; you cannot edit the configuration of shared sections when you have the local application's configuration open in the configuration tool. If you open the shared configuration in the configuration tool, ensure that the **Selected Source** property of that configuration is set to use the system configuration source.

You cannot share the contents of the **Application Settings** *section. This section in the configuration tool stores information in the standard* **<appSettings>** *section of the configuration file, which cannot be redirected.*

SCENARIO 6: APPLYING A COMMON CONFIGURATION
STRUCTURE FOR APPLICATIONS

In this scenario you have a number of applications or application layers that use the same configuration structure, and you want to inherit that structure but be able to modify or add individual configuration settings by defining them in your local configuration file. You can specify a configuration that inherits settings from a parent configuration source in a shared location, and optionally override local settings. For example, you can configure additional providers for an application block whose base configuration is defined in the parent configuration. The steps to implement this scenario are as follows:

1.   Use the configuration tools to add a suitable configuration source for your application to the **Configuration Sources** section. This configuration source should point to the shared configuration store. If you want to use a standard format configuration file as the shared configuration store, add a file-based configuration source. To store the shared configuration information in a different type of store, you must install a suitable configuration source. You can use the sample SQL configuration source that is available from the Enterprise Library community site at http://entlib.codeplex.com to store your configuration in a database.

2.   Set the relevant properties of the shared configuration source. For example, if you are using the built-in file-based configuration source, set the **File Path** property to the path and name for the application's configuration file.

3.   Set the **Parent Source** property in the properties pane for the **Configuration Sources** section to your shared configuration source. Leave the **Selected Source** property in the properties pane set to **System Configuration Source**.

4.   Configure your application in the usual way. You will not be able to see the settings inherited from the shared configuration source you specified as the parent source. However, these settings will be inherited by your local

configuration unless you override them by configuring them in the local configuration. Where a setting is specified in both the parent source and the local configuration, the local configuration setting will apply.

5.   To edit the contents of the shared parent configuration store, you must open that configuration in the configuration tools or in a text editor; you cannot edit the configuration of parent sections when you have the local application's configuration open in the configuration tool. If you open the parent configuration in the configuration tool, ensure that the **Selected Source** property of that configuration is set to use the system configuration source.

The way that the configuration settings are merged, and the ordering of items in the resulting configuration, follows a predefined set of rules. These are described in detail in the documentation installed with Enterprise Library and available online at http://go.microsoft.com/fwlink/?LinkId=188874.

SCENARIO 7: MANAGING CONFIGURATION IN DIFFERENT DEPLOYMENT ENVIRONMENTS

In this scenario, you want to be able to define different configuration settings for the same application that will be appropriate when it is deployed to different environments, such as a test and a production environment. In most cases the differences are minor, and usually involve settings such as database connection strings or the use of a different provider for a block. Enterprise Library implements this capability using a feature called environmental overrides. The principle is that you specify override values for settings that are different in two or more environments, and the differences are saved as separate delta configuration files. The administrator then applies these differences to the main configuration file when the application is deployed in each environment. To achieve this:

1.   Follow the instructions in the step-by-step procedure in the section "Using the Configuration Tools" in Chapter 1, "Introduction," which describes how you configure multiple environments in the configuration tools and how you define the overridden settings.

2.   Open the properties pane for each of the environments you added to your configuration by clicking the chevron arrow to the right of the environment title, and set the **Environment Delta File** property to the path and name for the delta file for that environment.

3.   Save the configuration. The configuration tool generates a normal (.config) file and a delta (.dconfig) file for each environment. The delta file(s) can be managed by administrators, and stored in a separate secure location, if required. This may be appropriate when, for example, the production environment settings should not be visible to developers or testers.

4.   To create a run-time merged configuration file (typically, this is done by an administrator):

- Open the local configuration (.config) file.
- Select **Open Delta File** from the **Environments** menu and load the appropriate override configuration (.dconfig) file.
- Set the **Environment Configuration File** property in the properties pane for the environment to the path and name for the merged configuration file for that environment.
- Right-click on the title of the environment and click **Export Merged Environment Configuration File**.

5. Deploy the merged configuration file in the target environment.

Enterprise Library also contains a command-line utility named MergeConfiguration.exe that you can use to merge configuration and delta files if you do not have the configuration console deployed on your administrator system. It can also be used if you wish to automate the configuration merge as part of your deployment process. Information about MergeConfiguration.exe is included in the documentation installed with Enterprise Library.

> *You cannot use environmental overrides with redirected sections or inherited configuration settings. You can only use them when the entire configuration of your application is defined within a local configuration source.*

For more information on all of the scenarios presented here, see the documentation installed with Enterprise Library and available online at http://go.microsoft.com/fwlink/?LinkId=188874.

Appendix E   Encrypting Configuration Files

Enterprise Library supports encryption of configuration information. Unless your server is fully protected from both physical incursion and remote incursion over the network, you should consider encrypting any configuration files that contain sensitive information, such as database connection strings, passwords and user names, or validation rules.

You can select any of the encryption providers that are included in your system's Machine.config file. Typically, these are the **DataProtectionConfigurationProvider**, which uses the Microsoft® Windows® Data Protection API (DPAPI), and the **Rsa ProtectedConfigurationProvider**, which uses RSA. The settings for these providers, such as where keys are stored, are also in the Machine.config file. You cannot edit this file with a configuration tool; instead, you must modify it using a text editor or an operating system configuration tool.

As an example of the effect of this option, the following is a simple unencrypted configuration for the Data Access block.

```
<dataConfiguration defaultDatabase="Connection String" />
<connectionStrings>
 <add name="Connection String"
      connectionString="Database=TheImportantOne; Server=WEHAVELIFTOFF;
                        User ID=secret; Password=DontTellNE1"
      providerName="System.Data.SqlClient" />
</connectionStrings>
```

When you specify the **DataProtectionConfigurationProvider** option, the resulting configuration section looks like the following.

```
<dataConfiguration
      configProtectionProvider="DataProtectionConfigurationProvider">
 <EncryptedData>
  <CipherData>
   <CipherValue>AQAAANCMnd8BFdERjHoAwE/Cl+sBAAAAc8HVTgvQB0quQI81ya0uH
     yTmSDdYQNdiSohA5Fo6bWOqhOR5V0uxdcfNUgKhUhuIAhl5RZ8W5WD8M2CdMiqG
     ...
     JyEadytIBvTCbmvXefuN5MWT/T
```

```
    </CipherValue>
   </CipherData>
  </EncryptedData>
 </dataConfiguration>
<connectionStrings
        configProtectionProvider="DataProtectionConfigurationProvider">
 <EncryptedData>
  <CipherData>
   <CipherValue>AQAAANCMnd8BFdERjHoAwE/Cl+sBAAAAc8HVTgvQB0quQI81ya0uH

     ...

     zBJp7SQXVsAs=</CipherValue>
  </CipherData>
 </EncryptedData>
</connectionStrings>
```

If you only intend to deploy the encrypted configuration file to the server where you encrypted the file, you can use the **DataProtectionConfigurationProvider**. However, if you want to deploy the encrypted configuration file on a different server, or on multiple servers in a Web farm, you should use the **RsaProtectedConfigurationProvider**. You will need to export the RSA private key that is required to decrypt the data. You can then deploy the configuration file and the exported key to the target servers, and re-import the keys. For more information, see "Importing and Exporting Protected Configuration RSA Key Containers" at http://msdn.microsoft.com/en-us/library/yxw286t2(VS.80).aspx.

Of course, the next obvious question is "How do I decrypt the configuration?" Thankfully, you don't need to. You can open an encrypted file in the configuration tools as long as it was created on that machine or you have imported the RSA key file. In addition, Enterprise Library blocks will be able to decrypt and read the configuration automatically, providing that the same conditions apply.

Index

W

X